Dirty Eddie's War

Based on the World War II Diary of Harry "Dirty Eddie" March, Jr., Pacific Fighter Ace

by
Lee Cook

Number 20 in the North Texas Military
Biography and Memoir Series

University of North Texas Press
Denton, Texas

©2021 Lee Cook
Foreword ©2011 William Landreth
All rights reserved.
Printed in the United States of America.

10 9 8 7 6 5 4 3 2 1

Permissions:
University of North Texas Press
1155 Union Circle #311336
Denton, TX 76203-5017

The paper used in this book meets the minimum requirements
of the American National Standard for Permanence of Paper for
Printed Library Materials, z39.48.1984. Binding materials have
been chosen for durability.

Library of Congress Cataloging-in-Publication Data

Cook, Lee, author.
Dirty Eddie's war : based on the World War II diary of Harry
"Dirty Eddie" March, Jr., Pacific fighter ace / Lee Cook.
     pages cm
  Includes bibliographical references and index.
  ISBN-13 978-1-57441-841-5 (cloth)
  ISBN-13 978-1-57441-851-4 (ebook)
  1. LCSH: March, Harry Andrew, Jr., 1919–1946—Diaries.
2. United States. Navy. Fighting Squadron VF-17—Biography.
3. Fighter pilots—United States—Diaries. 4. World War, 1939–
1945—Campaigns—Pacific Ocean. 5. World War, 1939–1945—
Aerial operations, American. 6. Guadalcanal, Battle of, Solomon
Islands, 1942–1943—Personal narratives, American. 7. LCGFT:
Diaries. 8. Biographies.

 D767.9 .C65 2021
 940.54/5973092 [B]–dc23
                    2021017334

Number 20 on the North Texas Military Biography and Memoir Series

The electronic edition of this book was made possible by the support
of the Vick Family Foundation. Typeset by vPrompt eServices.

For Harry, Elsa, Mary, and Dora

Contents

List of Illustrations

Foreword

I t really is a story that deserves to be told. Thanks to Lee Cook, it has been written.

I knew Harry "Dirty Eddie" March as a friend and squadron mate, a fellow member of *Fighting Seventeen*. We flew Corsairs together and spent countless hours in training and combat. Between battles, we all swapped wild sea stories in the isolation of our jungle ready room. Some of them were even true.

Thanks to Harry's letters reporting to the home front, his family preserved a very accurate picture of the man and his many adventures. Harry March's life may have been cut short, but due to the unstinting efforts of author and historian, Lee Cook, his true legacy will not be lost.

The surviving pilots of VF-17 who reunited in Oshkosh, Wisconsin in 1994 met Lee Cook, a young Englishman who had settled on "The Jolly Rogers" as a focal point for his interest in this period of history. He impressed us all with the amount of information he had gathered and was encouraged by us to write a book, but none of us realized just what that would entail. On his part, it has meant eighteen years of dedication to painstaking research and tireless communication, leading to three outstanding works of scholarly yet readable and entertaining history. It also meant that we, the men and families of VF-17, gained a faithful friend.

There are relatively few of us left who fought the battles of World War II. As one of the last "Jolly Rogers" standing, I believe I can speak for them all when I convey regards and respect to those, like Lee, who preserve our past. It's good to know that when we are gone and this generation's torch has been extinguished, our light will linger on.

Thank you, Lee and Godspeed.
William Lee "Country" Landreth
Commander, U.S.N. (Ret.).[1]

Introduction

T his book tells the war story of Harry "Dirty Eddie" March, as recorded in a journal addressed to his devoted wife, Elsa. However, this is much more than a wartime account by a fighter ace, it is also the story of a world-class athlete in the 1940s and a tale of his undying love for Elsa. Harry's unique journal has remained undisclosed for seventy-four years.

Disregarding official regulations, Harry March kept an unauthorized diary to record his experiences throughout his combat tours. This exceptional account includes all the major battles that he faced from June 1942 to April 1944, a long and arduous duty for an American fighter pilot. He details his personal experiences of combat air action, plus life on aircraft carriers and land bases in some of the key campaigns during two crucial stages of the Pacific War. Harry's diary documents the brutal campaign and primitive living conditions on Guadalcanal, dealing with the shattering loss of close friends plus the effects of combat fatigue. He captures the intensity of air operations over Rabaul and the stresses of overwhelming enemy aerial opposition. He expresses the rivalry between the services and candidly shares his point of view on the strategies of the higher command. The diary reveals the personal account of a pilot's innermost thoughts, both of the action he saw, the effects of his harrowing experiences and his longing to be reunited with his beloved wife back home. There is a devotion and tenderness throughout his account for the love of his life, Elsa. The story has human interest and unusual characters, all brought together at an extraordinary time in history.

There have been numerous personal accounts and memoirs from servicemen who fought in the Pacific War. In most cases, they are a retrospective look at events with experiences recalled with the benefit of hindsight and the passage of time. What is unique about the diary of Harry March is that it is a story of its time and his words are just as poignant now as when as he recorded them. These words provide a snapshot of the war as he saw and experienced it, at a time of cataclysmic world events.

....

The origins of the Pacific War are complex and were forged from a gradual escalation of Japanese ambition over many years. The Japanese saw themselves as major players in Asia, but expansion of their territories was dependent upon increasing their access to raw materials. Prior to World War I, Japan had already annexed Korea and defeated Russia in a war. At the Peace Conference of 1919 following the end of the First World War, Japan obtained a number of Pacific Islands that were previously German colonies.[1] The Limitation of Naval Armament Treaty (also known as the "Five-Power Treaty" or "Washington Treaty") of 1922 and 1930 resulted in a status quo in the Pacific with regard to the naval bases held by the United States, Great Britain and Japan. There was also an international agreement to safeguard the rights of China. The militarists in the Japanese government were unhappy with these settlements as they limited their expansion plans.[2] The Immigration Act of 1924 further inflamed relations between Japan and America as Japanese citizens were prevented from entering the United States.[3] The Great Depression, which had started in the United States in 1929, was also affecting Japanese exports.

In 1931, the Japanese Army invaded Manchuria, China, which was rich in coal and iron. The Chinese appealed to the League of Nations, and when their case was upheld, this led to Japan sensationally withdrawing from that organization in 1933. Tensions increased and the United States used diplomatic means to restore peace. However, in 1937, Japan undertook a full-scale attack on China. In fact, Japan wasn't strong enough to defeat China as it did not have the reserves in raw materials, particularly oil, to sustain a long-drawn-out war, but would lose face if it withdrew.

With the start of the war in Europe in 1939, Japan saw an opportunity to expand its empire further. After France had been defeated, Japan, with the Army strongly influencing government, moved into Indo-China. Following the unprecedented German advance throughout Europe, the Japanese assumed the same would occur when the Germans invaded the Soviet Union. They believed Great Britain and the United States would be preoccupied by the war in Europe and would have limited resources to allocate to Asia. Japan saw the opportunity to seize territory in the Pacific, giving it access to raw materials, such as rubber in Malaya and oil in the Dutch

East Indies. However, the nearby U.S. colony of the Philippines posed a threat to its plans.[4] America opposed this expansion and in response, moved the U.S. Pacific Fleet from San Diego to Pearl Harbor in the summer of 1940. From July 1940, the United States also placed Japan under a trade embargo, the first of several.[5]

The Japanese wanted a free hand in the Pacific and by increasing their influence, hoped that America would cede to their demands. Diplomatic solutions were sought by President Roosevelt, but no breakthrough was made. With the prospect of war looming, America planned to focus its efforts on defeating Hitler first, then concentrate on the Pacific, in cooperation with the British Empire. In September 1940, Japan formed an alliance with Germany and Italy by signing the Tripartite Pact. This was designed to discourage the United States from joining Great Britain and the Commonwealth against the Axis Powers.[6] Negotiations carried on, but secretly the Japanese were preparing for war with the United States. The Japanese military leaders planned a simultaneous attack on Pearl Harbor and the Philippines. Their aim was to inflict a decisive blow that would bring the Americans to the negotiating table suing for peace. Talks continued, but behind the scenes the Japanese strategy was to cease negotiations and declare war. However, as a result of a breakdown in communication within the Japanese diplomatic service, things didn't go to plan and this resulted in the Pearl Harbor attack proceeding without a declaration of war on December 7, 1941.

The Japanese had been planning the raid on Pearl Harbor for nearly a year and the naval forces involved had been training and preparing to eliminate the U.S. Pacific Fleet. With the American fleet crippled Japan would be able to control most of the South Pacific. The whole plan relied on secrecy and although the Americans suspected an attack was coming, they didn't anticipate that Pearl Harbor would be the target. Sunday was chosen as the best day to strike and the huge Japanese fleet, including six aircraft carriers, sailed to the north of the Hawaiian Islands and launched two assaults. The first wave consisted of 183 aircraft (two failed to take off) followed by a second wave of similar size. The attack was part of a number of simultaneous advances, as Japan also launched assaults on the Philippines, Guam, Wake Island, Malaya, Singapore, and Hong Kong on the same day.[7]

The world would never be the same following the aftermath of the Japanese sneak offensive at Pearl Harbor, which killed over two thousand Americans, as well as causing large scale damage to ships, planes, and shore installations. After being a bystander to the war in Europe, the situation changed immediately for the United States. The Japanese alliance with Germany and Italy meant the United States was now at war with them all. Although it was a victory for Japan in military terms, in other ways it was a catastrophe—they had chosen the quickest way to infuriate the whole country. The isolationists, such as "America First," were instantly sidelined as the country geared up for war, determined to avenge the unprovoked attack. This would change every part of the "Land of Liberty."[8] For the United States, one fortuitous aspect of the Pearl Harbor attack was that the three Pacific Fleet aircraft carriers, which were normally based there, the *Enterprise*, *Lexington*, and *Saratoga*, along with their escorts, were all out at sea. This would have major consequences for the Japanese Navy in the months ahead.[9]

After their attack on Pearl Harbor, the Japanese launched a lightning military campaign in the Pacific and their advance was a huge surprise. At the time, Japan outnumbered the United States in ships and air superiority. The American strategy after Pearl Harbor was based on defense until its forces could be built up again. The resources left at its disposal would have to be used wisely and only when necessary to counter the Japanese. Victory in Europe remained the first objective, the Pacific could be dealt with later.[10] By May 1942, the Japanese were still on the offensive and attacked Tulagi in the Solomon Islands. In response to this, the United States sent its carriers to engage with the Japanese in what would become known as the Battle of the Coral Sea and the result was what both sides would choose to call a victory. The United States lost one carrier and another was badly damaged, but for the first time, the Japanese advance was impeded.[11]

The next major engagement came at Midway in June 1942, six months after Pearl Harbor. By invading Midway Island, the Japanese knew the Americans would have to respond by sending their carriers into the attack. What the Japanese did not know was the Americans had worked diligently on breaking their codes and were aware of the impending attack. Unknown to the

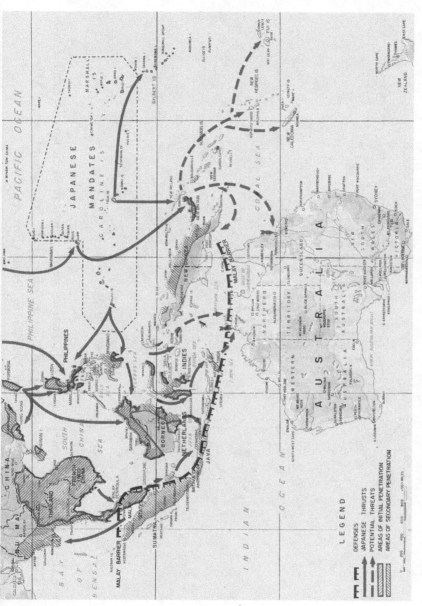

Map of the Imperial Japanese advances in the Southwest Pacific and Southeast Asia during the first five months of the Pacific Campaign in World War II. What is clear is the extent of the Japanese thrusts and their plan to defend their territories. *Source:* United States Army Center of Military History. *The Campaigns of MacArthur in the Pacific. Volume I. Reports of General MacArthur.*

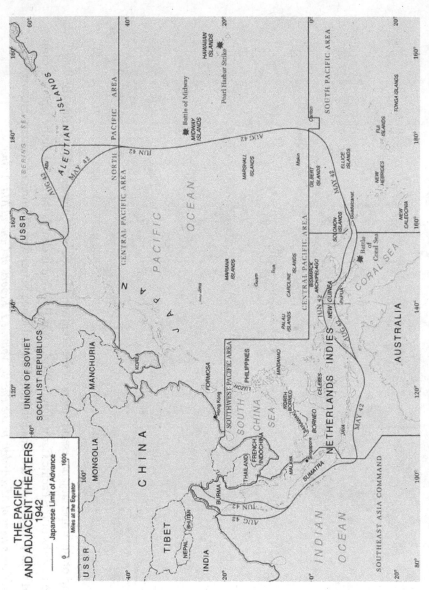

The Pacific and adjacent theaters in 1942. Featured are the boundaries of the Japanese Empire. Note key places, Pearl Harbor, Coral Sea, and Midway. *Source:* United States Army Center of Military History. *The US Army Campaigns of World War II.* Newell, Clayton R. 2003.

approaching Japanese task force, the U.S. carriers were already positioned to counter the assault. The eventual and monumental engagement culminated in the sinking of four of the Japanese Navy's frontline carriers, the *Akagi, Kaga, Sōryū*, and *Hiryū*, all of which had been involved in the Pearl Harbor attack six months earlier. Men and planes could be replaced, but the four carriers could not. Their loss permanently ruined what had been the most success-ful Japanese naval weapon system of the war, and hence must be ranked as far and away the most important material loss of the battle.[12] On the American side, the *Yorktown* was sunk by the Japanese;[13] however, the Battle of Midway was a crucial triumph for the United States and a turning point in the Pacific War. It demonstrated that carrier and air power would be key to victory in the Pacific.

Following the Battle of Midway, U.S. reconnaissance of enemy activity in the Japanese-controlled Solomon Islands continued. This revealed that an airfield was in process of construction on Guadalcanal Island and facilities on other nearby bases were being expanded rapidly. This threatened the supply lines from Australia to the United States.[14] The airfield was vital and the Allies had no choice but to immediately send a task force to take Guadalcanal before the Japanese airstrip was finished. The Americans were by no means ready to mount a major offensive and the Marines later dubbed it "Operation Shoestring." On August 7, 1942, American forces landed on Guadalcanal and started their legendary and bloody campaign.[15] They were only interested in capturing enough land to hold the airfield in the initial stages. After they had achieved this objective, the perimeter was strengthened then gradually, over many months, they gained control over the whole island. Once the Allies had eventually consolidated the island, the next phase was to nullify the Japanese stronghold at Rabaul. This heavily defended base on the island of New Britain had to be neutralized in order for the Allied forces to progress to Japan.[16] The Allied commanders initiated a huge air bombard-ment to bring Rabaul to its knees, resulting in its eventual isolation and enabling the Allies to leave it to wither on the vine and island-hop all the way to Japan. It was during these two momentous campaigns of the Pacific War that Harry March recorded his experiences.

....

Harry Andrew March, Jr., was born in East Liverpool, Ohio in 1919. He graduated from McKinley High School in 1936. Harry was a naturally talented, versatile, all-round athlete. He won the district junior tennis title in 1937 and became United States National Pentathlon Champion in 1940. At age twenty-one, Harry was one of the best 400 m hurdlers in the world, competing on level terms with future double Olympic Gold medalist, Roy Cochran. Had it not been for the advent of World War II, he would have represented the United States in the 400 m hurdles at the 1940 Olympic Games.[17] Unlike many of his competitors in the field of top-class athletics, Harry remains unknown, despite his considerable achievements. Many of his contemporaries went on to break records and achieve Olympic success. Unfortunately, Harry's career was to remain unfulfilled as his destiny was to be forever changed.

Harry March graduated from the University of North Carolina in 1940 and enlisted in the Navy on December 16, 1940. He had been based at the former Pacific Fleet base of San Diego at the time of Pearl Harbor and was finalizing his training before being assigned to his first fighter squadron. He qualified as a naval aviator and was commissioned as an ensign on August 18, 1941. Harry had known and possibly dated Elsa in 1937 when they were both studying at the University of North Carolina, Chapel Hill, but it wasn't until 1941, when they bumped into each other again, that they fell in love. They were married on February 10, 1942, at Coronado, San Diego.[18] After completing his flight training, Harry was ordered to the *Enterprise* on June 15, 1942, shortly after the Battle of Midway.

In 1942, few people in America had heard of Guadalcanal prior to the campaign there, let alone knew where it was. The Japanese fortress of Rabaul was similarly unknown when it became the focus of the Allied war effort in the South Pacific in 1943–44. However, these remote outposts were key to the United States' goal of defeating Japan.

Harry was one of the first pilots over Guadalcanal, flying an F4F Wildcat. After the *Enterprise* was bombed, he was transferred to serve on the *Saratoga*. When the *Saratoga* was torpedoed, Harry became land-based on the renamed Henderson Field with the "Cactus Air Force," defending the island against Japanese attacks. He was right in the thick of the action in the early days of one of the most significant campaigns of the Pacific War.

He obtained the peculiar nickname "Dirty Eddie" during his first tour of duty in the Solomons when he was so tired, he sometimes slept in his clothes and seldom shaved, resulting in him sporting a thick, black beard. After surviving the "Island of Green Hell," he returned home. After his leave between combat tours, Elsa shared the news that they were to have a child, and their only daughter, Mary Elizabeth, was born on September 29, 1943. He was assigned to VF-24, flying F6F Hellcats on the *Belleau Wood* and was sent out to the Pacific combat zone again in the summer of 1943.

Harry was involved in the attack on Tarawa in the Gilbert Islands on September 18, 1943, and upon returning to Pearl Harbor, a chance encounter with some Guadalcanal veterans led Harry to report to VF-17 on October 6, 1943. *Fighting Seventeen* were short of pilots with combat experience so Harry's expertise was sorely needed. He fought in the Bougainville campaign and finally the "hot box" of Rabaul, where he became an ace. Known by their pirate insignia, "The Skull and Crossbones Squadron" was the Navy's premier F4U Corsair unit and their name became famous, setting a Pacific record by shooting down 152 Japanese planes in seventy-six days.

In April 1944, Harry returned home and continued his naval career as an instructor for a year before being assigned to another fighter squadron, VBF-74. While there, he applied for a regular commission, which was accepted in November 1945 and he resumed his training in track and field to prepare for the 1948 Olympics in London.

Tragically, in March 1946, a swift and severe illness was to cut his life short at the age of only 27. He is interred in Arlington National Cemetery. His devoted wife Elsa raised their only daughter alone and never remarried. Harry March was awarded a Distinguished Flying Cross and numerous other awards for his gallant service, but may be considered to have been under-decorated particularly given the extent of his service and achievements.[19] Like in athletics, his wartime accomplishments were never acknowledged as they should have been. Details of Harry's citations and awards are provided in Appendix 1.

....

The origins of my fascination with the F4U Corsair go back to early 1993 when I saw a limited-edition print called *The Jolly Rogers* by Nicholas Trudgian advertised in *Flypast* magazine. In the summer of that year, I saw a signed copy of the print at an air show, loved it and bought it. I knew someone who was writing to fighter pilots in the United States and I found out that among his correspondents was Tom Blackburn, the skipper of VF-17, one of the four pilots who had signed the print. I started writing to Tom and he sent me a full roster of everyone from the squadron who was still alive. I wrote to the twenty-six people on his list and was later invited to the *Fighting Seventeen* reunion at Oshkosh in July/August 1994. Meeting the surviving pilots led me on a journey of discovery about the squadron's record-breaking achievements in the Solomon Islands and the challenge to record their history, resulting in the publication of three books on the subject. The picture on the cover of my first book, *The Skull and Crossbones Squadron—VF-17 in World War II*, was the one which I had bought at the air show.

My research has always focused on personal contact with squadron members and their families and they have been my primary sources. The best way to describe what I look for is the "shoe boxes in the attic." Through my research I have unearthed previously unpublished and unique material, stories and photographs. My next sources are official Personnel Records and Navy Operational Archives.

To find information about Harry March, one of VF-17's ace pilots, I obtained a brief biography from the U.S. Navy Operational Archives in Washington, D.C. This mentioned Harry's wife, Elsa, and their daughter, Mary, but I found that Mary had died in 1976 and Elsa in 2003. I spent many years trying to find Harry's two sisters, without success. However, I managed to locate Elsa's sister, Dora Taylor, and in 2008 I started corresponding with her for information and photos to include in the aces and photographic history books. I also contacted the National Personnel Records Center in St. Louis and obtained Harry's complete service record in 2009. Dora mentioned to me that she had a diary that Harry had recorded while he was in the Pacific, and this had been kept in the family after Elsa died. As soon as Dora mentioned Harry's diary, I was eager to find out more about it. Documents such as these are a mine of information for a researcher and historian such as myself. In 2009, Dora sent me a copy of the diary, Harry's flight logs, and some photos, which included Elsa and Mary, and gave me permission to use them. Ironically, it was as I was preparing the final manuscript for the book in June 2020 that I at last made contact with members of Harry's surviving family. Sadly, I learned that both Harry's sisters had passed away, JoAnn only the previous year, so the opportunity to learn more about Harry's early life had unfortunately been missed. However, correspondence with his nephew, Steve McAfee, and his wife, Mary Anne, resulted in receiving their full support for the project and they provided some details and photos I didn't have, some of which I am pleased to have been able to include in the book.

When I first started to write up Harry's journal, my original idea was to try and publish the diary in its original form. However, I found it didn't stand on its own as there were some time periods missing and some parts lacked context. The diary needed to be gradually pieced together with Harry's full military service record and his flight logs to corroborate key people, dates and events. I also wanted to explore other parts of Harry's life, particularly how important athletics was to him and to provide context and a wider perspective to some of the events and his comments about them. I decided it would work better if I included a narrative to enhance Harry's diary entries and make it into a more complete and coherent story. Some parts of Harry's original account have therefore been included in my narrative, supplemented by facts and additional information, which I have researched. The majority of the diary has been used, either in my narrative or reproduced verbatim. An examination of countless publications, war diaries, and aircraft action reports helped to describe and mold together the narrative. Although I have had to edit the diary to blend all his life together, conveying the complete story of this remarkable man has been the goal. I have worked on producing a manuscript on and off for more than eleven years.

For information on Harry's close comrades who died in World War II, I applied for their complete service records, which I was able to purchase due to the time that had elapsed since they died. The records were meticulously analyzed for all the key information and dates to further enhance the story.

There were several of Harry's close friends mentioned in the diary, such as Bill Wileman, Joseph "Dutch" Shoemaker, Johnny Kleinman, Donald "Stinky" Innis, and Jim Halford, and I have included brief biographies on them in Appendix 2. Some of Harry's buddies were recorded in his diary using first names only, and these have been difficult to identify, however, where possible, their identity, rank, and relevant dates have been researched and included in the narrative.

Harry's original diary entries are presented in italics to distinguish them from my narrative. Corrections have been made to his punctuation and spelling and some minor editing has been done to improve clarity. However, Harry's use of nicknames, slang, and his style of speech have been left as originally recorded. His language used in describing the Japanese enemy forces would not be considered acceptable in today's society, but this has been left as it was originally written, revealing the authenticity of this firsthand account. Unless marked with an endnote specifying the source, details in the narrative have been extracted from Harry's diary. Parts of the book also include information and quotes from Harry's sister-in-law, Dora Taylor. Harry's words of fondness and love toward Elsa have been retained for purposes of conveying his character and sentiments. However, some of the more personal passages of the diary I have omitted or handled with sensitivity out of respect for the family.

My only goal throughout this endeavor has been to perpetuate Harry's memory and those brave men who flew with him against the Japanese. I wanted to document their exploits and ensure that they will be remembered in the future for their many achievements. I have made every conceivable effort to contact all sources possible for information and to verify facts about Harry March and his squadrons, therefore regretfully any errors or omissions that remain are entirely mine.

Lee Cook

Acknowledgments

T his book has been a long time in the making and there were times when I thought that it would never come to fruition, however, I didn't give up. Somehow the Universe saw to it that all the right elements would fall into place at the right time to realize my dream of telling the story of Harry March's short but significant contribution to the world.

In the first place, this book would not have existed at all without the kind help and encouragement of Elsa March's sister, Dora Taylor. I am indebted to her for giving me her blessing to use Harry's diary and flight logs all the way back in 2009. Thanks too, to Lloyd Taylor for his help with copying the diary, documents, and photos. Dora has been an inspiration to me throughout the project and I offer my heartfelt gratitude to her and her family. My sincere thanks also go to Steven D. McAfee and Mary Anne Hampton-McAfee, Anne Hampton McAfee, Ashleigh Catharine Hampton McAfee, and their family for all their help with information and photos and Emilie Winters Mead, Chad Mead, Kimberly Buckland Mead, and the late Rhett Youmans Winters.

Since I first started researching fighter pilots in 1993, I have had the continued support, encouragement and help of a great many people. I would like to acknowledge the cooperation of members of Fighting Squadron Seventeen and their families, their assistance continues to this day. The late "Country" Landreth was a constant inspiration throughout my research. He took me under his wing and helped me to press on over the years and I thank him for his help, support, and faith in me.

My sincere thanks to Linda Landreth Phelps, Alexandra Bowers, Mike DeBorde, Dorothy and "Mac" Burriss, Kelly Burriss, Jay Burriss and the Burriss family, Christine Silengo, Randolph Soggs, Sidney Buff, Toni Sennott, Alida Christinaz, Lyle Herrmann, Jr., Kraeg Kepford, Del and Pat May, George Pillsbury, Joanie Diteman, John B. Kepchia, Rick Einar and Paul Matthews, Joni Logsdon Baker, Frances Kleinman Rowland, Mike Rowland, and the Kleinman family.

I wish to express my appreciation for the help of the late Tom Blackburn, Roger Hedrick, Alison Henning, Tom and Carolyn Killefer, George Mauhar, Wilbert Peter Popp, Lennard Edmisten, Joyce Wharton, "Hap" and Alice Bowers, Joy Anderson Schroeder, Harold Bitzegaio, Danny Cunningham, Ray and Milly DeLeva, Dale Logsdon, Boone Guyton, and Joseph Nason.

Researching a story of this type where the main protagonist and those who were closest to him are no longer with us takes a great deal of piecing together of records and information and I am grateful to many organizations for their excellent collation of statistics and data, including the USS Enterprise CV-6 Association, U.S. Navy and U.S. Marine Corps, the Watertown Historical Society and the USS Midway Museum.

I want to thank the following people at the University of North Carolina at Chapel Hill for their kind help, information and photos of Harry March, Chancellor Holden Thorp, Nancy Davis, Associate Vice Chancellor for University Relations, Tanya T. Moore, University Relations, Terry Roberts in the sports information office, and Jason Tomberlin. My thanks to the *Daily Tar Heel* for the mine of information contained in its pages during Harry's time at the University of North Carolina. I would also like to thank Tony Staley, Sports Manager for the A.A.U. and Garry Hill at Track and Field News.

I was lucky that others had already done much work to capture firsthand accounts from veterans who served at the same time as Harry March and I would like to thank Jeff Hohman of Kenwood Productions for his permission to use quotes from *Fighting Seventeen, The Jolly Rogers* DVD, 1990, and David Wechsler of RDR Productions for his permission to use quotes from *VF-17 Remembered* video, 1984. Great assistance was provided to me by Marc Levitt at the National Museum of Naval Aviation with information and photographs and also the Robert Lawson photograph collection.

I am in awe of historians like Frank Olynyk and thank him for his meticulous victory credit information and also Vought Heritage for their information and photos. Thanks to all the staff at the National Personnel Records Center in St. Louis, Missouri, the National Archives and Records Administration and U.S. Naval Historical Center, Operational Archives for the M. W. "Butch" Davenport Collection and the Naval History and

Heritage Command. Thanks to Kathleen M. Lloyd and Bernard F. Cavalcante of the Department of the Navy, Naval Historical Center, Operational Archives Branch, Washington Navy Yard, Washington, D.C. My thanks to the late Roger Mansell for his dedicated research and all his help with information about Allied prisoners of war at Rabaul. My thanks to Ron Chrisman, Director, University of North Texas Press, for all his help and advice to bring this book to fruition and Professor Eric M. Bergerud and Sharon Tosi Lacey for their constructive feedback.

Lastly, my greatest thanks of all go to my wife Michele, the love of my life, for having a look at my eleven-year project and giving her view on what I should do to turn it into something more readable. After taking it on the chin, I listened and with her unwavering dedication and attention to detail she worked with me to bring this book to a successful conclusion. I couldn't have done it without you.

I hope I have managed to include everyone who has helped, but to anyone who has assisted me that I have missed, a profound thank you. I have believed in Harry's story for eleven years and knew it needed to be told. Although I never met Harry, I feel I have grown close to him and got to know him over the years. To Harry and his many comrades, I wish to express my sincere appreciation to you all and I hope that in some small way this book does you all justice.

Timeline

Date	World Events/Pacific War	Date	Harry March
1939		**1939**	
Sep 1	Germany invaded Poland		
Sep 3	Great Britain declared war on Germany		
1940		**1940**	
Jun 10	Italy declared war on Great Britain and France	Jun 10	Graduated from U.N.C with A.B. degree in Physical Education
Sep 27	Germany, Italy and Japan signed the Tripartite (Axis) Pact	Jun 29	400 m hurdles—achieved 3rd best time in the world
		Oct 6	Won U.S. National Pentathlon Championship
		Dec 16	Enlisted in U.S. Naval Reserve, aged 21
1941		**1941**	
Jul 26	United States froze Japan's assets	Mar 6	Accepted on V-5 program as an aviation cadet
Oct 17	General Hideki Tojo became Prime Minister of Japan	Sep 23	Designated a naval aviator
Dec 7	Japan attacked Pearl Harbor	Nov 6	Accepted appointment as ensign
Dec 7–8	Japanese troops moved into Thailand and northeastern Malaya	Nov 29	Reported to Advanced Carrier Training Group, San Diego
Dec 8	United States and Great Britain declared war on Japan		
Dec 18	Japan landed troops in Hong Kong		
Dec 22	Japanese landed in the Philippines		
Dec 25	Hong Kong fell to Japan		

Date	World Events/Pacific War	Date	Harry March
1942		**1942**	
Jan 2	Japan occupied Philippine capital, Manila	Feb 10	Married Elsa Smedes Winters
Feb 8	Japan invaded Burma	May 26	Qualified as a carrier pilot
Feb 10	Singapore fell to the Japanese	Jun 15	Reported to VF-6 on *Enterprise*
Feb 19	Japan attacked Indonesia and bombed Darwin, Australia	Jul 15	*Enterprise* sailed for Solomon Islands
May 7–8	Battle of the Coral Sea	Aug 7	In the air over Guadalcanal—first aerial victory
Jun 4	Battle of Midway	Aug 24	Second aerial victory. *Enterprise* bombed
Aug 7	First U.S. land offensive against Japan in Solomon Islands at Guadalcanal	Aug 25	Transferred to *Saratoga*
Aug 12	Battle of Edson's Ridge	Aug 31	*Saratoga* hit by torpedo
Aug 21	Battle of the Tenaru River	Sep 2	VF-6 detached to Efate in Vanuatu island chain
Aug 24	Battle of the Eastern Solomons	Sep 11	Arrived on Guadalcanal "Cactus Air Force"
Sep 15	*Wasp* Sunk	Sep 13	Ens. William Wileman killed in action; Ens. Donald Innis shot down
Oct 11–12	Battle of Cape Esperance	Sep 29	Ens. Joseph Shoemaker killed in action
Oct 14	Japanese Battleships *Kongō* and *Haruna* bombard Guadalcanal	Oct 1	Promoted to lieutenant junior grade
Oct 25	Battle of Santa Cruz	Oct 6	Left Guadalcanal for Espiritu Santo (Codename BUTTON)
Oct 26	*Hornet* Sunk	Nov 18	Returned home on leave
Nov 12–15	Naval Battle of Guadalcanal	Dec 31	Reported to VF-24 on board the *Belleau Wood*
Nov 30	The Battle of Tassafaronga		
1943		**1943**	
Jan 22	U.S. and Australian forces defeated Japan in Papua New Guinea	Jul	VF-24 swapped FM Wildcats for new F6F Hellcats

Date	World Events/Pacific War	Date	Harry March
Jan 29	Japan began withdrawal of land forces from Guadalcanal	Aug 9	*Belleau Wood* arrived at Pearl Harbor
Jun 30	Allied forces invaded New Georgia in the Solomons	Sep 1–10	Flew combat air patrols over Baker Island
Aug 15	Allied forces landed at Vella Lavella in the Solomon Islands	Sep 18	Flew two combat air patrol sorties in attack on Tarawa
Aug 16	Allied air attacks on Japanese troops at Wewak, Papua New Guinea	Sep 29	Daughter Mary "Baby Skeex" born
Sep 1	Air Group 24 involved in occupation of Baker Island	Oct 1	Promoted to lieutenant
Nov 1	Allies invaded Bougainville	Oct 5	Reported to VF-17
Nov 5	Carrier strike on Rabaul	Oct 27	Arrived Ondonga
Nov 11	Carrier strike on Rabaul	Oct 28	First operations from Ondonga
Dec 10	Torokina airstrip on Bougainville operational	Nov 1	Flew air cover for the landings of U.S. 3rd Marine Division on Bougainville
Dec 30	Bomber airstrip (Piva Uncle) on Bougainville operational	Nov 6	Led section in escort for bombers to Buka Harbor. Squadron sank three ships
Jan 22	Fighter airstrip (Piva Yoke) on Bougainville operational	Nov 8	Shot down a Ruth for third victory
		Dec 2	Left Ondonga
		Dec 6	Sydney for R&R
		Dec 14	Left Sydney
		Dec 19	Rear area training
1944		**1944**	
Feb 17	Japanese withdrew all aircraft from Rabaul to Truk		Lt. John Kleinman, killed in flying accident
Mar 8	Japanese attacked U.S. air bases on Bougainville	Jan 24	First missions to Rabaul from Bougainville
Jun 15/16	B-29 bombers based in China attacked southern Japan	Jan 28	Shot down two Zeros over Rabaul. Now an Ace
Oct 20	Philippines campaign started	Feb 19	Last Japanese fighters over Rabaul
Nov 24	B-29s bombed Tokyo	Mar 8	Leave Bougainville

Date	World Events/Pacific War	Date	Harry March
		April 3	Arrived home
		May 6	Instructor at N.A.A.S. Green Cove Springs
		Jun 20	Lt. Donald Innis killed in flying accident
1945		**1945**	
Feb 19	U.S. forces landed on Iwo Jima, Japan	May 15	Reported to VBF-74
Apr 1	Allied troops invaded Okinawa	Jun 30	A.A.U. 400 m hurdles 6th place
May 8	VE Day (Victory in Europe)	Jul 7–8	A.A.U. decathlon 6th place
Jun 22	Okinawa captured by Allied forces		
Jul 5	Philippines liberation completed		
Jul 14	First U.S. Navy bombardment of Japanese home islands		
Aug 6	Atomic bomb dropped on Hiroshima		
Aug 9	Atomic bomb dropped on Nagasaki		
Aug 14	Japan surrendered		
Sep 2	Japan formally surrendered on the deck of the *Missouri*		
1946		**1946**	
		Jan 30	Commission approved
		Feb 23	U.N.C. track meet
		Mar 2	Died, age 27

Prologue

Living the Dash

His name was Harry. Her name was Elsa. Their lives would be inexorably joined through one of the gravest conflicts in history and their love would endure. Elsa was the love of Harry's life and Harry the love of hers.

Elsa Smedes Winters was born on April 5, 1918, in the "City of Oaks" Raleigh, North Carolina (named after Sir Walter Raleigh). Her parents were Dr. Rhett Youmans Winters and Elizabeth Washington Knox. The family on her mother's side were descendants of John Washington of Sulgrave Manor, Banbury, Oxfordshire, England. This made them distant relatives of George Washington, first President of the United States.[1]

Elsa's sister, Dora, remembers growing up in Raleigh in the 1920s and 1930s:

"I love the expression I once heard from a pastor at a funeral. He mentioned that there are two important dates on your tombstone—the year of your birth and the year of your death, but with a dash (–) between the two dates. How you lived that 'dash' was the important part! Elsa did live her 'dash' well.

"Elsa was the eldest child in our family, my brother, Rhett, Jr., came next and finally me when my sister was six. We were all born at home in

1

those days, with our grandfather delivering us himself. We were raised in Raleigh during the 'Roaring 20s' and 'The Great Depression.' Raleigh was a small town of about 35,000, but it was the State Capitol. Saint Mary's School and Junior College which we attended, was founded in 1842 by a great uncle, the Reverend Aldert Smedes, an Episcopal priest. Our father was from South Carolina and was Director of the Experiment Station at State College. Later, when the family relocated to Washington, D.C., his position was Administrator of Research for the U.S. Department of Agriculture.

"Elsa was a very caring and responsible person with a strong faith, even at a young age. Both the church and education meant a lot to us as a family growing up. We belonged to The Church of the Good Shepherd (an Episcopal Church, which was a part of the worldwide Anglican Communion) and were in regular attendance. In spite of 'The Depression' and money being tight, we never had the feeling of being deprived. There was always enough food and some to spare for the hobos who came by. No one would refuse them a plate of food and a place to rest on the back porch or in the kitchen. There was no fear of strangers then.

"Elsa loved to dance and was so good at it that all the boys vied to be her partner. Under her yearbook picture at Saint Mary's School was written this little note: 'With golden hair and turned up nose, she wears a smile wherever she goes.' She also loved the theater and when she was a student at Saint Mary's she performed in quite a few Shakespearean plays. Often, she would play a male part because she was so tall. Later, at Carolina she was a star on the fencing team. I guess her rhythm and skill at dancing were a real advantage for the strategies of fencing."

Elsa graduated from the University of North Carolina, where she majored in History. Elsa lettered in fencing and was on the first coed team to engage in intercollegiate games in the history of the University.[2] Among Elsa's university acquaintances was a talented young athlete named Harry March.[3] Elsa and Harry featured on the same front page of the University's newspaper, the *Daily Tar Heel* on March 23, 1939, with Harry being described as "the one-man track team" and Elsa noted for her win in a fencing match against Rollins College in Williamsburg.

....

Harry lived his "dash" well too. He was a skilled exponent of tennis, and a gifted all-round track competitor and he would go on to live a very packed "dash!"

On February 4, 1919, in East Liverpool, Ohio, Harry Andrew March, Jr., was born to Harry Andrew March, a steel mill worker and his wife, Lois Winfield Campbell.[4] He was the eldest of three children, his sister Marilyn Jean, known as Jean, was born in 1920 and the youngest, JoAnn in 1924. The family relocated to Washington, D.C., in 1928, where Harry received his elementary education. He went on to study at McKinley High School (named after President William McKinley) and graduated in 1936.

Harry developed a gift for handling a racket and by the age of fifteen he had become the number one man on the McKinley High School team and was ranked sixth best junior in the country in 1934. He later won the district senior men's singles, Middle Atlantic singles, the Maryland State singles and doubles,

Harry March (left), Junior Tennis Champion, Washington, D.C., 1936. *Courtesy the March family.*

and the District of Columbia playground singles and doubles tournaments.[5] One of the high points of Harry's teenage years was playing against the seven times U.S. Champion and three times Wimbledon Champion, William "Big Bill" Tilden in an exhibition match.[6] Tilden is now universally regarded as one of the greatest tennis players in the history of the game. In these days where everyone is termed "great," Bill Tilden can rightly be regarded as a legend. Although a largely forgotten figure, his momentous tennis achievements were overshadowed by his impropriety off the court. The openly gay Tilden was arrested twice, in 1946 and 1949, resulting in convictions for sexual misconduct with under-age boys. This caused worldwide scandal and as a result he was ostracized and his tennis career never recovered. In 1953, he died aged sixty, having squandered most of his money.[7]

Harry went on to study at the nation's first public university—the University of North Carolina, which he attended from September 1936 to June 1940. It was here that Harry first encountered his future wife, Elsa, as his sister-in-law Dora remembers:

"Although my family moved from Raleigh to Washington, D.C., in 1937, my sister Elsa was already at The University of North Carolina, Chapel Hill. The story that I remember was that Harry had cut her debutante picture out of the *Raleigh News and Observer* in 1937 and had told friends, 'I'm going to meet that girl.' In the fall of 1937, Elsa transferred to U.N.C. as a junior. Back then girls could only go for their junior and senior years to the University. Harry was already there and she may have started dating Harry in her first year. I'm not sure how Harry happened to choose Carolina, but he was always into sports, particularly track and tennis. U.N.C. was a part of the Atlantic Coast Conference in college sports, which has always been a strong sports conference nationally."[8]

In his freshman year, Harry's athletic talents were immediately recognized, as reported in the following article in the *Daily Tar Heel Sports*:

March Registers Four First Places
Turning in some good performances, the Carolina freshmen rolled up a total of 99 points to walk off with first honors in the Carolina's A.A.U. track meet at Fetzer Field yesterday. Harry March was the

Harry March (far right) competing in the 120-yard high hurdles in 1936. Harry was a hurdle specialist in three events ranging from the 120- to 440-yard hurdles. *Courtesy the March family.*

outstanding man of the meet, registering four first places and a second. March established a new freshman high jump record when he cleared the bar at 5 feet 11 inches.

In addition to his record-breaking mark in the high jump, March chalked up firsts in the broad jump (21 feet 4 inches), hop, step and jump (41 feet 7¼ inches), the 200-meter low hurdles (25.4 seconds) and a second in the 100-meter high hurdles.[9]

Harry responded to the outstanding coaches at U.N.C. and excelled in the "Tar Heel" athletic program, breaking many records.[10] In early 1939, Harry was noted as being a potential Olympic hopeful in the *Daily Tar Heel Sports*:

Big name runners who began pounding their annual track to glory last week in Boston will continue tomorrow, and on through the winter and spring in the hopes that somebody will deposit an Olympic invitation in their stockings some time in the middle of June 1940. Fred Fuller of Virginia, Hub Reavis of Duke, and Bill Corpening and Harry March of Carolina will all scramble. March, however, will probably try for the decathlon.[11]

At the Southern Conference Championship, March again demonstrated his skills and adaptability by achieving a new school and field best of 6 feet, 1½ inches finishing equal first in the high jump. Described as the "Iron Horse" of the Carolina track team, Harry March equaled or exceeded four University records during the season.[12] The victorious "Tar Heels" of 1939 conquered all-comers in this incomparable season and finished by winning the Southern Conference Championship for the second successive season. It was considered the greatest track team in the history of the University.[13]

In the spring of 1939, events in the Far East were starting to get attention in the United States. It appears that Olympic preparations were proceeding regardless and again, Harry was highlighted as a potential member of the American team:

The 1940 Olympic Games start off with two strikes. War has dogged the games from the very start. Japan was awarded the games, but the Japs, being too busy bringing civilization, light and gun-powder back to the Chinese, relinquished the whole business to Finland. The Finns are making great plans for the games, but the chances are that a war will blow up long before next summer and instead of tossing javelins, the boys will be throwing hand grenades around and running not toward a tape, but away from some alighting bomb.

It's very strange, but no-one in the United States is very worried that the Olympics will not be held, and instead are going ahead full blast with Olympic plans. The Olympic fathers in this country have set up times and distances in all track and field events, saying that the boys must hit these times before they can compete in the semi-final try-outs for the Olympic team.

Harry March, Washington's one-man track team, will be able to get under the wire in two events. March did 9.8 in the hundred and that's the qualifying time, and having hit 54 in the 440-yard lows, Harry beats the time the Olympic fathers have set up by a second.[14]

The year 1940 was Harry's breakthrough year in athletics and he showed his versatility in the Millrose Games at Madison Square Garden, New York in February 1940. The Millrose Games is the world's longest-running and most prestigious indoor track and field competition.[15] The day before his twenty-first birthday, Harry competed there in the Carolina's two-mile relay team, which came third. Harry led the team off with specific instructions from the coach and ran his half-mile in two minutes.[16] The Carolina's reigned supreme again in the Southern Conference. Harry climaxed his varsity track career with a great performance, winning three events; he tied for second in a fourth and led the individual scoring with eighteen points. Harry could always be relied upon to score points for the team and he thrived under pressure. After the meet, the team celebrated their outstanding achievements for the season.

Harry graduated from U.N.C. with a Bachelor of Arts degree in Physical Education in the class of 1940.[17] At that time, Harry March was one of the most versatile track athletes ever to represent the University of North Carolina. He competed in eight different events during his varsity career and in competition his achievements were considerable.[18] With Olympic selection looming, Harry's outstanding form in the season stood him in good stead for the A.A.U. National Championships which would be his biggest test to date. He only had a short time to prepare for a big weekend, as he had entered the A.A.U. National Junior meet on Friday, June 28, 1940, for those with comparatively little experience at national competition level. He finished second in the 220-yard low hurdles and fourth in the broad jump. The next day, Saturday, June 29, Harry gained nationwide prominence when he competed at the A.A.U. National Championships at Ratcliffe Stadium, Fresno, California. In the final of the 400 m hurdles he faced three of the best athletes in the world in this event. The finishing positions were as follows:

1. Carl McBain   51.6 (Personal best)
2. Roy Cochran   52.1
3. Harry March   52.2 (Personal best)
4. John Borican   (Time not available)

Carl McBain ran the race of his life and posted a world's best time to win the race. Roy Cochran was second and just a whisker behind, in a personal best time, was Harry March. Fourth was John Borican, who was best known at the time as two-time National Pentathlon Champion, 1938 and 1939.[19] This race produced the three best times in the world in an Olympic year and established Harry March as one of the country's five fastest quarter-mile hurdlers of all time.[20] The athletes Harry competed against were among the finest in the world and the results demonstrate that Harry was right in the mix to compete for world honors. The top performers from this Championship would almost certainly have been selected for the U.S. Olympic team. Unfortunately, due to the war in Europe, none of the athletes were able to compete in the 1940 Olympic Games, which were eventually cancelled.

In 1940, Harry had distinguished himself in national competition in his best event. He now turned his attention to training for the pentathlon, a notable multievent for all-round athletes, which at that time, consisted of the broad jump, 200 m, javelin, discus and 1500 m. The latter three disciplines were not on Harry's normal roster of events. Harry achieved the distinction of becoming the A.A.U. National Pentathlon Champion in Newark, New Jersey, on October 6, 1940. It was a stellar performance, with a score of 2981 points—an improvement on John Borican's winning total of 2947 the previous year.

The final positions were as follows:

1. Harry March   2981
2. William Gilligan   2942
3. William Burton   2910[21]

Harry March "the one-man track team" and world-class athlete. Harry ran the third fastest time in the world in 1940 in his best event, the 400 m hurdles. *Courtesy the family of Jean March McAfee.*

The culmination of Harry's superb 1940 season was being named on the All-America Track Team and qualifying for the U.S. Olympic Team in the 400 m hurdles.[22]

Harry's sister-in-law, Dora remembers his dedication to athletics:

"I believe he had a great deal of natural ability and his competitive spirit and discipline made him a winner. He had a fun-loving, boyish, sometimes mischievous way about him, but deep down I believe he was deeply committed to excellence and discipline."[23]

It is quite likely that these qualities would have stood Harry in good stead when he applied for aviation training in the Navy. At the time, there was believed to be a close link between sporting success and strength of character. He'd proven himself to be a team player at U.N.C. which fitted well with the requirements for a Navy officer and aviator. On his application, he listed athletic coaching and teaching experience in civilian life. It was noted by the selection board that he was "very good officer material, with an affable, sincere manner and a brawny, athletic appearance."[24] He passed the medical and on December 16, 1940, Harry, then twenty-one years old, enlisted in the U.S. Naval Reserve as a seaman second class.[25] Harry's ambition, like so many other young men at the time, was to become a Navy fighter pilot aboard an aircraft carrier. This would test the best of men as landing an aircraft onto an aircraft carrier was, and still is, considered to be the hardest task in aviation. VF-17 pilot, William "Country" Landreth, had seen it as the ultimate goal to try for when he'd applied to the Navy:

"The most selective, the most difficult to get into, the best training—was carrier aviation in the Navy. It was the most demanding, the toughest. I reported to duty at Fairfax Field in Kansas City for E-Base training. They gave us ten to twelve hours of dual flight instruction before solo. If you didn't solo by then, you were washed out and could apply for the Army Air Corps."[26]

Unfortunately, many candidates were unable to overcome the difficulties and obstacles involved in achieving such a goal. Countless energetic young men failed at various stages along the way. The Navy accepted only the best. Harry had always aspired to be the best!

Harry's application for flight training through the V-5 program was accepted and he became an aviation cadet. The greater number of Navy aviators came through the "AvCad" program. Harry began his elimination flight training on March 6, 1941, and reported to the Naval Air Station, Jacksonville for training.

Remarkably, Harry also found time to continue his passion for athletics. On June 29, 1941, in his last A.A.U. National Championships before the war, he achieved second place in the 400 m hurdles at Franklin Field, Philadelphia. He was beaten by Oris "Arky" Erwin who achieved a time of 54.5 seconds.[27] Oris "Arky" Erwin went on to win the A.A.U. National 400 m Hurdles title in 1943, 1944, 1945 and 1946. Sadly, his outstanding athletics career was cut short when he was fatally injured in an automobile accident on January 10, 1947, at the age of twenty-seven.[28]

Harry was detached from N.A.S. Jacksonville and ordered to N.A.S. Miami (Opa-Locka) for further training. He reported on August 21, 1941.[29] Harry, who was accustomed to the demands of athletic competition, threw himself into the program. He had to undertake preflight training for thirteen weeks, primarily fitness tests, with no aviation involved. This aimed to weed out any cadets who did not meet the physical requirements. Harry's superb fitness enabled him to sail through this aspect of the drills. After completing preflight training, Harry commenced primary flight training, with a typical aircraft being the "Yellow Peril" N2S Stearman. The Boeing Stearman was a biplane used for training the U.S. Navy and Army Air Forces. The six phases of primary flight training were flying a first solo, then advanced flying, aerobatics, review, formation flying, and then night flying. While having to pass each arduous aspect of the primary flight training, Harry was also expected to qualify in ground school that ran concurrently.

Harry March managed to negotiate all the intensive training despite receiving the sad news that his mother, Lois, had died aged 49.[30] He then progressed to two months of intermediate flight training. He flew aircraft such as the SNV Vultee BT-13 Valiant, nicknamed the "Vibrator," with fixed landing gear and the SNJ North American single-engine advanced training aircraft. During this phase of training, the cadets' aptitude and skills were assessed to identify the type of role they would be most suited to, that is, dive bomber, torpedo bomber, patrol flyer, fighter pilot, or reconnaissance flyer.[31] The training up to this point was classified as elimination training and many aviators were washed-out at this stage. Harry gradually progressed to flying more powerful aircraft and operational types. His ultimate ambition was to be a fighter pilot.

During a break in Harry's aviation training, a chance meeting (or divine intervention) on the street in his home town, Washington, D.C., brought Harry and Elsa together again. Elsa's family had recently moved there and she was working for an insurance company. Stumbling upon each other brought back fond memories of their university days together at U.N.C. Harry admired the tall, slender, young woman with golden blond, curly hair and large, hazel eyes. The unexpected encounter started a chain reaction of renewed friendship, then courtship, which led to their engagement being announced just before Harry left Washington for the West Coast to continue his training.

Society's views on marriage at that time differed greatly from today and it was seen not only as the natural order of things to settle down with a family but also something to aspire to. At the time, many servicemen wanted to have experienced married life prior to leaving for combat and it is telling that many unmarried men who had survived their first experiences of combat were married shortly after their return home on leave.

Harry and Elsa would eventually be married at Christ Episcopal Church in Coronado on February 10, 1942. Unfortunately, none of their immediate family was able to attend the wedding, but Harry's sister-in-law, Dora, remembers how they heard all about it:

"They were married by a priest in an Episcopal Church. It is bound to have been a small affair with Harry's Navy friends as guests. I believe there was a small reception or gathering at the Hotel Del Coronado in Coronado, California. Elsa loved that place and often spoke of happy times celebrated there."[32]

Harry passed the intermediate phase of training, received his wings, and was designated a naval aviator on September 23, 1941. On November 6, 1941, he accepted his appointment as an ensign to rank from August 18, 1941. Harry stood fourteenth out of fifty in his class with a total of 226 hours flying time. Harry's next step was operational training that would take a period of eight weeks.[33] This stage would determine what type of aircraft he was best qualified to fly. Operational flight training for fighter pilots such as Harry consisted of formation flying, fighter tactics, air to air gunnery, night flying, cross country navigation hops, aerobatics, glide bombing, carrier landings, and carrier checkouts.[34] Harry was not to be denied and got through all of

Harry March was appointed an ensign in August 1941. *Courtesy the March Family.*

the rigorous training required to become a carrier fighter pilot. He could now rightly be considered a "Top Gun."

The Navy pilots were considered top class as they had to fight in combat from a carrier, fly long distances, and then navigate back. They sometimes returned shot up, damaged and wounded, and had to land their aircraft on a carrier in rolling seas. It was a task that would test even the best of pilots. The last hurdle for Harry, as a carrier pilot, was at the Advanced Carrier Training Group, Pacific Fleet, located at N.A.S. San Diego. He reported there on November 29, 1941.

Throughout 1941, there were many potential Navy aviators going through training and among these were Bill Wileman, Joseph "Dutch" Shoemaker, Donald "Stinky" Innis, Johnny Kleinman, and Jim Halford. As these pilots progressed through their intensive training, close bonds formed that would last throughout Harry's combat career, and these characters would come to feature prominently in his story.

Chapter 1

A Date Which Will Live in Infamy

Yesterday, December 7, 1941—a date which will live in infamy—the United States of America was suddenly and deliberately attacked by naval and air forces of the Empire of Japan.

... Always will we remember the character of the onslaught against us.

No matter how long it may take us to overcome this pre-meditated invasion, the American people in their righteous might will win through to absolute victory.

... Hostilities exist. There is no blinking at the fact that our people, our territory and our interests are in grave danger.

With confidence in our armed forces—with the unbounding determination of our people—we will gain the inevitable triumph— so help us God ...[1]

The above passages from President Franklin Delano Roosevelt's speech galvanized the nation. Immediately after the announcement, Americans volunteered in droves for military service. "Remember Pearl Harbor" was the rallying cry. The whole country geared up for war and the might of the U.S. industrial machine swung into action. America was now at war.

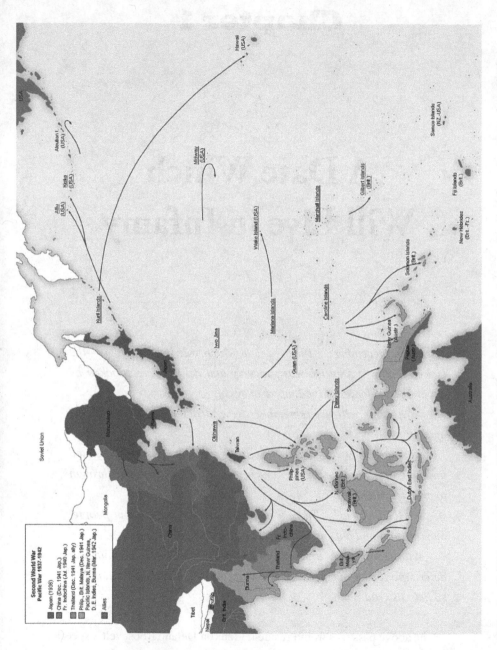

The Pacific War, 1937–1942. What is evident on this map is the vast distance from Japan to the islands

In May 1942, the United States had repelled the Japanese offensive in the Coral Sea, which was the first carrier-based air battle, and although American forces had suffered significant losses, it was the first time the Japanese advance had been stalled. On June 4, 1942, the momentous Battle of Midway saw the destruction of four of Japan's frontline carriers and turned the tide of the Pacific War America's way. The *Enterprise* came through this battle undamaged and returned to Pearl Harbor on June 13, 1942, for overhaul and a period of rest for its crew. Its next mission would be part of the U.S. strategy to halt the Japanese expansion in the Solomon Islands.

For Navy aviators like Harry March, based at San Diego at the time of the Pearl Harbor onslaught, the war became an immediate prospect. Close to completing his final training, it would not be long before he would be sailing into the crucible of war. Harry qualified as a carrier pilot on the *Saratoga* on May 26, 1942, with seven successful landings, although only five were required.[2] This was the closing chapter of his Navy aviation training. He had made it! Harry was ordered to Fighting Squadron Six (nicknamed the "Shooting Stars") based on the *Enterprise*.

The *Enterprise*, known as "The Big E," was named to commemorate six U.S. Navy ships that had previously carried the name.[3] Launched on October 3, 1936, and commissioned on May 12, 1938, the *Enterprise* sailed on her shakedown cruise from July 18 to September 22, 1938. After some early teething problems, the *Enterprise* was based in San Diego and later Pearl Harbor. On November 28, 1941, the *Enterprise* sailed to Wake Island to deliver Marine Squadron VMF-211 to the island. On the return voyage she was delayed due to bad weather and was therefore saved from the Japanese attack on Pearl Harbor on December 7, 1941. "The Big E" had also taken part in the famous "Doolittle Raid" on Tokyo in April 1942.[4]

Harry reported for duty on June 15, 1942, shortly after the Battle of Midway, along with his good friend, Ens. Joseph Donald "Dutch" Shoemaker.[5] Shortly before Harry departed Pearl Harbor he started his diary to record his adventures for his cherished wife, Elsa. Diaries were not permitted for reasons of security, so, as a way around this, he wrote his journal in letter form to Elsa, chronicling his exploits while he was away from home.

View showing the stern quarter of the ship as the carrier *Enterprise*
steams in the Pacific during 1942. Ens. Harry March was assigned
to *Fighting Six* on the *Enterprise* on June 15, 1942. *Courtesy National
Museum of Naval Aviation.*

The night before the *Enterprise* sailed, Harry noted in his diary:

> *Spending the night on board tonight. Leave early in the morning and
> fly on board later in the day. This seems to be the real thing this
> time. I feel that it's either to Wake or someplace down by Australia.
> Let's hope we have plenty of luck!*

On Wednesday, July 15, 1942, the *Enterprise* and Harry, along with
Fighting Six led by Lt. Louis Hallowell Bauer, departed for the Solomon
Islands.[6] Harry had been with the squadron for just over a month and would
soon be in action:

> *First day out. Scuttlebutt has us heading for Tongatapu. Shoved off
> from Pearl today. No telling how long we'll be out. Looks like some-
> thing big may be cooking after we get there.*

After a couple of days at sea, the *Enterprise* was getting closer to the equator:

Wonder what's cooking on the other side of it?

Harry was missing Elsa, his bride of under five months:

Really feel lonesome for the little woman. It's going to be the most wonderful day of my life when I hold her in my arms again.

The *Enterprise* crossed the equator at 1000 on Sunday, July 19, 1942, and the traditional "Crossing the Line" ceremony took place where the "Pollywogs" became "Shellbacks." The "Pollywogs" were sailors who had not crossed the equator before and the "Shellbacks," sometimes called "Sons of Neptune," were sailors who had previously crossed the equator. It was a long-established naval custom to initiate the "Pollywogs" with all manner of dastardly deeds, many of which would by today's standards be considered rough treatment. By July 21, the *Enterprise* was approaching the Samoa Islands, close to Pago Pago:

I've read about this place for years but never thought that I'd get this near to it. Wrote to the little woman today. Just makes me love her all the more. I miss my baby something terrible. Boy, do I love that girl!

By the next day, they were only four hundred miles from Tongatapu and at about 0900 they passed within sight of Tau Island of the Samoa group. The pilots spent the day making shoulder holsters for their guns which they thought would come in handy sometime in the future. The scuttlebutt was still prevalent on Thursday, July 23:

We're pulling in tomorrow morning, filling up with aviation gas and shoving right out again! Must be something to it if they're getting out of there so quick. I think that eventually we'll meet the Wasp, Saratoga and Hornet.

Also heard from a guy in VS-5. He said that the Japs have some carriers (three or four) due down here in this area on August 21. We'll just have to wait and see!

Beautiful moon tonight. It's like the last Saturday night you and I were together in Coronado. When we went down to the rocks together. Gosh, you're a wonderful little woman!

The *Enterprise* docked at Tongatapu at 1030 on Friday, July 24. After swift refueling they left at 1530 with no time wasted. "The Big E" was heading for a rendezvous with Task Force Eleven that included the carriers *Saratoga* and *Wasp*, plus escorts.

This'll be the biggest naval force in the history of the Navy. We may be going to try and take Tulagi and then to Rabaul. It'll be mighty big anywhere we go! Just so I get to see my honey before too many months are up, I don't care where we go—but I hope we really do the job!

Harry was impressed by the size of the force, but the reality was the Americans were not prepared for a large campaign in the Pacific at this time.[7] By Sunday, July 26, it was apparent that a major engagement was imminent:

Boy, are things going to pop! We rendezvoused with the Wasp and the Saratoga and their escorting ships. I counted seventy-three ships in all including us! We even have the Australian three-stack cruisers and some destroyers.

We have at least twenty troop transports with us and mine layers, tankers and oilers. We're probably going to Tulagi. Although it almost looks as though with this force, we could go right up the streets of Tokyo and pay the Emperor a visit.

We're getting pretty near to enemy range, it appears to me. Might meet up with some Jap patrol planes very soon. Boy, it's certainly an awesome sight to see all of those ships out there!

Harry heard what was to become of them on Monday, July 27. The objective was to attack and capture Tulagi and some other islands in that group. The operation was important enough to have the distinguished Adm. Ernest J. King directing it. *Fighting Six* was assigned the job of combat air patrol over the entire fleet when the attack commenced on Tulagi. The other two fighter squadrons were detailed to protect the bombers and strafe land installations:

We're supposed to have the most experienced outfit so we draw the . protection job. Don't know where they get the idea we're experienced! I think it'll happen in about a week. Let's hope the old March luck holds up. Especially with a "Mrs" at home waiting for me!

Harry, despite being a well-trained pilot with 483 flying hours under his belt by the start of July, was, as he admits, inexperienced in aerial combat. The procedure for the next couple of days was for the pilots to standby on alert as the armada of ships was approaching hostile waters. The closer they got, the more inevitable encounters with the enemy became. When they reached the south of the Fiji Islands, they carried out a "dress rehearsal" attack on Koro Island, which was one of the group:

Sure hope it goes off ok. My division drew the combat patrol hop over the task force. On the day, we'll probably have the same job. Heard a very good rumor from a darn good source (no kidding this time). If this raid turns out successful, "The Big E" will go back to Bremerton Navy Yard and all hands will get about thirty days leave. If that's so, I hope we're included in on it. Sure would like to see my baby!

On Thursday, July 30, in preparation for the upcoming operation, Harry flew combat air patrol over the carrier for two and a half hours and then went in to fly support for the transports for nearly two hours while they landed their barges in a practice attack in the Fiji Islands area. It was a very busy morning:

Don't know exactly how things went today, but I hope everybody got something out of it to profit by "Dog Day."

Harry and the squadron practiced gunnery on Saturday, August 1, and received the word that "Dog Day" was to be the following Saturday. This led him to think about whether he would come through it and of his dear Elsa:

Did I ever tell you how much I love you my darling? It's more than you ever thought anyone could love you, I'll tell you that.

Fighting Six lost a pilot on Monday, August 3. Mach. Clayton Allard tried a slow roll at around three hundred feet, misjudged it and went straight into the sea.[8] For naval aviators, accidents were part and parcel of normal operations.

Getting closer to "Dog Day." It may be Friday instead of Saturday. My section flies combat patrol over the ship in the early morning and then we cover the transports later in the morning.

By Tuesday, August 4, tension was growing as the attack force was only four hundred miles from Tulagi. It was apparent to all that they were getting near to enemy action:

Still haven't spotted any enemy planes. We're on combat patrol tomorrow though and I imagine we should meet some four-engine patrol planes. Hope we get as close as we can without being spotted. It'll give us a much easier job of it on "Dog Day." Everyone's in good spirits. Maybe it'll be a little forced from now on. "Dog Day" will probably be Friday now.

A state of heightened awareness was building by Wednesday, August 5, the closer it came to "Dog Day." They would have to take on and beat Japan's battle-hardened Zero pilots. This would be the day that all the training, drills and practices would come to fruition.

At the start of the Pacific War, there were training techniques employed to help pilots gain the experience necessary to counter the highly acclaimed

Japanese Zero. Intelligence obtained from the "Flying Tigers" in 1941 had been fed back to the United States and the brilliant fighter tactician Lt. Cdr. John S. Thach used the information to devise ways to beat the Zero. His now legendary "Thach Weave" was tried successfully at the Battle of Midway and as it proved so effective, was adopted throughout the Navy.[9] The F4F Wildcat was the main Navy fighter at the time. The aircraft was more durable under fire than its counterpart the Zero, thanks to the addition of armor for the pilot and the engine. Six .50-caliber wing-mounted machine guns provided the firepower and self-sealing fuel tanks made the aircraft more resistant to small arms and machine gunfire. However, the lighter, faster, and more agile

Grumman F4F-4 Wildcat fighter of Fighting Squadron Six (VF-6) has its six .50 caliber machine guns tested on the flight deck of the *Enterprise*, April 10, 1942. Note open gun bays in the plane's wings and markings below the cockpit (6F9 with no dashes between letters and numerals). When Harry March was assigned to VF-6 in June 1942, he flew this type of aircraft. *Courtesy National Archives.*

Zero could outclimb and outmaneuver the Wildcat. To stay alive in air-to-air combat, F4F pilots continuously refined their strategies and techniques, relying on teamwork, and accurate marksmanship.[10] For many of the aviators, it would be the first test of whether they were up to the task.

For Harry March and his fellow pilots aboard the *Enterprise*, the nearer their objective, the more the pressure and excitement grew, as did the increasing risk of the task force being discovered by the enemy and attacked at any moment. The uneasiness of the situation was starting to take its toll by Thursday, August 6. The fleet sailed on through a storm, with mist and haze reducing visibility to three miles. By this stroke of good fortune, the aim of remaining undetected by the enemy was achieved:

We've been really lucky! Don't think we've been spotted yet. We're launching tomorrow morning about thirty-five miles from Tulagi. It'll be a plenty busy day too. Eight of us are going to go to Guadalcanal after we capture and set up a squadron with eight from the Saratoga. We're to hold it 'til the Marines come to relieve us. We all volunteered for it. Figure that any place (ship or shore) will be hot from now on.

Won't be long now my pet! We've got most of the dope for "Dog Day" now. Boy, all the VSBs are carrying 1000 lb. bombs. They should really shell that place to pieces. It's going to be a really big day. Our first real offensive movement of the war, I think. It's the biggest naval fleet in history too. I'm glad I'm going to be able to try and do my part honey. The better the job we do, the sooner I'll be home to you—and do I love you!

Chapter 2

I Got One of 'em!

On August 7, 1942, U.S. forces landed on Guadalcanal (codename CACTUS), a name which was unknown at the time, but became legendary by the end of the grisly campaign. The island was of immense strategic importance, it had to be captured. Therefore, ready or not, the decision was made to invade. The island itself had not been part of the original U.S. strategy in the Solomon Islands and was considered of little importance, until they learned in July 1942 of Japan's construction of an airfield on Guadalcanal. This development, together with increased activity in Eastern New Guinea, clearly indicated that Japan was attempting to establish and maintain command of the air and sea in the Solomon Islands area. Securing such control would put the Japanese in a position to launch a seaborne thrust at Port Darwin in Australia and would seriously threaten the Allied communication and supply lines to Australia and New Zealand, as well as to the island bases in the New Hebrides, New Caledonia, and the Fiji Islands. This expansion immediately changed the U.S. operational objectives. The U.S. priority had been the European theater first, then the Pacific, so there were limited ships, aircraft, and supplies to allocate to the Pacific area until the huge industrial might of America got to work.[1]

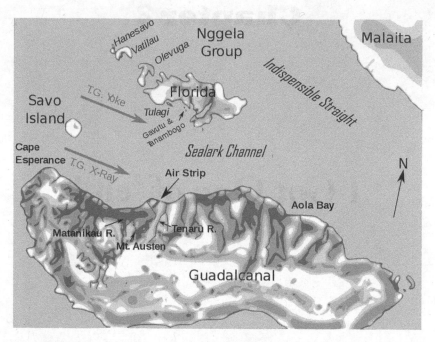

Route of Allied landing forces to Tulagi and Guadalcanal islands,
August 7, 1942. Task Group (T.G.) X-Ray was designated to land at
Guadalcanal and Task Group (T.G.) Yoke to invade Tulagi and Florida
Island. *Source: History of US Marine Corps Operations in World War II.
Pearl Harbor to Guadalcanal.* Hough, Frank O.; Ludwig, Verle E., and
Shaw, Henry I., Jr. (Unknown date).

The hastily planned operation, later nicknamed "Operation Shoestring,"
was put together with what resources were available. The Allies had no option
but to attack the island and Operation WATCHTOWER began. The airfield
was key and the plan was to take what later became known as Henderson
Field (named after Maj. Lofton R. Henderson, the first Marine pilot killed
at the Battle of Midway), then defend it as best they could. Once the U.S.
forces had captured the airfield, they formed a strong defensive perimeter to
protect it. They didn't need to take the whole island initially, just enough to
enable them to make the airfield operational and gain control of the skies in
this area.[2] In the battles that followed, the 1st Marine Division bore the brunt
of the action until December, when they were relieved. The Marines would

gain legendary status and turn the unknown name of Guadalcanal into front-page news in the States for months.

Harry, as a member of *Fighting Six*, was one of the first fighter pilots over Guadalcanal. At the spearhead of the attack, the squadron's role was vital because air cover was paramount to the success of the landings. Harry's task in the hostilities was flying three separate sorties of over two hours each. This led to his first encounter with the Japanese in aerial combat:

August 7, 1942. Today was the day! We took all the islands with very little opposition. I was over Guadalcanal for two hours on my first flight and saw no signs of Japs at all. They probably took to the hills!

In the afternoon, they had some aircraft in on us probably from up Rabaul way. Some of the boys met twenty-two twin-engine bombers and about ten Zeros. We got two bombers and one Zero—possibly more.

May be a big day tomorrow, honey. Hope I get through for you. I love you so much darling.

Oh yeah, my hop met some dive bombers and I got one of 'em. He was practically on the water trying to run away. Don't let anyone tell you that a fellow doesn't get scared when he goes in to something either, honey! It's a funny feeling to kill someone—it's either you or him though.

Harry's flight engaged a large force of enemy bombers. During the ensuing action his flight of six F6Fs shot down six Aichi D3A1 Type 99 dive bombers (later given the code name Val). Harry was officially credited with a dive bomber shot down on this date, which he recorded in his logbook. Considering Harry was a rookie in air combat he had acquitted himself well in his first foray against the Japanese. Harry was flying the F4F-4 Wildcat and the following action report from "The Big E" on August 8, 1942, gives an indication of what he was up against:

The F4F-4, considering equality of pilots, is no match for the Japanese Zero fighter in a dogfight, plane for plane, due to the superiority of the

Zero in climb, speed, maneuverability and endurance. However, in its ruggedness, ability to "take it" and fire power, the F4F-4 is superior to the Zero. These factors of superiority, combined with an apparent superiority of our pilots in deflection shooting, give the F4F-4 a reasonable chance of attaining a successful outcome in an engagement in which there are several fighters involved on both sides. The principal weaknesses of the Zero are (1) inability to absorb hits, and (2) ineffective fire power. The modification of the design of either airplane toward that of the other probably would result in a fighter superior both to the F4F-4 and the Zero.

It is now believed that the best defense for F4Fs against Zero attack is for each plane of the two-plane element to turn away and then turn immediately toward each other and set up a continuous "scissors"; Thus, when a Zero bears on one of the F4Fs the other is in position to fire on the Zero ("Thach Weave"). A short accurate burst from the F4F is generally sufficient to knock down the Zero whereas the F4F can absorb almost unbelievable punishment from the Zero.[3]

During this engagement Harry's squadron-mates, Ens. Earl W. Cook, Mach. Patrick L. Nagle, Mach. William H. Warden, and Mach. Julius A. Achten were listed as missing.[4] This led to the rest of the squadron waiting for news on whether they had survived. These would be the first of numerous comrades to be listed as missing in action.

The day after the landings on Guadalcanal, August 8, 1942, VF-6 were again in the thick of the action and Harry flew another two arduous sorties, resulting in over five hours of flying. His good friend "Dutch" Shoemaker also opened his account with his first victory:

"Dutch" got one today. A type 97 bomber which had dropped a torpedo. Don Runyon (Mach. Donald E. Runyon) *got one and a Zero and Will Rouse* (Ens. Wildon M. Rouse) *got two 97's. Makes fifteen for us all together.*

Still no word about any of the boys missing from yesterday. All we can do is hope. The islands still aren't completely taken yet. Don't know yet whether we're going to the island or not. Think the fleet's leaving tomorrow, so if we don't hear any word tomorrow, looks like we'll stay aboard.

This is really tiresome flying honey. Gosh, I've never been so completely exhausted in all of my life. If we do go to that island, I'll really have some stuff to put down in this book!

On Sunday, August 9, 1942, the *Enterprise* departed—the Navy did not want to risk one of their remaining carriers in an area where they were vulnerable to Japanese aircraft and submarines. This formed a vital part of their strategy to conserve the carriers with a "hit and run" philosophy:

We left the battle scene last night. Just in time too—the Astoria was sunk by a sub when she was still there.

We're heading SE. We're fueling soon and then gosh knows where we'll go next. I don't feel that we're strong enough to head for Rabaul. Never can tell though.

Honey, we will have been married six months tomorrow! A fellow never had a sweeter wife either!

Really had a scare today. They picked up some bogeys on the screen and passed the word to stand-by for an air attack. Boy, my heart dropped clear to the deck (so did everyone else's too). It was really wonderful news when they were identified as B-17s. This doggone war is too nerve-wracking.

On the following day, Monday August 10, 1942, the *Enterprise* refueled and sent mail out. Harry had been married six months and he had been awaiting news from home for some time. He was hoping in a month or two to celebrate his anniversary with his dearest Elsa. It was not clear to Harry where the squadron would be going next and what would happen. The scuttlebutt was that they would form a fighter squadron and be transferred to fight from the island. The intensity of the situation heightened his yearning for Elsa:

Sure wish we were together right now. Baby, I love you more every day—if that's possible. It took me a long time to fall in love, but when I really did fall—boy, I fell!

Four VF-6 pilots pose beside a Grumman F4F-4 on board the *Enterprise*,
August 10, 1942. They were credited with shooting down eight Japanese
aircraft during the Guadalcanal-Tulagi operation a few days earlier. From
left to right: Mach. Donald E. Runyan, credited with four planes; AP1c
Howard S. Packard (one plane); Ens. Joseph D. Shoemaker (one plane);
and Ens. Wildon M. Rouse (two planes). Note shoulder holster rigs
for .45 pistols. Shoemaker was one of Harry March's closest friends.
Courtesy National Archives.

For the next couple of days there was no flying for Harry and life consisted
of reading, catching up on sleep and fun playing poker at night with the skipper, "Dutch" and his buddies. Always in his thoughts was Elsa:

*Am getting an enlargement made from your picture, honey. One of the
fellows at the photo lab is doing it for me. I can't be with you right
now, but I sure do like to have your pictures around me. I love you my
darling—more than anything else in the world.*

The next two weeks brought a period of combat air patrols, awaiting developments, false sightings of Japanese aircraft, the inevitable scuttlebutt, and the prospect of being attacked at any moment. The duty of the *Enterprise* and her pilots in this period was to patrol the southwest area of the Solomon Islands. This positioned the ship ready to intercept any enemy aircraft heading to strike Tulagi.[5] Along with the usual nightly poker game came the uncertainty of what would happen the next day and where the pilots would end up. The recent combat and the prospect of more always led to thoughts of his treasured Elsa:

> *Looks like we may go on up to Bougainville or Rabaul soon. Boy, it'll really be tough going in that case, honey. All the time I think of you though, so everything'll come out ok.*
>
> *Dispatch stated that the field at Guadalcanal was ready for fighters and that the Long Island was bringing a squadron of Marines to Espiritu Santo, but that they were inexperienced and that it would take several weeks of training to get them ready to come into Guadalcanal.*
>
> *I almost feel certain now that we'll go in and operate there 'til they come down. It'll be pretty rough, honey—they'll bomb the place every day!*
>
> *I got the photo lab man to "blow up" your picture for me. In fact, I'm getting two of 'em made. Want to see you all of the time my sweet! Boy—just wait 'til I really do see you again.*
>
> *We're really in dangerous waters though—only 300–350 miles from Tulagi all the time. I love you more with every day—if you only knew how much!*

On August 17, the squadron was delighted to hear that Bill Warden had been picked up after six days in his rubber boat.

> *Everyone was tickled at the news as he is one swell guy.*

Due to the length of time at sea, by the middle of August rations were starting to be reduced with only one egg for breakfast, although the *Saratoga* was worse off—on the *Enterprise* they still had plenty of canned food. "The Big E" refueled and the squadron received the welcome surprise return of another pilot, Mach. Julius "Joe" Achten on August 18. There was no word as to what had happened to him until he returned to the ship. Achten related his lucky escape after he and three other pilots had spotted twenty-five bombers:

"We jumped them and a few minutes later became aware that sixteen Zeros were nearby. The other three planes making the attack were able to get into a rain squall, but I was on the wrong side of the bombers and could not get any protection."

Six Zeros concentrated on Achten and his plane was severely damaged. He managed to land in the sea, near Tulagi, where Marines were being landed by Higgins boats. He brought the battered aircraft down near the boats and was picked up soon after. He was transferred to a transport, and a total of eleven days after he was shot down, he was back on the *Enterprise*. Meanwhile, his wife was sitting in a California motion picture theater and saw a newsreel that showed him being brought aboard a ship. She had not yet been informed that he was alive. It was a bizarre experience and she was overwhelmed with joy at learning of her husband's recovery, even if the circumstances were somewhat strange. Achten injured his neck in the landing, which made it necessary for him to return home for hospital treatment and he was reunited with his wife.[6]

With Achten's recovery, the squadron's average score went up to thirteen planes with the loss of only three pilots. Ensign Cook and Machinist Nagle, listed missing on August 7, were never seen again. Achten saw the fighter cover get nineteen torpedo planes on August 8. "Dutch" and his flight accounted for four of the six that got away.

For all servicemen, whether they were away training or in combat areas thousands of miles from home, the mail was a vital factor in maintaining morale. Its importance could never be overstated. Sometimes, due to the vast area where personnel were deployed, mail took many weeks to catch up. Whenever mail arrived there was a buzz and thoughts of home and loved ones were brought altogether closer:

August 18, 1942. Darling, I wrote you another letter today and it'll go out tomorrow. Better get ready for bed now. Gosh, I'm sick of sleeping by myself—I want you to cuddle up to.

We got mail aboard today. Boy, I got three letters from you today! They were written after the ones I last got at Ewa. Gosh but it's great to hear from you my darling. It makes me miss you so doggone much. We're getting more mail soon, I think. There should be lots more letters from you then. We were married twenty-seven weeks ago tonight, honey. Do you ever regret it?

We lost three heavy cruisers on the 9th and an Australian cruiser. The Astoria, Vincennes and the Quincy. The 'Limey' ship was the Canberra. Pretty big price to pay. I love you darling.

The action Harry was referring to was the Battle of Savo Island. The Japanese response to the U.S. landings on Guadalcanal had been to send a task force to the island, resulting in the first naval engagement there. In the action that followed, they decimated the Allied cruisers protecting the troop transports. Savo Island was a tiny island off the north coast of Guadalcanal and by the end of the war, so many ships had been sunk around there that the nearby waters became known as "Iron Bottom Sound."

August 19, 1942. Four of the fellows went up on a scramble this afternoon, but the bogeys turned out to be B-17s. We may get action soon though—surface vessels are shelling Tulagi and land-based bombers from our bases in the New Hebrides bombed 'em. They were probably Army planes though, so we can't hope that they did any good. The great General MacArthur's Army airmen were supposed to have bombed Tulagi four days running before we got there too—they didn't even show up! Boy, it really makes a fellow see red.

Speaking of the Army, twenty P-39s already in the air failed to even contact twenty-four enemy bombers over Port Moresby.

It's evident from the comments in Harry's diary that he had two major gripes. The first was lack of mail, which was common to all men serving overseas, the second was the Army. There was always rivalry between the services—Army, Navy, and Marines. Rumors were rife during the war and servicemen would not always have access to the facts. However, some of Harry's criticism might be attributed to the pressure he was under and the

Elsa. *Courtesy the March Family.*

natural need to find someone to blame for his frustrations. As his stress in combat intensified, his exasperation with the Army increased, but his mood was always tempered by thoughts of Elsa:

> *Honey, I got two pictures of you from the photo lab today. They turned out doggone well. Now I have more and larger pictures of you to look at! Gee, but you're cute—and I do love you!*

On August 20, 1942, the first aircraft arrived on Henderson Field to support the land forces there. The U.S. Navy had retreated due to the constant threat of the Japanese Navy as they couldn't risk their few remaining aircraft carriers. The aircraft were the only source of protection for the

Marines on the island and they became known as the "Cactus Air Force" after the code name for the island. The "Cactus Air Force" consisted of Marine, Army, and Navy units that included VF-5 under the command of Lt. Cdr. LeRoy Coard Simpler from the *Saratoga*, along with eight pilots from VF-6. When the *Saratoga* was damaged, her air group was assigned to Espiritu Santo and Guadalcanal.[7] The Japanese were desperate to retake the island. The U.S. forces were drastically outnumbered but had to hold on. The daily routine was one of constant air attacks, sea bombardments, shortage of supplies, shelling from land forces, and poor living conditions, which resulted in the spread of tropical diseases.

The *Enterprise* was positioned well away from Guadalcanal but was still too close for comfort to the enemy forces. On Thursday, August 20, 1942, enemy ships were reported as being in the area:

> *General Quarters sounded about 1400 and sent six of the fellows up to investigate bogeys on the screen. Nothing came of it though. We're really in a hornet's nest here. We're one hundred and eighty miles from Tulagi today and our search planes sighted an enemy cruiser, two destroyers and two submarines.*
>
> *Don't know how long we'll stay around this hornet's nest. I'd like to get back to Pearl soon 'cause maybe then I'll get a chance to go on back to the States. Wouldn't that be wonderful honey? Gee but I'm lonesome for you!*

It was inevitable that contact would soon be made with the enemy as recapturing Henderson Field was of vital importance to the Japanese. By Friday, August 21, 1942, it was clear to Harry and all aboard the *Enterprise* that action would soon be upon them. General Quarters sounded at 0620 and combat air patrols were undertaken all day. The tension was mounting with every hour and the apprehension turned Harry's thoughts to Elsa and whether he would survive the ensuing encounter:

> *Something may be up tomorrow, honey. Today the Japs tried unloading troop transports at Guadalcanal (the Marines killed 680 and*

captured 20 out of 700!) and tomorrow we're expecting a follow up of it.

We're pretty close to it again and hope to do a little damage to the fleet of the Rising Sun tomorrow. Hope there are no carriers—we shall be able to massacre 'em if there isn't.

Darling, I think about you more every day. Just can't wait 'til the day when I'll be back with you—once more in your arms and loving you and having you love me. Goodnight for now and always remember that I love you more than anything.

What became known as the Battle of the Tenaru River was the first major Japanese land offensive at Guadalcanal. The American 1st Marine Division was dug in, well-prepared, and ready for the attack.[8] They proved they were more than a match for the much-lauded Japanese who were annihilated, losing 800 men. The U.S. Marines lost 34.[9]

Despite the anxiety of the previous day, no sightings of the enemy materialized at all, even though they were only 60–65 miles from Guadalcanal in the morning. There was some good news, however, as Lt. Albert Ogden "Scoop" Vorse, Jr's., section was vectored out after a bogey and it turned out to be a Japanese four-engine patrol plane. "Scoop" Vorse shot it down using only about twenty-five rounds of ammunition. That raised his total to five and made him an ace.

Throughout the war in the Pacific, there was a constant threat from enemy submarines and aircraft carriers were a key target. The *Enterprise* was the victim of an attack by a submarine that fired a torpedo at 1800. Fortunately, it missed, but it was one of several alerts:

Just hope they keep on missing. I'd give anything to be with you now! That time will come though, won't it? Gee but I love you my darling.

With hostilities inevitable, a Japanese force heading in their direction was reported by a patrol boat on Sunday, August 23. Two cruisers, three destroyers, and seven transports were due to hit Tulagi by 0200 the following morning. The trepidation and pressure of forthcoming combat were starting to tell on Harry:

Looks like the higher-ups dropped the ball. We messed around until it was too late to launch an attack group. The Saratoga did and it was supposed to land at Lunga tonight. The group had two hundred and seventy miles to go to attack and the weather was bad as heck. We may have a tough time tomorrow.

What was later to be called the Battle of the Eastern Solomons or the Battle of the Stewart Islands emerged the next day, August 24, 1942. The *Enterprise* had so far avoided any battle damage, despite being in the danger zone for some time. Her luck finally ran out when "The Big E" was involved in a battle with a large Japanese task force heading for Guadalcanal. For Japan, the situation at Guadalcanal was becoming desperate. The U.S. forces had gained a foothold on the island and had begun to intensify their operations. The Japanese stronghold at Rabaul would be susceptible to an air offensive if they didn't retake the island. The Japanese launched a full-scale attack and their strategy was to finally defeat the American carriers that had so far evaded them. Their other objective was to land additional forces on Guadalcanal and finally secure the island. They sent ahead the light carrier *Ryūjō*, along with escorts, to cover the troop transports heading to Guadalcanal. This was in advance of the main carrier task force, consisting of *Shōkaku* and *Zuikaku*, two of the six carriers involved in the Pearl Harbor attack. They also launched bombers with fighter cover against the U.S. carriers.[10]

U.S. Intelligence in the Solomon Islands had gathered information by the afternoon of August 24, which indicated that an attack was imminent. The Grumman F4F Wildcat fighters of Fighting Squadron Six were assigned to protect the U.S. Task Force in what would be one of the most significant battles for Guadalcanal. "Twenty-seven Japanese planes downed in single action by pilots of *Fighting Six*" was how the actions of the heroic pilots of VF-6 were described in reports received by the Navy Department after the attack.[11] *Fighting Six* lost two pilots and four planes in the altercation and one plane had to make a water landing due to lack of fuel, although the pilot was rescued.[12] A press release at the time stated:

Navy Pilot from D.C. Assists in Felling Eight Japanese Planes.

Ens. Harry March, Jr., of Washington was mentioned in a dispatch as one of a group of four American pilots who shot down eight Japanese torpedo planes in the Solomon Islands in action late in August.

According to reports, Ens. H. A. March, Jr., "let a tentative burst go at long range at a torpedo plane and caught it square and down it went."[13] Harry was one of only five fighter pilots available to defend the *Enterprise* against a dive-bombing and torpedo attack. The attack was successfully repulsed and Harry was officially credited with one Nakajima B5N2 Type 97 torpedo bomber (later code-named Kate). It was Harry's second confirmed victory:

Hell of a day today. We attacked Jap carriers and they got us. I think we sank one and possibly two of theirs. They hit "The Big E" about four times and a couple of near misses. Quite a lot of damage. A big hole in the side right at the water line—twenty-five guns washed out and the crew killed—about seventy-five dead and one hundred wounded. It's really hell, honey.

My flight was on combat patrol and after several bad vectors we jumped on eight VTs and VBs about sixty miles from the ship. They were very low and going like hell. We got six of 'em and chased the other two 'til they were about 90 miles away from the fleet.

Both sides suffered losses and neither could claim a decisive victory. As a result of the battle, the Japanese reinforcements to Guadalcanal were delayed, and this gave the Americans time to prepare for the next assault on the island. After this frantic engagement, the pilots returned to find chaos aboard the battered ship:

We came back and landed. We only have nine pilots here, don't know how many are on the "Sara." "Dutch" isn't here and neither is Bill. Sure hope they're okay. "Bud" (Lt. (jg) Henry E. Hartmann) *is back okay. I think we're retiring now—which suits me fine. I love you darling—that's what keeps me going!*

Chapter 3

Torpedoed!

Although the Japanese were repulsed and had lost the light carrier *Ryūjō*, the *Enterprise* was also seriously damaged and had to return to Pearl Harbor for repairs. The devastation on "The Big E," meant it would take until October before the *Enterprise* was ready for battle again.[1] The aftermath of the battle had serious consequences for the VF-6 pilots who, as the *Enterprise* was out of action, were deployed to the *Saratoga*. The *Saratoga* was an old carrier, originally converted from a battlecruiser to a carrier in the 1920s.[2] Compared to the *Enterprise*, the facilities aboard the *Saratoga* were antiquated:

> *August 25, 1942. Yesterday was the bluest day I've had since I left you. They told me to fly over to the Saratoga and to come back two hours later. Well, I did and they kept me on this damn tub. They kept all of VF-6 that was here on it and eighteen of 'em landed here last night after the attack.*
>
> *The skipper's going back and taking our Engineering Officer with him. A destroyer's picking up our gear tonight and bringing it over here. Gosh, all the fellows are really sore. We had such a wonderful*

outfit—and the one on here is so lousy. The ship itself can't hold a candle to "The Big E" in any way. The skipper was broken up pretty badly too 'cause he had gotten to think a whole lot of his outfit.

"The Big E" may go back to the States, but I sort of doubt it. They can probably fix her up at Pearl. I'm in some dump. Slept last night on a lounge in the wardroom. Most of us did that. The only thing that's any good about the whole set-up is that they're going to let all of us old VF-6 bunch operate together.

There was no comparison between "The Big E" and the *Saratoga*, which had taken on board many pilots from the *Enterprise*, so it is little wonder that Harry was unhappy about his new, cramped quarters. Despite his success in the air two days previously, Harry's mood was no better on Wednesday, August 26, 1942. He was scheduled to fly four hours combat air patrol after practically no sleep for the last two nights. When he landed back on the ship, he was weary and blue:

What a hell hole this place is! Practically no food aboard—everyplace is hot as hell—and the way they operate the thing can't come near "The Big E's" crew. Right now, I'm in a hot, stuffy, one-man room with two of us in it. The water is running off of me and I'm still bitched off (excuse the language my darling, but it's the way I feel). "Dutch" doesn't even have a room! He's stuck off in a room with six other guys. Since I'm the Senior Ensign I happened to get this room with one of the other boys.

I'm getting tired of fighting—want to get back to you. I'm glad some of my gear got over here 'specially all of your pictures. I feel better now that you're here with me. Better go to bed now, darling—am pretty tired.

There was some welcome news for Harry the following morning, with the arrival of more of his personal items, on Thursday, August 27. This led, as always, to thoughts of Elsa:

There's nothing to do on this tub, like there was on "The Big E." And boy, is it hot here! "Dutch" and three others flew some planes over to the Wasp today. They're to stay for a day or two. If they get to stay for good, they'll get a break. Checked up on my gear and I got most of it ok. They didn't send me my maps though. I had some maps on which I charted our course and put the battles in, etc. I'll have to make up another for you to see now.

Gosh honey, it'll be such fun to go over a lot of this stuff with you. I hope to have a lot of money by then to put with what you have now. We'll really get along in good shape, won't we? I love you too, my baby—or do you already know that?

Friday, August 28, was an early start for Harry and his division and resulted in nearly four hours of combat air patrol, even though they weren't

L-R: VF-6 division consisting of pilots Harry March, William Wileman, Patrick Nagle, and Harold Rutherford in July 1942. William Wileman and Harry March had been good friends since training together. *Courtesy National Museum of Naval Aviation.*

originally scheduled to fly. They were launched at 0700 after being on stand-by and were sent out after bogeys, one of which turned out to be a B-17. After landing, it was then time to reflect on what his buddy "Dutch" was doing and his sweetheart Elsa:

"Dutch" is still on the Wasp. Bet that rascal is having a picnic over there. Listened to some good records after supper—fell asleep and then came up to write you a letter and then to bed as soon as I finish this. I haven't had as much of this war as a lot of the fellows, but I've had plenty. The quicker they let me get back to your arms, the better I'm going to like it. We'll get along okay though, won't we my sweetheart? I love you—gooood-night!!

Following two sorties, resulting in over six hours of combat air patrol on Saturday, August 29, 1942, Harry and his buddies blew off steam and had a great time in the evening raising their glasses for "Dutch's" twenty-second birthday:

We celebrated "Dutch's" birthday tonight. Bill broke out a bottle and we had a good bull session. Looks like Fighting Six is the only outfit that can fly on this tub. The hell with it—the only time I feel like anything is when I'm in the air now anyway. I'll fly all day now if they want. Landed on the Wasp after our first hop. Met a lot of the old boys. Found out that two of my buddies from E-Base are gone now. Good boys too.

Baby—I love you so doggone much. Gee, when you said you'd marry me, that was when my life began. When you read this book, honey, you'll really have in writing how much I love you, won't you? Better get some sleep now.

Further combat air patrols were scheduled for the following day and Harry was assigned to fly as wingman to Ens. Bill Wileman, who had previously been awarded the Navy Cross at the Battle of the Coral Sea.[3] Along with "Dutch" Shoemaker, he was one of Harry's closest friends. Harry,

although downcast about being on the *Saratoga*, would find things going
from bad to worse:

> *Doggone but it's hot on this tub. When we get near "The Big E" again,*
> *I'm never going to leave it out of my sight. Gee, we all really miss that*
> *ship. Oh yes—since I came on board this tub, I haven't shaved! Don't*
> *give a damn how I look. Shaved the day after the battle—25th—will*
> *shave again the night before we hit some port.*
> *Sweetheart, I love you so much. I have $172 now and a pay day*
> *tomorrow with $130 due. I'll have plenty of money for you, sweets!*
> *We may hit the Japs again soon—we're heading north.*

There followed a period of intense unpredictability after VF-6 had
departed the *Enterprise*. Harry, along with his buddies, waited to see what
would happen next:

> *August 31, 1942. Two things happened today, honey. We had butter*
> *with our meals and we were hit by a torpedo!*
> *Had General Quarters at 0400 this morning and nothing came of it.*
> *At 0745, three or four torpedoes were fired at us and one caught us on the*
> *starboard and damaged our electric engines very badly. We were dead in*
> *the water and listing badly for a long time. We're darn lucky we haven't been*
> *hit more. The way our "high-priced help" has been running this thing!*

In hostile waters, the threat of being attacked by submarines was a
constant danger. It would not have been an easy maneuver for a large carrier
like the *Saratoga* to take evasive action to avoid three or four torpedoes.
The extent of the damage necessitated the *Saratoga* to return to port as a
matter of urgency. Two of the squadrons based on the ship, VS-3 and VT-8,
took off and went to Espiritu Santo to operate from there. What would happen
to the fighter squadrons was undecided:

> *Things are so messed up we don't know what we'll do. Gee, wouldn't*
> *it be wonderful if this goes back to Bremerton and I get to stay on it!*

Darling, that would be the most wonderful thing that could happen. Better close now and get some sleep. I love you, sweetheart.

The feeling was that if they were ordered to one of the islands, particularly Guadalcanal, life would be rough for sure and there was no telling how long they would be there. It seems this was enough to make Harry appreciate the limited comforts of the *Saratoga*. The twenty-two guys in the squadron cut the cards and Harry drew the ace of hearts, which meant he would be the first to stay on the ship. A letter to Elsa and a game of cards were all that made up that evening's entertainment:

Have been playing poker again and still winning some. Just play little games, but I had $94 on August 15 and I have $184 tonight and didn't draw any pay yesterday. If I keep up like that, I'll have

The *Saratoga* under repair at Tongatapu, Tonga Islands, in September 1942. She had been torpedoed by a Japanese submarine on August 31, 1942. Note: The list seen in this photo is probably deliberate, to bring the damaged part of *Saratoga's* hull out of the water. She had been hit on the starboard side, amidships. *Courtesy National Archives.*

a little extra money for you. I love you my sweetheart—more than you can imagine.

The torpedo hit to the *Saratoga* resulted in VF-6 being detached again and ordered to fly to Efate, in the Vanuatu island chain. The squadron took off at 0930 for a hundred-mile flight and after eventually finding the island, they landed and were taken to Iririki, a few minutes ferry ride from Efate. For *Fighting Six* it would prove to be an ideal place for some much-needed R & R:

We're all living in tents on the side of a hill. No modern conveniences, but it still feels good to relax. Don't know how long we'll be here—or where we'll go from here. Saw a movie for the first time since we left Pearl. We have real good, substantial food and have nothing special to do. Really should be a good rest.

Once they had settled in, the ensuing day was an eye-opener for the pilots of VF-6. They went into town, shopped for some souvenirs and bought some French and English notes and coins:

Had a good day today. Gee honey, I wish I had a camera to get some real pictures for you. Boy, you should see the natives around here!

Got cold as heck last night. It's fine to sleep through and see daylight though—something different from what we're used to.

I want to hurry up and come home to you though, honey. "The Big E" is on its way home now, I think. It must be fate or something that caused me to have to fly to the Saratoga. Otherwise, I'd be coming home to you.

The *Enterprise* returned to Pearl Harbor for over a month of urgent repairs to the damage sustained in the Battle of the Eastern Solomons. The pilots spent their time relaxing and taking it easy, which they would come to be grateful for, considering the grueling duty that was awaiting them. One downside was the start of the rainy season in the area, although despite the downpours, Bill, "Dutch," and Jim (Ens. James Alexander Halford, Jr.)

went fishing. Halford had come through the Battle of Midway, for which he was awarded a D.F.C.[4]

Until confirmation of their next assignment came through, there was some apprehension about what was to follow. Information as to where the squadron would be going was still shrouded in secrecy. The *Kitty Hawk* dispatched aircraft and men and transferred them to the *Long Island* and thirty-five fighters flew in to Guadalcanal from there. In the next few days, a bunch of the men, along with Harry, went to town to try to find (by begging, if necessary) some heavy shoes, which would be the best thing to wear in the torrential rain. But they had no luck. They were able to pick up some little trinkets, such as a bow and arrow from some of the local inhabitants, which they used for shooting fish. After the day's activities, the attention turned to a bull session and watching a movie, which was the same for two nights running. Even though it rained during most of the show, it didn't deter the men who all stayed out in the wet weather and saw the whole thing through. The usual letters to Elsa were on hold due to the erratic nature of the post from this island and the uncertainty as to where the squadron would go next. Harry loafed around all Sunday morning, September 6, and then went over to the airfield in the afternoon. At last, he managed to scrounge a pair of big shoes and won twenty-three dollars shooting crap. The scuttlebutt was that one of the Marines at the airfield had just made first lieutenant. He said an All-Navy Circular came out saying that all commissions dated August 30 or before were advanced, which meant Harry may have been promoted to lieutenant junior grade, but didn't know it yet. He had to wait to find out the answer, but the prospect of eighty dollars more a month was most appealing. There was still no word as to what the squadron was going to do or when they would be assigned new orders.

While Harry was at the airfield, four fighter pilots from the *Wasp* flew in from Noumea (WHITE POPPY) to take four of the squadron's planes to replace their damaged aircraft. This would leave the squadron short of planes. The four reassigned aircraft were going to the *Wasp* in the morning, which led Harry to wonder:

Maybe they'll take our planes away and send us home on the Kitty Hawk—wishful thinking!

With the situation as it was on Guadalcanal, it was wishful thinking indeed. Pilots were sorely needed to defend the island from constant enemy attack. The subsequent day, Monday, September 7, entailed going over to one of the islands to get the laundry sorted and the evening duty revolved around a double-feature movie, which again was the same as the previous night. There was still no word as to what was going to happen or where they would be going:

We're still the lost battalion!

The squadron should have made the most of the easy life they had in the rear area, because the time was drawing near when they would give anything to be back there again. Eight planes and pilots were sent to Espiritu Santo on Tuesday, September 8, with the intention that they would leave the planes and then return to Efate. The squadron had the opportunity to blow off some steam on Tuesday afternoon, as some pilots from the Army's 26th Bombardment Squadron challenged them to a softball game at midday. After the game, their major invited the men to their barracks for some drinks and it was a pleasant surprise for Harry:

Doggone if they didn't have real American stuff! The first real blow-out any of us have had in two months. Most of the Army guys were pretty good eggs. They admit that they can't hit any surface vessels with their B-17s.

The latest scuttlebutt on Wednesday, September 9, was that six mechanics were being sent up to CACTUS and something about planes and pilots going up the following week. Those in command of the operations to secure Guadalcanal made every effort to ensure Henderson Field was completed and operational at the earliest opportunity. Rumors about the mechanics proved to be accurate, as the planes arriving there had to be kept in flying condition at all costs. They also had to secure the area and improve defenses around the airfield so that operations could be maintained and missions intercepting the Japanese bombers could be undertaken. Due to the grim state of affairs at Guadalcanal, any Army, Navy, and Marine aircraft that were available were called upon to repel the Japanese attacks.

As a result of the incessant rain, Harry spent the whole day reading and in old-fashioned bull sessions:

This whole tent will be a bunch of jabbering idiots if this is what it's going to be like in the rainy season.

After supper, the guys had a bridge game until the order came for lights-out when five unidentified ships were spotted near the island. Harry just wanted to get on with the war and was missing his darling Elsa:

Still no dope as to what we're going to do yet. Washington probably doesn't even know that we're here! Don't care where they put me as long as I get home to you before very much longer. Sweetheart, I think of you so much now—dream of you almost every night.

On Thursday, September 10, Harry and Elsa had been married seven months:

Our anniversary today, my sweet. Gosh, this island is a hell of a place for me to be spending it, isn't it? May the next one or two months bring me home to you—wishful thinking!

Honey, I think often of how nice it'll be when we're together again. If I can only get shore duty when I get back. That'll be a so much nicer life for you too. And honey, I've been thinking over the prospect of my not staying in the Navy as we first planned. After this is all over, we should have quite a sum of money saved, and putting it with the five hundred dollars a year that they'll give me when I leave active duty, we'll have a nice nest egg. Settle down in a little place and I'll start coaching and we'll live a quiet life. That'll be better for you, my baby.

After reflecting on his anniversary and his future plans with Elsa, Harry spent the morning reading and then was preparing to fly after lunch. The flying was curtailed as the ceiling closed in and it started raining, so it was called off until the following day. Harry's division was a close-knit unit led by "Larry" Grimmell (Lt. (jg) Howard Laurence Grimmell, Jr.) with "Dutch" as his wingman, and Bill Wileman, with Harry as his number two. The rumors surrounding the defense of CACTUS came to fruition:

> *Looks like we may be elected to go up to Guadalcanal try to do the job that the Army should be doing. A few Marines have been doing all the flying there and attacks come over every day—thirty-six bombers with thirty-six Zeros. Not a nice thing to think about.*
>
> *Because of the Army falling down on their job we may lose that place. No Army reinforcements have gone in yet. Boy, is MacArthur and his men dropping the ball! They really are over-rated and haven't helped the Marines or Navy one bit.*
>
> *We'll do our best to all come back to you all, honey.*

Harry's notion of the campaign was formed from his view of a small part of the overall strategy. In actual fact, the Guadalcanal Campaign was a naval operation.[5] The Navy had to use all the resources at their disposal, but they were in short supply. Harry had no idea what awaited him and his comrades in the coming weeks as operations progressed. When Harry left the United States, he had probably never heard of Guadalcanal. By the time he left the "Island of Green Hell," it was a place he would never forget!

Chapter 4

"Dirty Eddie"

During September 1942, Guadalcanal was besieged from the sea and shelled by Japanese naval vessels, bombed by enemy aircraft and subject to the constant threat of troops and snipers.

Leading the squadron into the devastation at CACTUS was Lt. Cdr. LeRoy Coard Simpler, a native of Lewes, Delaware, who would later be awarded the Navy Cross for "extraordinary heroism" for his time at Guadalcanal[1]. After more than a week spent relaxing at Efate, the pilots of VF-6 would become land-based and attached to VF-5, along with many other units, to support the defense of Guadalcanal. The squadron flew from Efate to Espiritu Santo and then into Guadalcanal, where they arrived at 1600 on Friday, September 11, 1942:

> *Wish me plenty of luck my baby. Boy, they really were happy to see us come here. It's been plenty tough going all the time. No living conditions at all here, honey—really nature in the raw. Probably have our first air raid on land tomorrow. I'll be thinking of you always.*

Prophetic words indeed. The next day, as predicted, Harry was in the thick of the action. After flying missions to ambush enemy aircraft, they were

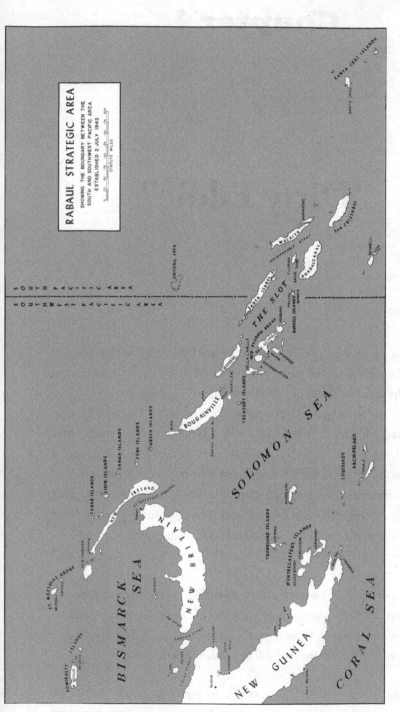

Rabaul Strategic Area, August 1942-February 1943. During the Guadalcanal Campaign the Japanese had air bases at Rabaul, Buka, Buin on Bougainville and Munda, New Georgia. The Allies' "Cactus Air Force" was based on Henderson Field, Guadalcanal.

Indicated on the map in New Georgia Sound is "The Slot" which was a narrow channel named by the Allied forces due to its shape and the large number of ships which used it.

In order for the Japanese to re-supply their forces on Guadalcanal, they sent in ships under the cover of darkness so they faced with potential attacks from land, sea, and air. Combined with the primitive living conditions, it was a matter of surviving as best they could:

September 12, 1942. Air raid today about noon. We were in the air but hit 'em just after they dropped. We were at 28,000 feet—they were at 25,000. We got eleven bombers and three or four Zeros. I didn't get any. A Zero got on me and I didn't know it 'til one of the guys yelled to me. I turned in to him and he ran.

This is some place here, darling. Two meals a day and an air raid or two every day plus shelling by surface vessels on a lot of nights. It's pretty tough though 'cause the "high-priced help" just seem to forget about the place. Really could use reinforcements in both planes and men. Japs are on the island here and the front line is only two or three miles from here.

Baby, when I get out of here, I'm sure going to come home to you.

Harry recorded in his diary a song that summed up the feeling of the pilots who flew at Guadalcanal, that was written by a Marine ace, 2nd Lt. Charles Kendrick of VMF-223, who was credited with shooting down five Japanese aircraft before he was killed in action on October 2, 1942:

To the tune of "The Road to Mandalay":

By the old Guadalcanal Pagoda
Where the Generals and Colonels hide
They've cooked up a tough assignment
For Fighting Squadron Five
As the wind howls thru the palm trees
You hear operations say
Fill the belly tanks with juice boys
Take the scouts to Gizo Bay (repeat)

Chorus:

Hit the road to Gizo Bay
Where the Jap fleet spend the day

You can hear the duds a chunkin
From Rabaul to Lunga Quay
Pack a load to Gizo Bay
Where the float plane Zeros play
And the bombs come down like thunder
On the natives cross the bay
Take us somewhere east of Ewa
Where the best ain't like the worst
Where there ain't a Doug MacArthur
And a man can drown a thirst
For the Army takes the medals
And the Marines they take the prize
But the ones who take the rookin'
Are the boys of Fighting Five

The gratitude of the men at the sharp end was illustrated by another ditty written for Fighting Squadron Five by a Marine (private first class) at Guadalcanal. He wrote it on the frontline and brought it up to the squadron ready tent. Harry copied it into his diary:

To the Tune of "Ramblin' Wreck from Geo Tech":[2]
We are Fighting Five and man alive
We're really destructive guys
We're rootin', tootin', hootin', shootin'
Masters of the skies.
We saw the yellow fellows
Just where they all can go
So they head pell-mell
Right straight for hell
Instead of Tokyo
Now if we had a penny Mac
For every slant-eye we've shot
We'd have a pile of "Jack"
To cover a city block
So when those pesky slant eyes

Bring their aircraft out to play
We will slap the Jap out of the skies
For the good old U.S.A

The reaction of the men was not surprising, as Harry was to quickly experience for himself. A major land battle ensued the day after his arrival on Guadalcanal (September 12, 1942), later known as the Battle of Edson's Ridge (named after the Marine Commander, Lt. Col. Merritt Edson), or the Battle of Bloody Ridge. As night fell, some of the fiercest fighting for the island took place, with shelling throughout the night. The enemy forces were repelled within a few hundred yards of the airfield. This was the closest the Japanese came to capturing Henderson Field.[3] From this point on, Harry and his comrades were subject to a gradual physical and mental deterioration. The loss of many friends and fighting men was to become commonplace and for many men serving there, it was more than they could cope with. After Guadalcanal, life would never be the same, as Harry was to shortly find out:

September 13, 1942. Sunday evening. Hell of a day today. They shelled us all night last night and we had a 0530 take-off this morning. Two attacks came in. Bill was in trouble and tried to get home and spun in while landing. Gee, it was like losing a brother to lose that boy. This is really hell, honey—don't see how a man can stand so much of it.

Wasn't up with Bill, but didn't contact anything. Did see lots of Zeros, but we didn't bother them and they didn't bother us. Don't know when Bill got in trouble. He was having engine trouble and couldn't get up very high.

Spent most of last night in the foxholes dodging shells—will do so tonight too. They have a big task force going to attack us, I think. The people back home will never believe what the guys on this place are going through. We're all so damn tired—just seems that no matter how hard we fight, it won't do any good—we'll get no help and a great number of us won't make it.

I'll have to write to Dorothy—it'll be tough to do. Good night for now, my darling—I'll always love you.

Bill Wileman was shot down and killed on September 13, 1942, a few days after arriving at Guadalcanal. He was one of Harry's best friends. Lt. Cdr. Simpler wrote to Bill's wife, Dorothy Connors Wileman, with the sad news:

Dear Mrs. Wileman,

It is with the most sincere regret that I must inform you of the death of your husband, William Wolfe Wileman, who died as result of injuries suffered when his plane was damaged in action with the enemy so that he was unable to avoid a crash landing. Bill had taken off on a flight at 0930 with other pilots of the squadron to intercept an attacking group of enemy planes. Upon returning at or about 1120 his plane was seen to be partly out of control from damage to it. His attempt to land his plane upon the field was unsuccessful and he crashed just short of the field. He was thrown clear and help arrived within thirty seconds of the crash, but he died immediately without regaining consciousness.

Every man in the squadron has felt the loss of your husband as a personal friend, including myself, and I can sincerely and truthfully say that your loss is our loss. Bill was an excellent pilot and distinguished himself in his profession as a naval aviator. While I sincerely appreciate how deep must be your grief because of his loss, I do hope that some solace may be afforded you in the knowledge that your husband lived as you would want him to live and that he was a credit to the Naval Service.

Speaking for Fighting Squadron Five, for myself as well as for the officers and men, I again express our heartfelt sympathy to you in the loss of your husband.[4]

The same day as the loss of Bill, another of Harry's close friends, Ens. Donald "Stinky" Innis, was engaged in air combat against Japanese aircraft. He was struck by gunfire from an enemy plane and his aircraft burst into flames, resulting in first- and second-degree burns to his face, neck, arms, and legs. "Stinky" survived but was admitted to hospital for an indefinite stay. Harry also learned that Ens. Charles E. "Ike" Eichenberger had been killed and another close friend, Ens. Richards Llewellyn "Dick" Loesch, Jr., had been shot down.

In just two days, he had experienced a major land battle, Bill and "Ike" were dead, and "Stinky" and "Dick" were missing. This was just the start.

The next day, the situation on Guadalcanal was still grim. A feature of the Japanese offensive was to use a bomber known as "Washing Machine Charlie" to attack at night. The engines were out of synchronization and had a particular characteristic sound (hence the nickname), the aim being to disrupt the sleep of the U.S. forces.[5] Snipers were also evident and this, together with the incessant night bombing, had a significant effect on Harry's morale:

While I'm writing this our 75mm howitzers are firing over my head—air raid alarm just came over—oh well, so it's an air raid. I don't seem

The men of VF-5 in September 1942 on Guadalcanal. "Dirty Eddie" March is fourth from left, back row and Jim Halford is in the front row 5th from left, with his helmet in front of him. *Courtesy James A. Halford collection.*

to give a damn anymore. Last night at this time (1800) two float-type
Zeros came over and shot down two SBDs in the landing circle and got
away. Very poor on our part. Four of 'em came over today and we got
'em all. I've just been sick (I'll finish this in the morning—I'm using a
flash light and Jap snipers are very close).

From his comments, it's clear Harry was suffering. He seemed to have
stopped caring and this may have led to him obtaining his nom de guerre.
According to Ens. Wilbert Peter "Beads" Popp, Harry reputedly got the nickname "Dirty Eddie" due to his lifestyle on Guadalcanal. He didn't change
his clothes and seldom shaved, resulting in him sporting a thick, black
beard.[6] Harry later related his version of the story to a war correspondent:
"There didn't appear to be any reason for getting particularly slicked up, and
after an unusually tough day of flying I had slept in my clothes. My buddy
took one look at me the next morning and said 'My God, Dirty Eddie!' and
the nickname just stuck."[7]

The next morning the constant shelling and the effects of sleep depriva-
tion were taking their toll on "Dirty Eddie":

Felt like hell all Sunday night. No sleep and had to throw up. Heavy
battle in the woods all night. Japs broke through our lines and snipers
were in the trees alongside the field.

The last two nights I have slept in foxholes, or at least, stayed in
foxholes—no sleep. This air raid that just happened made the third
today. I didn't fly any—too sick. About fifteen sea planes came over and
did some glide bombing on us. One bomb hit about thirty yards from
the hole I was in. Our boys knocked down ten of 'em. "Dutch" got his
plane shot up, but he didn't get hit any.

Everyone is so tired around here. When the raid came over this
evening (Monday) I was with Major Galer—skipper of VMF-224. He just
said to let the raid come—he'd jump in a hole. He said that the pilots are
all too worn out. He's been here three weeks—the other Marine outfit
longer than that—and we were all at sea for two months before coming
here. Why in the world can't the big boys realize that a flyer can stand so

much and that's all. No sleep, not much to eat, no bathing for two or three days at a time. Gosh, it's really a hell of a war.

Maj. Robert E. Galer was awarded the Medal of Honor at Guadalcanal for "conspicuous heroism and courage above and beyond the call of duty." His citation, in part, was as follows:

Leading his squadron repeatedly in daring and aggressive raids against Japanese forces, vastly superior in numbers, Major Galer availed himself of every favorable attack opportunity, individually shooting down eleven enemy bomber and fighter aircraft over a period of twenty-nine days. Though suffering the extreme physical strain attendant upon protracted fighter operations at an altitude above 25,000 feet, the squadron under his zealous and inspiring leadership, shot down a total of twenty-seven Japanese planes. His superb airmanship, his outstanding skill and personal valor reflect great credit upon Major Galer's fighting spirit and upon the U.S. Naval Service.[8]

The situation was not much better on Tuesday afternoon, September 15, 1942, and "Dirty Eddie" was still experiencing the physical effects of combat stress:

Tojo hasn't made any raids so far today. Maybe he's getting tired of losing so many of his planes. We had two false alarms, but not the real thing so far. Doggone it, I still can't hold anything on my stomach. Yesterday I had half a dozen prunes in the morning and same number of peaches in the afternoon. This morning I had a cup of hot chocolate and just had another. I can't seem to hold anything else in my stomach. Get cramps all of the time.

Last night I had my only night's sleep—went out in the middle of the field and slept with some enlisted men by their guns. The troops were firing all night, but I had a good sleep anyway. We're still hoping on getting relief soon. Maybe the big boys will realize before long that we're not a fresh outfit by a long sight. Let's hope for the best anyway.

By Wednesday evening, September 16, 1942, "Dirty Eddie's" mood was starting to improve and he took the opportunity to clean himself up:

Feel much better today. Just came back from the river. That's the only part of the day a man looks forward to round here. You get so doggone dirty during the day, and then after the air raid, you get a chance to go to the river and get clean. Tojo didn't come today. It was a little cloudy and they turned back quite a way from here. We got the dope that the Wasp was sunk last night—torpedo. That's plenty bad if it's true. Two Marine VF squadrons are on their way here—maybe we'll get relieved. Let's hope that we'll see each other soon, my baby.

The sinking of the *Wasp* on September 15, 1942, was another devastating blow for the U.S. Navy. The *Enterprise* was still being repaired, as was the *Saratoga*, leaving the *Hornet* as the only operational carrier in the South Pacific.

The incessant shelling, relentless bombing, round the clock risk of snipers, and sleeplessness all took their toll. Even after only a short time on Guadalcanal the strain was evident. Regardless of all the ordeals, things were improved by the welcome reappearance of a friend:

September 18, 1942. Am writing this Friday morning—no time yesterday. Took early hop with the Captain, Paul Mankin (AP1c Lee Paul Mankin) *and "Sandy" Crews* (Lt. Howard William Crews) *with orders to carefully search all little inlets, etc of islands around here. Finally located an enemy sea plane base on NE end of San Isbel. We strafed it and came home. Saw two bombers sunk off shore. Apparently, some of the bombers we hit here make it back to there and then crash land.*

"Dutch" and I felt a little bad later and went to the hospital. They gave us some pills to settle our stomach and some opium. We dozed all afternoon there and then went back to the squadron. We sent four planes two hundred and twenty miles to Geisel Harbor

Guadalcanal Campaign, 1942. Wreck of a Grumman F4F Wildcat fighter, victim of a Japanese bomb, September–December 1942. Photographed by Cpl. L. M. Ashman, U.S.M.C. *Courtesy National Archives.*

with an attack group—they went up on an Army contact report which, as usual, proved to be wrong! Luckily, they all got back, landing after dark.

No raids at all—think the weather has been too bad between here and there. Let's hope that it keeps up like that. "Dick" Loesch turned up! He had been hit, taken to the hospital and then flown to Efate. Boy, it sure is wonderful news.

Baby, I love you so much—just keep praying with me for the day when we'll be together again.

"Dick" Loesch was severely wounded on September 13, 1942. He recovered from his injuries and later served in the Attu campaign in the Aleutians and was acknowledged to have been the first pilot to shoot down Japanese aircraft in both the F4F Wildcat and F6F Hellcat.[9]

With conditions on the island so severe, hope for the future and thinking of home was what kept the men going and was a feature of all the servicemen's aspirations and dreams. This was clear from "Dirty Eddie's" diary:

September 19, 1942. Am writing this Saturday morning—no time yesterday. No raid again—gee, let's hope that they finally gave up and feel that this is too hard a nut to crack.

Flew a three-hour patrol over seven transports unloading on the beach. Supplies and some reinforcements were being unloaded. Didn't get a chance to go to the beach 'cause of the convoy being here—too much chance of the Nips coming in. Last night, about midnight (Friday night) a cruiser plane dropped flares and they started shelling us—boy, we really dove in a muddy hole! One hit close. Our naval vessels began opening up on them though and we got back in bed for more sleep.

"Dutch" and I really shot the fat yesterday evening about you girls. Gee, my darling, if you only knew just how much your love means to me. You're the only thing that keeps me going. Just the thought that sometime I'll be back in your arms makes everything else seem so insignificant.

The guys serving on the island felt isolated, neglected, and they were literally just hanging on:

September 19, 1942. Just got through fixing up my mosquito netting. Been too busy to even clean up our tent. No raid again today— wonder why they're letting us alone. Maybe the Army is finally doing some bombing and helping us some. Some new troops went back in the lines today. Gee—the boys coming out really looked whipped down. They're really doing their part. If the people back home only knew how horrible this war really is here. I love you sweety—boy—I love you!

An early flight and a scramble kept "Dirty Eddie" busy in the morning, but his thoughts were with his late mother on the anniversary of her death:

It's been a full year hasn't it honey. Remember one year ago—mother died just one year ago. Gee, it would be wonderful if she were still with us, wouldn't it? We'll never forget her though, will we?

September 20, 1942. Had the dawn patrol this morning. Took off at 0515—quite a bit before daylight. Nothing happened and we landed at 0700. Then at 1015 we had a scramble and finally ended up looking for three float-type planes over the northeast part of the island. Nothing turned up there either. It's 1430 now and it looks like they're not coming over. That suits me—once a day up to 26,000 feet or over is plenty. I talked to "Dutch" up that high and darn if it almost didn't poop me out.

Understand that the ship that's bringing the Marine relief squadron is due to hit Noumea today. Hope they come up soon and relieve us all. Gee, honey, I want to see you so badly. I gotta keep my spirit and pep up though, that's the best thing to do, I guess.

Had a good night's sleep last night—no shelling again. Living here is almost normal when they let us get some sleep. God bless you my precious.

After some much-needed rest, "Dirty Eddie" was feeling better, although mourning the loss of his friend Bill and missing Elsa:

September 21, 1942. Scrambled again today, but it was a false alarm again. They sure have let us alone lately. Good battle in the hills last night though. The Japs came close again last night—even sniped at our dawn patrol this morning. Got Bill's gear together too—didn't feel too good doing that. Gee, it still doesn't seem possible that he's gone.

Feeling better lately, but still would like to get out of here. I want to see you so badly my darling. Gee, I love you.

It was clear that going through Bill's personal effects evoked painful memories for "Dirty Eddie" and his death must have had a profound effect on him. Thoughts of returning home kept him going and while waiting for his plane to be repaired due to mechanical problems, "Dirty Eddie" was able to catch up on the latest scuttlebutt, which encouraged his hopes:

> *September 22, 1942. Another quiet day today. My plane was out for a while so I went visiting up in the lines. Heard rumors of a dispatch to Buttons which said for all carrier pilots to go back to the States. Gosh honey, I hope that's good dope. I sure want to see you, honey—I love you too much.*

"Dirty Eddie's" aircraft was still being repaired on Wednesday, September 23, which gave him time to devote to the heart-rending task of writing to Bill's widow, Dorothy. After completing the letter, it reminded him of how lucky he was to have Elsa and the hopes he had of being with her again soon:

> *Not much today. They let us alone again. We've heard some scuttlebutt about the Army finally doing something and bombing Rabaul and Bougainville. My plane was out of whack most of the day and I took her up for a little test when they fixed her up. The only flying I did today.*
>
> *Wrote a letter to Dorothy Wileman a few minutes ago. Gee, that was some job. I'd give anything if I didn't have to do that—if Bill were only here with us yet.*
>
> *If things can only keep up this way, honey—we may get some relief before long. Gosh, just stop in Pearl long enough to get my gear together and then straight across that big, blue Pacific to you! Darling, that will be the most wonderful thing that I can imagine. Won't we have a wonderful time together though! Baby, I love you more than any man ever loved his wife!*

On Thursday, September 24, "Dirty Eddie" had the day off, his first since he had been based on CACTUS. He was scheduled to have an early start the following morning after catching up with his laundry:

Spent three hours down at the river doing my washing. Boy, I'll really be a good husband when I get home, honey.

No Japs again today. Some ships are supposed to be coming this way—may have some shelling tonight. Having a little drink tonight in the Captain's tent. Just a little one helps the bull sessions go good. Better stop now—have the dawn patrol tomorrow. I love you my darling.

For the second consecutive day there were no enemy planes to encounter, which usually meant that something was brewing and the next action was imminent:

September 25, 1942. No Japs again today—maybe they've given up just like the Germans did over England in the fall of 1940. Sure will be swell if that's straight dope. Speaking of dope—our personnel officer just came up from Buttons and he said the Chief of Staff said to Admiral Fitch that VF-5 is doing a good job here and that in a month at the latest we'll be heading back for the States. That'll really be swell though if it's right. I need to see you soon, honey—the sooner the better. Night honey—I love you.

In recognition of their efforts, *Fighting Five*, received a letter from Admiral Halsey for "Outstanding Performance of Duty—Congratulations," stating:

You, by your courage and skill and utter disregard of personal safety contributed greatly toward the success of Fighting Squadron Five in action with the enemy as recognized by the Commander South Pacific Area and South Pacific Force. By your unyielding courage and desire to make every possible contact with the enemy you contributed greatly to the squadron spirit, presenting an outstanding example to all as a fighting pilot.[10]

It is evident from "Dirty Eddie's" diary entries that there was a deterioration in his outlook since Bill's death and he vented his frustrations on the things going on around him. A recurring theme was his view on the poor effort of the Army pilots:

September 26, 1942. Just finished supper and the rains started—looks like we may have lots of rain now. "Dutch" and I and two others flew up to one of the northern islands this morning.

Our scouts have been getting jumped by Jap float planes quite often, so today he acted as bait and we stayed three to four thousand feet above and behind him. Maybe they saw us—anyway we didn't have any action.

We'll all have a real bitch today though, honey. Here it is—the Army is getting all the credit for what we're doing and they are doing nothing themselves. In fact, they even decorated their bomber crews for the work they did bombing this place before we came in—and advanced them all a rank. All that and they didn't even hit the place!

Well, this afternoon, eight B-17s landed here coming back from bombing Geiso—an enemy port north of here. They dropped eight bombs each from 8000 feet—a total of sixty-four bombs—and didn't make a hit! And their targets were twelve ships that were anchored in the harbor. Gosh honey, it makes a guy feel really disgusted to think that they can't do any better than that.

I'm writing this so you can see in black and white just how bad they really are. We had some good news, though—it's straight dope now that they're going to send all carrier pilots back to the states as soon as relief can be arranged. Maybe they're going to finally give us new planes.

Gee, honey—as soon as I leave here, I'll be coming back to you— isn't that wonderful!

The ensuing day was one of peace and relaxation until the Japanese interrupted events just after lunch. However, they paid the price for the disturbance:

September 27, 1942. We were having a quiet day today, 'til old Tojo showed up about 1330. Fifteen or twenty bombers and twenty-two

Zeros. Sent my bunch down to 5000 feet to protect the ships in the harbor against torpedo attacks. We only got four Zeros and the Marines got four bombers and one Zero. I didn't get into 'em though today. Maybe they'll come back tomorrow.

We're having "choir practice" now, honey. Our quartet is warming up as usual at this time. They have me singing a poor baritone. "Dutch" is second tenor. The best thing though, honey will be when I get back to you. Let's hope that it'll be soon. Good night my sweet.

The Japanese returned again the following day, Monday, September 28, which was to prove eventful for "Dirty Eddie":

Tojo came again today—just as I went back on duty. Gee, we really were in position for 'em. There were sixteen of us together and just as I started to use my oxygen at 10,000 feet my mask came apart. Had to come in and land. We got ten of 'em and the Marines got seventeen and one Zero. Went up on another scramble right after the first one when I had another mask but made no contact.

Nothing much else today—except it's not so good on the ground during an air raid—I'd rather be in the air. At this moment ten new SBDs and four TBFs are landing. Maybe our new fighters will come in tomorrow. It's getting tough, honey. The planes as well as the men can only take so much.

Chapter 5

This War Is Really Hell

T he Japanese were making a major effort to retake Guadalcanal with nightly runs by ships to reinforce their troops and resupply them. The Allied forces had to defend the island, regardless of the cost, and hold it until the battle was won. The Navy couldn't risk their last remaining carriers, and both aircraft and spare parts were in short supply.[1]

The extent of the fierce fighting involved in the battle for Guadalcanal meant that "Dirty Eddie" knew there was an ever-present risk that he and people close to him could get killed at any moment. His diary entry of Tuesday, September 29, 1942, was therefore particularly poignant:

> *Well honey, our "Dutch" got shot down today. Gee, I'm still in a daze from it. I was on the ground where he was supposed to be. We were off from 1300–1600, but he stayed around here while I went down to the river. The raid came and I came back to the field. "Dutch" had taken a plane that one of the other fellows didn't want to fly. He's yellow clear through and caused "Dutch" to get killed. Something must have gone wrong with the plane and he headed for the field to land. He had his wheels down and two Zeros jumped him at about 5000 feet. I don't*

*think he even saw 'em, honey. The first burst must have gotten him
'cause he just went right on down and hit the water. If I could have been
with him, maybe I would have saved him.*

*I feel just empty inside—to lose Bill and now "Dutch"—darn I feel
sorry for Mary. This war is really hell, Elsa. The sooner they take me
away from here the better it'll be. Old Joe Russell came around this
evening. Wanted to make sure that I was okay after today. Baby, keep a
stiff upper lip and remember that I love you.*

To have lost both his best friends when they were shot down and killed
had a profound effect on "Dirty Eddie," who was devastated. In this same
short time, his other close pals "Stinky" and "Dick" Loesch were also shot
down but had survived and were wounded in hospital.

The war of attrition was taking its toll on "Dirty Eddie." It is clear
from his diary that he had been suffering for some time from sleep depri-
vation and was physically and mentally exhausted. The loss of his close
friends intensified his deteriorating condition and his disillusionment
became more apparent:

*The whole outfit is all messed up—just a bunch of glory-grabbers, all
but a very few. More than half of 'em are claiming planes they never
saw fall—just want to get planes to their credit and are fighting among
themselves to get 'em. I say the hell with it—when I fly through the
pieces, I'll claim him. All I want out of this affair is to have your arms
around me just as soon as possible.*

What was known then as combat fatigue or shell shock, now commonly
known as "Post Traumatic Stress Disorder," would affect many of the men
who fought at Guadalcanal. The constant shelling from enemy ships, the threat
of land troops and snipers, even without going up to fly in aerial combat, told
on the pilots and the stresses would show on all who served. To raise morale,
Adm. Chester Nimitz visited the squadron on Wednesday, September 30:

*Raining like hell right now—looks like it may keep up for days. Admiral
Nimitz is just coming in—he's to pin medals on some of the men for*

purposes of morale. They're picking four of our boys now. I understand that all of the fellows with two planes or more will get the D.F.C.—I'd like to get one for you, my sweet.

"Dirty Eddie" was promoted to lieutenant junior grade on October 1, 1942, although he did not find out until a few days later. There was respite from Japanese attacks that day and as always, Elsa was in his thoughts:

Tojo didn't come today. We thought he would do. Nothing much else happened to write about. Right now, our SBDs and TBFs are landing. They went out to hit some cans that are supposed to be heading this way. Hope they did some good. Baby, when your old man gets back to you—is he going to love you! More than you ever thought a guy could love you!

Trying to stay alive and cope with the stresses of aerial combat required extraordinary effort, but was helped by any positive news, especially lost pilots suddenly turning up after being listed as missing in action:

October 2, 1942. Had some good news a minute ago—to make a hell of a day a little better. Last night, Alan Divine (Lt. (jg) Robert Alan Divine) *didn't come back from that attack. Just got the word that he and two others missing are on one of our cans coming into the harbor here. Gee, that's really wonderful.*

Today though, we lost one man (Ens. George Jasper Morgan, Jr.) *and the Marines lost four and only got one Zero. The bombers didn't come in. I didn't go up—it was my time off.*

Had a little bombing last night. Some of those planes from Rekata Bay must have come down. They dropped half a dozen or so bombs but didn't do much damage. I moved from the coconut grove out here to a dugout by the hill. A little safer than back in the grove for a shelling.

They say we're not supposed to have diaries now. This is my letter to you though, honey—not a diary. I love you my darling—be good.

There was the feeling that despite their sterling efforts, they were forgotten by their leaders. They just had to hang on:

October 3, 1942. Scrambled today, honey. Nine of us got to 30,000 feet and waited for the bombers. We saw twenty Zeros at about 10,000 feet directly below us. We let 'em go and waited for the bombers but they never came in. Found out today that the big boys only gave this place thirty-six hours on the 13th of last month and they still haven't done anything for us. Boy, it sure is discouraging to see the way they forget all about us. Looks like another Bataan—let's hope not.

Baby, you just keep things going back there and your old boy will take care of himself for you out here. I love you, my precious and think of you always.

"Dirty Eddie's" mention of the Battle of Bataan may give a clue to his scathing comments about the Army and MacArthur. This battle in the Philippines was one of the most devastating defeats in U.S. history with 76,000 (66,000 Filipinos, 10,000 American) troops surrendering to the Japanese on April 9, 1942. Gen. Douglas MacArthur had been the overall commander.[2]

Although "Dirty Eddie's" promotion ranked from October 1, 1942,[3] he did not find out until Sunday, October 4, 1942, and along with this he also had some encouraging news:

Am writing this by flashlight by the edge of a big bomb shelter. Had some good news today, my sweet. First of all, I found out that I made JG yesterday and the best thing of all is that it looks like we'll finally get out of here!

The skipper sent a dispatch to COMAIRSOPAC and told him we needed relief immediately—that the squadron is fast reaching the stage of exhaustion. He's sending "Sandy" Crews and "Benny" Currie (Lt. (jg) Benjamin Franklin Currie) to Buttons tomorrow and will send us out a couple at a time 'til we're all out. Gee honey, isn't that wonderful?

Last night our boys hit a force and sunk two cans and one cruiser.
Seven cans got in and unloaded troops. No raid today, thank goodness—
I felt like hell all day and feel not much better right now. My eyes, head
and stomach bother me most.

Better get to bed now—have the dawn patrol. Goodnight my sweet-
heart, I love you.

The next day, Monday, October 5, the scuttlebutt was that "Dirty Eddie"
and the squadron would soon be relieved. By the notes in his diary, it is clear
that he was suffering from combat fatigue and needed a well-deserved rest.
As usual, thoughts of Elsa kept him going:

Well, my darling, I really have news for you tonight. Out of a clear
sky this afternoon the skipper told Mark (Lt (jg) Mark K. Bright) *and*
I that he was evacuating us out tomorrow. Four VF-71 pilots came up
today and we're going out. Gee, it's hard to believe isn't it—no more air
raids, night shelling, Zeros, Japs on the ground. I won't know what it is
not to start getting jumpy between 1030–1500 every day.

I think the skipper picked me 'cause of Bill's and "Dutch's"
deaths. They naturally hit me harder than anyone else and Mark
says he's noticed a change in me lately—that I don't seem as full of
life as I was. He says my eyes have looked dull and that I seem to be
in a daze lately.

I admit too, honey that lately I've noticed a change. For the
longest time I haven't been able to concentrate on a book or anything
like that. In the last few days, I've been jumpy as hell just at Tojo-time—
sort of wondering whether it'll be my time or not—whether I'll be the
one to get it today or not. That's a hell of a way to get, baby—when a
man gets to be that way honey, he's ready for a rest.

The prolonged time away from home, the unrelenting barrage on the
ground, and the perilous nature of the aerial operations all told on "Dirty
Eddie." The loss of his closest buddies was the turning point and he had
reached his limit. On Tuesday, October 6, 1942, "Dirty Eddie" along with a

few of his comrades, finally left Guadalcanal for Espiritu Santo, codename BUTTON. The relief was clear:

> *Baby—I'm at Buttons right now. It almost seems like a dream! Mark and I can't seem to get it through our heads that we got out of the "Island of Green Hell." Here it is, we're on our way out of the war zone instead of going into it like we have for the last three months. Mark and I are going down to the Curtiss to see about getting home. It seems unreal to walk around and not worry about anything.*
>
> *None of that nerve-racking waiting between 1015–1400 to wonder whether or not Tojo is coming and if he comes, to wonder whether or not you were going to get it that day. That's where it got me toward the last, honey. After "Dutch" went, I began to get too jumpy and started to think that maybe I wouldn't come back from one of the hops.*
>
> *When a man gets to feeling like that, he's no longer any good as a combat flyer. Gee, I tried to fight that feeling off, but all I could see was Bill crashing and those two Zeros jumping "Dutch." Darling, things are getting tougher up at Cactus. An enemy fleet of three cruisers, seven cans and two transports are heading that way. If the big boys don't hurry up and realize that some help is needed there, it'll fall. Those flyers can't possibly last more than a week longer.*
>
> *I love you and a few weeks with you'll fix me up though, my baby.*

He took the opportunity to find out the latest scuttlebutt by visiting the bomber field on October 7. The only word was that he and the other men who had departed CACTUS would have to wait at BUTTON until the rest of the squadron had flown out of the combat area, then await further orders. Despite being clear of the front line, "Dirty Eddie" showed the strain of the ceaseless daily bombing, shelling, and aerial combat which he'd had to endure:

> *Didn't sleep much last night. It seemed too quiet and I was restless as hell. I still seem to be jumpy and my eyes and head bother me a little all the time. I'll get over that soon though. Gee, it's wonderful not to worry about Tojo-time every day.*

To know that there's a darn good chance of being home with you by Christmas—wouldn't that be heaven. Baby, anything you want to do is what we'll do. We'll make my leave our honeymoon and two happier kids you'll never find, will you? Gee my darling, I love you so much.

For the first time in weeks, "Dirty Eddie," along with his comrades, started to reap the benefit of being out of the battlefront. A quiet day (October 8) started by sleeping late and just fooling around until lunchtime. Then a little reading and more sleep, followed by a movie, then bed. "Dirty Eddie," although content to be away from the frontline, was physically affected by his new conditions:

I got sick last night—my stomach isn't used to so much food, I guess. Right now, it still aches a little. Sure wish that they'd relieve the other boys up at Cactus so we'd be able to start home. Baby, just wait 'til you see how much your old man loves you!

Since flying out of the inferno of Guadalcanal, "Dirty Eddie" was adjusting to the relative comfort of the rear area. He flew a fighter over to the bomber strip, and for the first time in months he felt free from the anxiety of enemy air attack. He managed to obtain some candy and towels and a few other personal items. After his successful trip, his thoughts were, as always, of Elsa and also his comrades who were still awaiting their salvation from Guadalcanal:

October 9, 1942. Another good day today, honey. Came back here and played a little poker in our tent. I won again. There must not be anything to that "lucky in cards, unlucky in love" stuff!

Sure wish that they'd relieve the other boys up at Cactus so we'd be able to start home. The skipper of VF-71 cracked up and killed himself this evening—tough luck but that's the way things go. I love you, sweets—so much.

Even though "Dirty Eddie" was based in the relative safety of BUTTON, he was still thinking of the war close by and remembering his fallen shipmates. It wouldn't be long before he would be sailing home to Elsa:

October 10, 1942. Eight months ago today, honey—remember? With any luck, I'll be with you on our ninth or at least our tenth anniversary. No kidding honey. Our fellows are coming out of Cactus on the 15th and they say we'll head for home soon after.

We went to Mr Strickler's (Lt. Cdr. Robert Lawrence Strickler) *funeral this afternoon. Since Bill and "Dutch" couldn't have a funeral, I said a little prayer for 'em there today.*

Just got back from the movie and am going to write you a big, long letter now. Gee, hun—won't it be great to be together again? It's so much of a relief to be coming out of the war zone instead of going in. Good night, my pet—I love you.

The next day, he bumped into an old buddy, which led to dinner with a Navy construction outfit. This followed with time on the *Curtiss*, a seaplane tender. Once the men found out "Dirty Eddie" had been flying fighters at Guadalcanal, he was immediately the center of interest. The guys wanted to know all about his ordeal in the battle zone:

Most of that stuff I want to forget, but fellows keep asking questions.

After the primitive living conditions "Dirty Eddie" had been used to, the contrast of Espiritu Santo made a real difference to his morale, and the simple things made him really appreciate his time there:

October 11, 1942. Am spending this night between clean sheets for a change, honey—and in a real bed too! Took a real hot shower. Gee, if you only knew how good it felt. Baby, you're going to have a heck of a time getting me out of that shower when I get in it back home there.

For anyone who fought in the Guadalcanal Campaign, life would never be the same again. The loss of close friends and the constant shelling, bombing, and sniping had transformed those who survived. They suffered more than most men could endure and the events would stay with them for the rest of their lives. In "Dirty Eddie's" case, he had become disillusioned and felt let down by the higher command:

October 12, 1942. Went to a meeting today—they had a big battle up at Cactus last night. We did fair. Looks like Tojo may be starting after that place. I think he can just about take it if he wants it to. That's bad to say, but the big boys just don't seem to give a damn whether we hold this place or not. These people can't seem to get it through their heads that a war's going on! Gee, I'm afraid that I'm going to be quite changed when you next see me. This experience has given me quite a few different ideas and viewpoints. I'll probably get in plenty of arguments back home.

The Japanese had sent a supply convoy to Guadalcanal and in the action "Dirty Eddie" referred to in his diary, which was to become known as the Battle of Cape Esperance, both sides lost ships, but the U.S. Navy kept the Japanese at bay. The fight for Guadalcanal still raged on and for the Allies, it was hanging by a thread. In reality, the higher command, with their limited resources, were doing everything they could to hold on to the island.

"Dirty Eddie's" comrades still fighting at Guadalcanal were never far away from his thoughts, even when he and his buddies had a get-together:

October 13, 1942. Came back to camp after lunch and we had a big party tonight. Twenty-three fellows from Colonels on down were in here at one time. Felt good to unlimber for once.

A dispatch came from the big place saying the field was out of commission and from what we can gather, the boys had it plenty tough up there today. Let's hope that all of 'em came out ok.

There was some good news the day after the party, as a number of "Dirty Eddie's" buddies had survived the bloodshed. The bad news was that all the pilots were suffering the effects of their supreme courage and endurance and were no longer able to continue flying in combat:

October 14, 1942. Mel Roach (Ens. Melvin C. Roach), *"Cash" Register* (Ens. Francis R. Register) *and Jim Halford got out today. They all looked bad. The doctor had grounded 'em and sent 'em out over the General's protest. The stupid General had wanted to keep 'em there. The sooner this country begins treating their fighter pilots as fighter pilots the way England does, and stops treating them as dogs, the better off everyone's going to be!*

According to the boys, things are in bad shape up there. Tojo's sending over two waves of bombers now and they're hitting. We only have eight to nine planes in the air to meet 'em. They have artillery set up and shell us even in the day-time and last night, twin-engine bombers bombed and cruisers shelled. They all say that the way things are going, we'll lose the place.

Well, we got orders today that we're all grounded indefinitely on doctor's orders. The boys today said the skipper ordered that. Tomorrow we're going to go to the Curtiss and see if we can't get out. Not a one of us will go back up there to fight. We feel it's not fair—it's asking too much from so few men. Three VF squadrons have been fighting this war out here and even though they tell us that Fighting Five has made a wonderful name for itself, they'll never get those of us that are out now to go back up.

We're going to demand they send us back to the States for a rest. Right now, we have a report that an enemy carrier is heading this way and that we may expect an attack in the morning. If those yellow rascals plan a coordinated attack on here and Efate and knock us out, they can walk right into Guadalcanal.

Let's hope our trip to the Curtiss brings us luck, Sweety and I'll be able soon to tell you I love you and not just write it.

It was clear at this time that the American Forces were just hanging on at CACTUS. Things were as miserable as they could be with the Japanese still trying to recapture the island. Prior to landing on Guadalcanal, the Americans knew they had to take the airfield and hold it, whatever the cost. To the guys at the sharp end, it would have appeared that no one cared and little was being done, but they had no choice but to keep fighting.

October 15, 1942. Boy, it seems that everywhere we go anymore we run into trouble. This afternoon, they spotted a carrier 400 miles north of us heading south. They would be 100 miles from here by 0400 tomorrow. We're not flying, but let's hope nothing happens.

We got a little good news today and sure hope that this hubbub doesn't "jim the works." We went to the Curtiss and saw the Admiral's Secretary and he took our names and said he'd see the Chief of Staff and would call us in the morning. He seemed to think we had an excellent chance of getting out of here. Just let him give us orders to 'Frisco and we'll get there!

Things look black as hell, right now. I firmly don't think we'll hold Cactus. The Japs have not one, but several task forces, including transports, all heading for Cactus—and we have one battleship (coming tomorrow), four cruisers and not enough destroyers to beat 'em off with. The field up there is in very bad shape and can't operate the planes too well. Gee, things look bad for our boys—we sort of feel that they're doomed and that we only got out because we were destined to.

Gee, it's disheartening when we see what's going on here—to see how completely unready we were for this supposedly big push. And still the people back home are being fed the goo about how rosy things are and what a great job the Navy is doing when we're right here and are seeing our Navy get their tail licked.

Let's just hope that everything turns out okay and that we get orders home tomorrow and then I can live like a normal human for a while, baby—and show my wife how much I love her.

Whether they realized it or not, many of the guys had to endure the slow anguish of combat fatigue, which was best described by Roger Hedrick, who would feature later in "Dirty Eddie's" story:

"I recall some who were unable to keep going in combat, and that taught me that you cannot with any certainty predict a person's reaction to lengthy stress. I believe we all have our limits. Some are more fortunate than others, can keep going longer, but at some point in time, I think we all would probably break."[4]

A regular feature of "Dirty Eddie's" thoughts were the failings, in his eyes, of the Army pilots to do the job he thought they should do. Keeping his spirits up by thinking about being with Elsa soon raised his morale, although it is clear he was in a bad way:

October 16, 1942. Spent a typical Guadalcanal night last night—and yet there were just a lot of scares—nothing happened. Yet I was so damn jumpy all night—my nerves must be shot. Didn't get our orders today— but did hear that we may wait 'til our boys come out and go with them.

Heard tonight real dope on the situation up there and it's bad. This Major who told us went in on an AP with his "Big Boat" and got it with his fish. He says that VF-5 has one plane left and that we're getting out tomorrow. That's something kid—a squadron stays 'til it runs through twenty-four airplanes!

During the Guadalcanal Campaign, the Japanese sent ships at night from Rabaul down "The Slot" to Guadalcanal delivering troops, supplies, and equipment to reinforce their army. The Allied nickname for this was the "Tokyo Express." The Americans were well aware of this enemy activity, but following the Savo Island disaster, they were reluctant to commit their remaining ships to counter the Japanese forces.

The Japs are unloading troops right off the field—just west of it. And doing it in the day time too! They've unloaded seven of 'em and have between 20–30,000 troops. We just can't do anything about it—we simply have no Navy, it looks like.

Something that really burns me up is this, too, honey: B-17s came over to bomb those ships unloading and yet are too damn yellow to come down low enough to do any good—so they bomb at 20,000 feet with no opposition, with thousands of men's lives depending on 'em— and don't even get a hit! And yet one Marine Major (Maj. Jack Cram)

*takes his old tub of a P-boat—a literal "Flying Coffin"—and goes in
with fish and sinks a transport—and then can't go out that night after
the cruiser shelling 'em like he wants to 'cause his plane was so shot
up with holes!*

Maj. Jack Cram was awarded the Navy Cross for his extraordinary
heroism in the sinking of a Japanese ship.[5]

*It makes you sick to see how the Army continuously falls down on
their jobs and the stupid persons who are running this show bungle
things and kill off our men who want to fight, if they'd only get a
little help.*

*It gets to you sweetheart—and I'm tired of it all. I want you and need
to get away from all this stuff. Let's hope we'll be together soon.*

Chapter 6

Never Have So Few Been Dumped On by So Many

On the night of October 13, two Japanese battleships, *Kongō* and *Haruna*, shelled Henderson Field in the most ferocious naval barrage ever directed at American forces in any war.[1] This was later to become known by Guadalcanal veterans as "The Bombardment."[2] They had suffered one of the most terrifying experiences that U.S. forces had to endure.[3] "Dirty Eddie" and the other members of his squadron who escaped from Guadalcanal with their lives were lucky indeed. VF-5 evacuated a few men at a time to Espiritu Santo, where they were safe from the perils of combat. The next stage further improved their hopes of returning home when "Dirty Eddie" and some of his squadron were moved to Efate, an island south of Espiritu Santo, and were settled there by Saturday night, October 17. Fittingly, one of the islands close by was called "Tranquility Island" (Moso Island).

Well, maybe our long trip homeward started today—let's hope so anyway.

"Dirty Eddie" and his buddies had suffered the effects of combat fatigue from their experiences at Guadalcanal, and once they were safe in the rear area, Halford, Roach, and Register shared what had been happening on the

"Island of Green Hell." The sense of relief that the squadron got out safely
is evident:

*We heard that all our boys came out last night, so we went to the bomber
strip and ran into most of the men. We got a ride on a B-24 and all the
pilots and some of the men got out to Efate. The skipper and some of
the men are on a destroyer and should be here by tomorrow or the next
day. It sure was good to hear that all the fellows and our men got out
okay 'cause things were getting pretty hot.*

*They told us of how things were the last couple of days—I certainly
wish all the people back home knew what the men there are going
through—and with the Army giving 'em no help. Three of the men in
the Army regiment that came in a couple of nights ago shot themselves.
How 'bout that—couldn't even stand for a few days what the Marines
and Navy went through for weeks. A lot of the boys are showing it
though, they say.*

*Many of the men—officers too—are shell-shocked bad and
"Morty" Kleinmann* (Ens. Mortimer Valentine Kleinmann, Jr.), *one
of our flyers broke up and had to be sent out to a hospital. All those
boys we lived with in the gun position on the field, except the Sergeant
in charge and one of the older boys, cracked during the shelling. Just
broke down and began sobbing. One Sergeant in one of the gun crews
beat his head against the bulkhead and fractured his skull. Gosh, no one
can realize how hard a shelling can be on you. The Japs' battlebuggies
and cruisers were throwing 14" shells at the boys all night. No wonder
some men went crazy. A British officer told "Cash" that he had been at
the blitz at London, at Dunkirk and at Crete and that Guadalcanal was
worse than any of 'em. And he was only there about three days!*

*You can't imagine how wonderful it is to be back here at Iririki and
not have the knowledge that we're going into a fight—we're heading
out now, honey—back to you! It'll be great to get out of this part of the
world though—this climate really runs a man down. It is better here
though 'cause we don't have the vicious flies that are a little further
north. Gosh, they drive you crazy!*

Iririki was a tiny island close to the capital of Efate, Port Vila, and offered a retreat for the men to recover from their ordeal while waiting for the remaining men to arrive. To be able to do normal, everyday things was what they looked forward to. George Mauhar, who served as a crew chief in the Pacific Theater, said the thing he missed most was a home-cooked meal.[4]

A few of the guys decided to go to church on Sunday, October 18, but arrived late, as locally the services started earlier than they were used to. After the service had finished they went inside, and for "Dirty Eddie" it was the first time he had been in a church since he had attended with Elsa in Coronado:

It's a beautiful place and it's a wonderful feeling to be inside a church again.

The afternoon was spent just loafing around in his tent, as it rained most of the time. He managed to secure some newspapers from the States, including a *Washington Post*.

All we're waiting for now it seems, is for the skipper to get here. All our men are gradually getting here to Iririki, so we'll be ready to leave. Gee, honey, looks like we may all be together for Christmas yet. That would make all of this being apart seem not so bad, wouldn't it?

Monday, October 19 was a similar kind of day to the previous one. Since being withdrawn from combat, the squadron was still getting used to the absence of almost daily attacks from the Japanese:

It's really great to know that around noon-time you won't have a visit from Tojo. This is all very fine, but we all wish the skipper would hurry up and get down here and get things moving for us to get out of here. Too much chance of catching Malaria around this island.

All of us in the tent had the usual bull sessions yesterday. We decided that we, as a squadron, were in a better position than anyone to know what our new planes should do. And if they don't come up to snuff, we should be able to say something about it. Also got to talking about combat and such.

We decided that the planes one shoots down are greatly due to luck. Planes are where you find 'em. Even though I only have two knocked down, that's just the way it goes. I'll get my chance later on to get some more. Two or twenty-two, it's all the same as long as everyone's doing his part.

Although it appeared that the squadron was going home, events transpired that there was still work to do before the time came to finally leave the area:

October 20, 1942. The skipper came in today. He brought word that we have to go out to the field and man the planes 'til we're relieved on November 15. All the boys are pretty well on the bitching side again 'cause they feel we may have to go back to Cactus. Let's hope that doesn't happen, honey.

Thoughts of returning to Guadalcanal were not received well and in "Dirty Eddie's" case, he was not keen to step forward. Deep down he was desperate to get home:

October 21, 1942. Well, some of the boys did go up to Cactus this morning, very early. They said they needed twelve planes up there and they'd return immediately. They still may keep 'em though. I didn't go 'cause it was volunteer and when I got in this outfit, I was told to keep my mouth shut, eyes open and never volunteer for anything!

We're over to the field now, though and have to stand by these planes here. We won't fly though, only when it's necessary and it should be okay if we can hold out 'til the 15th. We all feel that VF-5 is really getting kicked around and one of the boys put it very nicely by stating that "Never have so few been dumped on by so many." Very good, we thought.

I love you my baby and will be home with you by Christmas, if everything goes well.

Still no news of going home. The rains came and the wait continued:

October 22, 1942. Nothing doing today—stood by in the ready tent all day—we passed the time by playing "Monopoly." Lots of fun. The boys came back from Cactus today. Will Rouse had to land in the water on the way up—about twenty miles from the field, but it was pretty dark. Don't know whether they got him or not. Sure hope so, 'cause there is one real swell guy. (Ens. Wildon M. Rouse was listed as missing on October 21, and not seen again).

"Sandy" is going over to Iririki tonight—seems that Dave stopped on the Curtiss on the way back and he must have some word for us. Let's hope that it's good. I'm getting plenty tired, honey. Think the rains are here for good too. This is no rest around these parts here. We all need to get home before we'll be ready to do any fighting again. Then I can tell you how much I love you!

The rain and the lingering seemed to have no end and by now all that was needed was the order to go home:

October 23, 1942. Rain again mostly all day today. Damn, if this isn't slowly driving a man crazy. Just loafed around the ready room and our tent all day. We played poker tonight and doggone if I don't think that all of us are crazy. We all seem punch drunk. I felt just like I did when I used to stay up all night before exams at school. If this rain keeps up, I'm afraid we'll all get Malaria. Our resistance is too low to do anything against it.

Four of the boys got orders to fly back to Pearl though. The skipper picked out the four who were in the squadron the longest. Looks like that may be the beginning of all of us getting back.

Just how important letters were in raising morale was clear when the mail finally caught up with "Dirty Eddie" on Saturday, October 24. To hear from his beloved Elsa was just the tonic he needed. Although the wait to go home seemed eternal:

Baby, I finally got letters from you today! One of the boys brought it over from Iririki to us. Darling, I feel like a million dollars now that I've heard from you. Gee, you write wonderful letters! It's a great feeling to know that you love me so terribly much too my darling. Nothing can ever happen to a love like ours.

It makes me sick to think of "Skeex" (Mary Shoemaker) and Dorothy (Wileman) though. To think that they were all so happy too! I love you, my precious and will always do so.

The squadron intelligence received information that a Japanese attack was imminent. VF-5 were pressed into service and had to ensure their planes were flown back to BUTTON at the earliest opportunity. An engagement was looming, which turned out to be one of the last Japanese assaults to retake Guadalcanal:

October 25, 1942. Well, we're on the move again! We're back at Santos tonight. Yep—old Fighting Five gets the dirty work again! Got the word about 1600 that a big Jap push was on and heading toward Santos, so we had to fly our planes up here. Got here after dark. Mark and I landed over here at the fighter strip, while the others went to the bomber field.

The boys were glad to see us—really good boys. The word came from the Curtiss that this Marine squadron has to furnish eight pilots tomorrow to go to Cactus. If we can only get rid of the rest of our planes, we may stand a better chance of getting home, honey. Have to be up at 0430 tomorrow, in case the Japs continue this way and throw a carrier attack at us. I'm tired of fighting now though, honey—just plain tired is a good way to express it. I love you though, my sweet—more than you ever thought possible, I bet!

"Dirty Eddie" was referring to the Japanese launching a ground and naval offensive that culminated in the Battle of Santa Cruz on October 25, 1942. The Japanese had four carriers to the Americans' two (*Hornet* and *Enterprise*). The United States won the land battle, but both sides incurred losses at sea. After this major carrier battle, the Japanese withdrew from the area. Both of the American carriers sustained hits and the *Hornet* was ultimately sunk.[5] On the morning of October 26, as the *Hornet* burned just over the horizon, the *Enterprise* became the last operational U.S. carrier in the Pacific. A bold sign appeared in the hangar deck, "Enterprise vs Japan" reflecting both the desperate nature of the situation, and the resolve of the *Enterprise's*

With tailhook down, an SBD-3 Dauntless of Scouting Squadron Ten flies over the aircraft carrier *Enterprise* prior to recovery aboard the carrier. The *Saratoga* steams in the background. Note that the wartime censor has blocked out *Enterprise*'s radar equipment. The aircraft pictured, with Ens. Charles Irvine at the controls, played a notable role in the Battle of Santa Cruz on October 25, 1942. Irvine and another pilot discovered and attacked the Japanese carrier *Zuihō* during the battle. *Courtesy Robert Lawson Photograph Collection, National Museum of Naval Aviation/U.S. Navy photo.*

men. Not until December 5, when the repaired *Saratoga* arrived at Noumea, would the men on the *Enterprise* see another friendly flat top.[6]

For "Dirty Eddie," the aftermath of the Battle of Santa Cruz wouldn't become clear for a few days. He was still not well and what he needed was rest and recuperation and some time at home with Elsa:

October 26, 1942. Well, nothing happened today. Only four planes got off to Cactus. We stood on alert all day and will tomorrow, too. Don't know how long they'll keep us here—'til the scare's over, I guess.

Baby, I miss you so much—damn, but I want to get home to you. This damn climate and the continuous unsettled conditions we're operating under will knock us all out, I'm afraid. I'm under the weather tonight—we all have touches of Malaria, I think. Gosh, I took a hop yesterday before we came up here and doggone if just going up to 27,000 feet didn't make me feel woozy—had to use emergency oxygen lots of the time. I guess I'm just a worn-out aviator, hun—all I need is you though—you're all the tonic I need! Better close now and get some shut-eye. Night my darling!

The ensuing day (Tuesday, October 27) revolved around the usual poker game, shooting crap and some cribbage. There was still no word of going home:

Rained all day—just like all the other days around these islands. May go back to Efate tomorrow and let someone else come up in my place. Today, fifty of our men and three officers had a chance to leave on a ship at noon for the States. Don't know whether they got away or not—it was down at Efate. Looks like we're gradually getting away though, honey—and I think we'll fly out if there's any chance at all. That would really be a lot better than on a ship. I'd get to you much quicker! And then I'd be able to tell you how much I love you!

"Dirty Eddie" finally heard news of the fallout from the Battle of Santa Cruz on Wednesday, October 28, when he discovered the casualties the Navy had sustained, including the loss of the *Hornet* and damage to his old carrier, the *Enterprise*:

Mark and "Cash" went back to Efate today—I should go tomorrow or next day. The Hornet air group's around there now—what's left of 'em! She and "The Big E" were in a big battle with three Jap carriers a few days ago. The Enterprise VF outfit lost eleven in combat and the Hornet lost eight. Boy, that's really rough. The Hornet was hit badly and they had to scuttle her. "The Big E" was hit too.

He still had no news of getting home, although reminders of his darling Elsa at the evening movie helped his mindset:

Hello there, Kitten! Just saw a movie tonight ("Meet the Stewarts") with William Holden and Frances Dee—he called her that and I liked it so much and she was so cute and reminded me of you, that I decided that from now on, you're my "Kitten."

At the time, Frances Dee was hailed as one of the most beautiful women in motion pictures.[7]

Oh my darling, I love you so much. All that's ever in my mind, morning, noon and night, is you. I think of you all the time. I'm going to go nuts if I don't get home to you soon. Just to look at you and to hold you in my arms again—that will make me the happiest man in the world. Good night now Kitten, I love you.

"Dirty Eddie's" two friends, Mark Bright and "Cash" Register, secured flights out to Efate, which led to the hope that his time would come soon:

May get lucky and get out of here for home. We're trying to decide what day and date it is. Some say it's Saturday, 30th. But Saturday would make it the 31st. I still think it's only the 29th and this is Thursday. That gives you a good idea of life out here though Kitten—don't even know the day or date!

I do know that I love you, though—that's one thing I never get messed up on!

The following day, Saturday, October 31, "Dirty Eddie" was still yearning to leave. For some reason, the pilots who were supposed to fly home were subject to a delay and were still waiting:

We found out that none of the men got out on that strip the other day. The dispatch was held up in some way. That's really too bad—it

*would have been swell if some of the men could have gotten out.
We just keep on hoping though and figure that we'll get out when
Marine Air Group Eleven get here. We can at least hope for things
like that.*

Although the waiting was tiresome, "Dirty Eddie" had some light relief
when he went into town on Sunday:

*November 1, 1942. Went to the church in town today. It's quite a feeling
to see so many different types of people all in the same church worship-
ping God together. There were French, English, Americans, Tongans.
A big native sat in front of me, bare feet and holes in his ears for his
earrings and tattoos on his face. It's a wonderful sight though—makes
a man feel real good inside. Went to the movie this evening. Nothing
else to say, except that I love you.*

There was finally good news, as sixty-five men and four officers
(Mark Bright, "Cash" Register, Jim Halford, and "Benny" Currie) left
for Noumea. Unfortunately, this didn't help "Dirty Eddie" as he wasn't
among them. All he wanted was to be on his way home:

*The men go straight to San Diego, but we have to stop by Pearl
Harbor. If they keep us there and send us back out that would really
be a kick in the pants. I'm way down on the list to leave here—
apparently, I "look like one of the healthiest ones of the outfit!"
Some of us are even scheduled to go back to Buttons next week. Let's
hope I get out of here by then.*

*Baby, I've looked forward so much to getting home to you that
I think it would be too much to take if they'd keep me at Pearl
Harbor and then send me back out. I'm afraid I'd do something
pretty drastic. In fact, Kitten, I think I'll simply refuse to come out—
tell 'em I'm unfit to fly in combat for a while. Well, let's hope I don't
have to do that—we'll just wait and see what happens when we
get there.*

After what appeared an age of waiting, "Dirty Eddie" finally received the news he had been hoping for:

November 3, 1942. Well Kitten, things happened today. Mel and I were over to the field getting the doctor's okay for our JG when the word came that we were to go to White Poppy (Noumea) *and from there home! We got our gear together and all our men and we officers that were left flew there—got out to the Lurline, a former Matson luxury liner.*

Gee, you should see it, honey—what a palace! Elevators on it, big dining rooms, etc. The darn thing looks like a hotel. They say it's going straight to the States. If that's so, I'll be in 'Diego fourteen days after we leave here.

While waiting for the *Lurline* to depart on Wednesday, November 4, "Dirty Eddie" heard that yet another close friend was lost in combat. There was also the nagging worry that they would return to the combat area:

Baby, "Cookie" (Lt. (jg) Morrill I. Cook, Jr.) *got it in the last carrier battle. He got shot down while escorting one of the attack groups. Seems that we're losing all our best buddies, doesn't it, honey? If that country of ours would only wake up and stop being so damn selfish and get things moving back there, the two hundred-odd pilots fighting this war out here might get some relief from the thousands of pilots they're supposed to be training every month back there. Let's hope that before it's too late, they eventually wake up.*

Maybe the rest of the fellows will get here from Buttons if we hang around long enough. It all seems too good to be true though, and we all want to get under way. Afraid that someone will pull us off of this thing. We especially don't want to go by Pearl. They're really liable to clamp on to us. We found out that practically all the fellows who stayed on "The Big E" and Saratoga had to come back out from Pearl. All the fellows got a raw deal.

Kitten, before long I'll be holding you in my arms again. I keep thinking of that all the time.

Still no word on Thursday, November 5, of his departure, but there were some positives aboard the liner:

Still here, honey—don't know how long this thing will stay here before we sail. Hope it's soon so we won't have any chance of them taking us out of here. Gee, the biggest thing that we like here is the wonderful food we're getting. After two-and-a-half months of spam, rice, Vienna sausages and corned beef, the change is wonderful. We have eggs for breakfast, chicken and all fresh meats and ice cream almost every day. We're all gaining back the weight we lost.

Finally, after so many false starts and endless waiting, on Friday, November 6, the *Lurline*, with "Dirty Eddie" aboard, was heading for home. Although, the excitement of this event was tinged with sadness, as yet another of "Dirty Eddie's" buddies was posted missing in action:

Well Kitten, I'm on my way to you. We shoved off this afternoon about 1700. It seems to be either to 'Diego or 'Frisco. They say it'll be Wednesday morning, the 18th. Won't be long 'til we're together, baby.

All our other boys got aboard today. Things seem to be working out okay. One thing isn't good though, honey. Found out today that Mike's missing up at Cactus. It happened the 29th. Damn, why is it all the good boys here get it? It makes me wonder what kept me alive when I think of Paul, Bill, "Dutch" and Mike.

He was on an attack hop to Rekata Bay and apparently ran into heavy anti-aircraft fire while strafing. He didn't come back and all the others are shot up badly. There's still a chance that he may have had an oil line shot off and made a forced landing and got to some natives. Let's pray for that, honey. He's too fine a fellow to go like that.

For the next twelve days, the *Lurline* sailed home and life aboard simply involved loafing around, reading, eating, and sleeping, but despite this he was still anxious. His fingers were crossed that the liner didn't turn north in the first three days of the voyage—this would mean that they would be heading home. "Dirty Eddie" was still concerned on Tuesday, November 10, that the ship would head to Pearl Harbor and back to the war:

> *Heading about 030°. Sure wish we'd hurry and get past Pearl Harbor, so we wouldn't have to worry about going there. Pray that we'll be together soon, my Kitten. I love you so much. Tonight makes nine months since you made me the happiest fellow in the world. And one month from now we should be together. It's a heck of a feeling not to be sure though—I still can't keep from thinking that they may head for Pearl Harbor. We should know tomorrow.*

Tomorrow came and "Dirty Eddie" figured that Pearl Harbor was not part of the itinerary. Each day that passed now meant one day nearer to being with Elsa again:

> *I think we're safe in assuming we're coming home now. We've been heading about 040° all day. That puts us on past it. Darling, we should be in port in one week. I think I'll look okay to you 'cause I've had lots of rest and wonderful food in the last few days. Such food is putting on weight for me. I'm feeling good too, Kitten—all except missing you so much.*

"Dirty Eddie's" experiences since he left San Diego many months ago had changed him and the loss of so many close friends weighed heavily on his mind:

> *Another day closer to you my sweet. It doesn't seem possible that I'll see you soon. We'll really be happy, won't we?*
>
> *All that I've been through and all that I've seen since I left you seems like a horrible nightmare. And yet, when I think of "Dutch," Paul, Bill, "Cookie," Mike, Mary, Dorothy, Becky, Mother Herbert and think that there are thousands like them, I realize how horrible this thing really is.*
>
> *Baby—won't it be wonderful to be together again? I've longed for you so much in the last few months. I never knew I could miss anyone as much as I do you.*

The news that he had a definite date to disembark was well-received, but "Dirty Eddie's" thoughts dwelled on his lost comrades and on seeing Bill Wileman's widow, Dorothy, and "Dutch" Shoemaker's widow, Mary. He felt he owed it to his shipmates to see their grieving widows in person:

We should get in Wednesday morning, November 18. Whether I call you right away or not depends upon what "cooks" when we get in port. If we get leave right away, I'll go to Los Angeles see Aunt Nell and Dorothy Wileman—then fly to Kansas and see Mary—call you from there and then get right home. I'd call you from the coast, but this way I'll be home almost as quickly as you could come out. I should stop and see Mary and I could do it this way. See, I haven't written her yet and she'll want to know everything about what happened. I only wish it were such that the little man was here so he could go home to his Mary himself.

Two days to go before putting in to port, the restless "Dirty Eddie" was eager to get home:

Doggone if I'm not getting more impatient than ever. Now that I'm getting so close to you, the time seems to pass slower than ever. By this time on Wednesday though, I should have gotten a call through to you. Boy, you'll be surprised to hear my voice, I'll bet.

We'll be in tomorrow morning. Couldn't sleep at all last night, just stayed awake 'til 0400 this morning thinking of you. A lot has happened since I first started this little letter to you, my sweet, but through it all, I was always thinking of you.

The night before he returned to American soil, "Dirty Eddie" reflected on what he had been through. He had been away for nearly five months. He left as a fully trained pilot, although a novice in aerial combat. He returned an experienced aviator, credited with shooting down two Japanese aircraft. He'd been through hell and survived, when so many of his other squadron-mates and colleagues had given their lives for their country. He had played his part in the vital battle to hold Guadalcanal, but also paid the price, having to suffer the misery and torment that would become the legend of that campaign. He was one of the lucky ones. He would not forget.

In November 1942, the Japanese made one last-ditch bid to take Guadalcanal. They sent a large naval force to destroy Henderson Field. The Naval Battle of Guadalcanal was a decisive victory for the U.S. Navy, resulting in substantial losses of ships for the Japanese. Although the Japanese had lost the engagement, they were not finished and two weeks later defeated the Americans in the Battle of Tassafaronga, where they sank one heavy cruiser and put another three out of action for nearly a year. The 1st Marine Division received a Presidential Unit Citation for their valiant efforts repelling constant enemy attacks on Henderson Field and they were finally relieved in early December. Later that month, the U.S. forces would mount a successful land offensive on Guadalcanal. Finally, in February 1943, after months of fighting, the last of the Japanese surviving troops were evacuated and the island was secured. Thus ended one of the most intense and bloody campaigns of the Pacific War.[8]

Chapter 7

A Young Man of Action

While the fighting to secure the island continued on Guadalcanal, "Dirty Eddie" was on his way home. He had planned to see Dorothy Wileman and Mary "Skeex" Shoemaker, but he was also desperate to get home to Elsa. Once the *Lurline* docked in port, he was dependent on what transport he could find. From the evidence in his flight log, he was not able to see his late comrades' widows. For the next few days, he worked his way across the country on a convoluted series of flights to get home. Starting at San Diego on November 20, he travelled to Phoenix, then on to Dallas, and from there to Corpus Christi. The following day, he flew to New Orleans, then to Pensacola. From there, to Jacksonville and then to Norfolk. He made the short flight home from Norfolk to Washington, D.C.,[1] to be finally reunited with Elsa.

"Dirty Eddie" was home at last, trying to recuperate from the brutality and carnage of Guadalcanal. He had to recover his senses after the loss of so many close friends and come to terms with the fact that he had survived the conflict and returned. He was due a well-earned leave and time to find himself again. He was grieving inside and the war had changed him. "Dirty Eddie's" sister-in-law, Dora Taylor, recalls that too much free time

Harry showing Elsa a Japanese flag when he returned home after his tour of duty in the South Pacific in November 1942. *Courtesy the family of Jean March McAfee.*

was not good for him and he had to keep on the go after his return from Guadalcanal:

"As I remember, Harry, for the most part, was laid back, fun loving, warm-hearted and outgoing. My sister Elsa, in later years, shared that when he was home on furlough from the Pacific, he was quite high-strung and 'hyper.' He needed to be doing something every minute. If they had an engagement in the evening, he would need to plan something else to do, such as going to a movie first, in order to not have too much down-time. I guess that was his way of not thinking about some of the horrors of war he had encountered. I remember him with great affection—he had his own brand of charm. He was very special and all my family loved him."[2]

A short while into his leave, "Dirty Eddie" received instructions: "On or about December 7, 1942, you will proceed to Baltimore, Maryland for temporary duty in connection with public relations duties. Upon the completion thereof, you will return to Washington, D.C., and resume your leave status."[3] As a champion athlete and veteran fighter pilot of the Guadalcanal Campaign, he was perfect for Navy public relations duties and it would not be the first time he was chosen for these assignments.

On December 19, 1942, "Dirty Eddie" was detached from Fleet Air Command, West Coast, and ordered to Fleet Air Detachment, N.A.S. New York, then on December 31, 1942, to Fighting Squadron Twenty-four (VF-24), based on the *Belleau Wood*.[4] It had been over two months since "Dirty Eddie" had flown in a fighter. On January 7, 1943, with his new squadron, he was in the air again in the sturdy F4F Wildcat, the aircraft in which he had scored his two air combat victories in the South Pacific. The squadron was still flying the outmoded F4F and the pilots were eagerly awaiting the arrival of the new Grumman F6F Hellcat, which was due to replace the squadron's Wildcats in the summer of 1943.[5]

The *Belleau Wood* was an Independence-class, small aircraft carrier that was built at Camden, New Jersey. It was originally built as a light cruiser, *New Haven* (CL-76) and was converted to a carrier prior to launching and commissioning in March 1943. Her hull number was changed from CV-24 to CVL-24 in July 1943.[6] When "Dirty Eddie" was assigned to VF-24 in January 1943, a new squadron was being formed in Norfolk, Virginia. They were to fly the powerful Chance Vought F4U Corsair, a fighter that was unproven to the Navy.[7] They were soon to become famous as "The Skull and Crossbones Squadron," led by Lt. Cdr. Tom Blackburn, and would come to feature prominently in the story of "Dirty Eddie's" war.

During his assignment to VF-24, "Dirty Eddie" was still carrying out public relations duties and was interviewed for a radio show in February 1943. Fortunately, a transcript of the interview survives, which gives a flavor

View of a formation of F4F-4 Wildcats of Fighting Squadron 24 in flight near Naval Air Station, Floyd Bennett Field, New York. Established on December 31, 1942, the squadron eventually transitioned to F6F Hellcats. *Courtesy National Museum of Naval Aviation.*

of the time and the importance to the country of the morale-boosting public relations duties which combat veterans like "Dirty Eddie" were asked to participate in. It's clear from some of the passages that there was a strong message about the Navy and its training, to encourage young men to enlist in this branch of the service:

> Interviewer: Good morning, folks. Today we have the privilege of presenting a young man of action—Lt. Harry A. March. Lt. March is a Flight Officer of the United States Navy—and he has just recently returned from the hot spot of the Pacific, Guadalcanal. Lt. Harry A. March, U.S.N.R.
>
> March: Thank you. It's a real pleasure to be here with you.

Interviewer: According to the record, you are credited with knocking quite an impressive number of Japanese out of the air. Apparently that occupation agrees with you.

March: Why do you say that?

Interviewer: For one reason—you're here to tell the story. Furthermore, you look like you're in tip-top health.

March: I feel tip-top. I ought to because all I've been doing since I got back to the States has been taking it easy.

Interviewer: Can't complain about that, can you?

March: No complaints—but I have got a little guilty conscience.

Interviewer: From what?

March: I've got a lot of good friends out there in the South Pacific. I know what they're doing right this minute. I know how tough it is.

Interviewer: And knowing that, you can't go on living the life of Riley here in New York without—well—without thinking about them. Is that about it?

March: That's it exactly. Anyway, I guess it won't be very long before I'll be back there—so what am I worrying about.

Interviewer: You mean you really want to return to the South Pacific?

March: Those pals of mine aren't having any picnic. I promised 'em I'd be back to help out—and I will. They need all the help they can get.

Interviewer: I take it you have no quarrel, then, with my description of the place being the "hot spot of the Pacific."

March: (Lightly) Well, that's one way of putting it. I'm afraid my way of putting it wouldn't sound too good over the radio.

Interviewer: Lt. March—I don't suppose there's any doubt in your mind why we asked you to appear on this broadcast. Our listeners, like all Americans at home, are intensely interested in hearing about what's going on out there in the Solomons—and we particularly want to hear about it from men like yourself, who have actually participated in combat. So, let's move along and have your story. First of all, how old are you?

March: Twenty-four, just a few days ago.

Interviewer: Did you attend college?

March: Yes, I graduated from the University of North Carolina back
in 1940.

Interviewer: Any special degrees?

March: I was after a degree in Physical Education, but I settled for an A.B.

Interviewer: Why?

March: Because that's when I decided to enter naval aviation.

Interviewer: Immediately after graduation?

March: That's right.

Interviewer: I understand you were quite a track man in college. Did
you win any particular recognition in that line? You could be a
champion for all I know—so happens I don't follow track activities in the papers.

March: I think you'll find in the records, that I was National Pentathlon
Champion.

Interviewer: I sort of put my neck way out on that one, didn't
I. Anyway, I think that's fine, Lt. March—apparently the qualities which gave you recognition as a winner in that field have
been carried over into naval aviation. Now you say you entered
the service right after you graduated from the University of North
Carolina. When was that?

March: I was enlisted as a Cadet on December 16, 1940. I was twenty-
one at the time.

Interviewer: Where did you start your flight training?

March: I started my primary at the Naval Reserve Air Base at Anacostia.

Interviewer: That's just outside of Washington, D.C. Then where did
you continue?

March: I was then ordered to the Naval Air Station at Jacksonville.
I was there about five months, went from there to Miami, where
I got my wings and was commissioned an Ensign.

Interviewer: Did you state a preference for any particular type of duty?

March: Yes, I did. I asked for fighter duty aboard a carrier—and got it.

Interviewer: That, of course, is in keeping with the Navy's policy
to assign men where they want to be—and for which duty they

are best fitted. Of course, not every man is fortunate enough to get the duty he wants. The needs of the Navy at a given time must be considered as well as the man's fitness for such duty he requests, as shown in his training record. Anyway, evidently both you and your instructors felt the right spot for you was behind the controls of a fighter plane. Have you ever regretted your choice of duty?

March: I should say not. If I had it to do over again, I'd still ask for fighter duty.

Interviewer: Where did you take your operational training, Lt. March?

March: San Diego. There we trained for every conceivable type of operation. Then I was assigned to a squadron destined for further training at Pearl Harbor. We arrived there just about the day after the Battle of Midway.

Interviewer: In other words—sometime in June 1942.

March: That's right. We trained pretty carefully for about a month, operating with other squadrons, practicing landing operations—strafing—in fact, everything in the book and a lot more.

Interviewer: When did you personally have your first contact with the Japs?

March: I was just about to come to that. Actually, my first contact with the Japs came on August 7th. Our mission was to act as air support for the Marines going in to take the airport and soften up the harbor defenses set up by the Japs at Tulagi.

Interviewer: Now wait a minute Lieutenant, it has been my understanding that the Marines took over Henderson Field at Guadalcanal on August 7th.

March: They did. But it is also a matter of record that we were in the air protecting the landing parties before the Marine fliers came. Our skipper Lt. Lou Bauer, from Philly, led us on that first strafing attack on August 7th.

Interviewer: I stand corrected then. Tell us more about that first attack. How did you feel about meeting the enemy for the first time in the air? Were you scared?

March: I was plenty scared. And anybody who says he isn't scared in a situation like that is either abnormal mentally and emotionally—or he's a liar.

Interviewer: What kind of plane were you flying at the time?

March: A Grumman F4F.

Interviewer: For the benefit of our radio audience, the Grumman F4F is the Navy's single seater fighter plane, more popularly known as the Wildcat. The naval aviators who pilot this type of aircraft have to do their own navigation, handle the radio, and fire the .50-caliber guns.

March: That's the general, idea. It's strictly a one-man operation.

Interviewer: Tell us about it.

March: Well I was, as I said before, plenty scared—and a little nervous at first—but then when I found myself right square in the middle of things, I was kept too busy to think about myself. And that's the time that I thanked my lucky stars I had trained in the Navy.

Interviewer: How do you mean?

March: Well, it's pretty hard to explain.

Interviewer: I think I know what you're trying to say—and that is—when the real test came, you were able to meet it squarely and confidently, as a result of your training in naval aviation. You were trained so well and disciplined to such an extent that when the time actually came to prove what you really knew—it was a little like a practice maneuver.

March: Exactly, excepting this time—unlike a practice maneuver—I had to be right or else. Everything I did that first time came instinctively and easily. I had the comfortable feeling of knowing what to do and precisely when. This may sound a little boastful—but that's not the way I mean at all. What I'm trying to say is that I consider the training I got in naval aviation the best in the world. I felt I had an advantage—a big advantage over every Jap—because of my training. After all, the proof of the pudding is in the eating—there were thirty-six of our fighters altogether in that attack—and we lost only three in actual combat, recovering two of the pilots at a later date.

Interviewer: How'd you make out? That is, how'd you make out personally?

March: That's a pretty hard question to answer. Officially I was credited with knocking down an enemy dive bomber during one of the actions.

Interviewer: I'd say that's a mighty fine record for the first time up to bat. When did you actually move in over Guadalcanal?

March: Early morning about 0530.

Interviewer: Then you yourself were one of the first men to fight in the air over Guadalcanal.

March: Right. We started off the battle at 0530. The Marines landed not many hours later. And what a job they did on those Japs when they did land. No, those Marines, make the "Dead End Kids" look like a gang of sissies. They're really tough—and I mean tough! That goes for the land troops and Marine flyers as well.

Interviewer: At this point, let's not fail to remind our audience that all Marine Aviators are trained by the Navy. The training they receive is identical to that of the naval aviator. Tell me, Lieutenant, how do the Grumman Wildcat's stack up against the Jap Zero fighters?

March: Well, of course, it's well known that the Jap Zero is a much lighter plane. That means they can fly level faster—they can climb faster—and they can, by and large, out-maneuver us. On the other hand, they're pretty flimsy craft—they can't pull out of a fast, deep dive without something going wrong—and once we hit one, it usually blows up right in the air. The Grumman Wildcat, while not as fast, is well-protected—can take a lot of punishment and they can dive.

Interviewer: According to all reports, our success in knocking Zeros out of the air has been phenomenal. Can you elaborate on that a little?

March: I don't know what the actual odds are—but I'd guess there are about eight Zeros knocked down to every one Wildcat.

Interviewer: That's a high percentage—eight to one.

March: Well, take this case, for example. On August 24th our squadron alone knocked off twenty-seven Jap planes in the vicinity of the Stewart Islands—that's northeast of Guadalcanal. We lost only two planes—that's a percentage of a little over thirteen to our one. The total number of Jap planes knocked down by all of our operations that day was ninety-six.

Interviewer: Ninety-six in one day! I guess you'll never forget that occasion.

March: Not likely. Then about the 11 September, my squadron was transferred from the carrier to Henderson Field. We were based there and we lived there.

Interviewer: Operating with the Marines.

March: Yes, and I'll never forget that occasion either. There they were with only eight planes—going up to fight four and five times a day against always a superior number of Jap planes—every day—day in and day out. They were really whipped down. And then when we arrived with twenty-four planes to add to their eight, you should have seen the reception we got. We were like an answer to their prayers—and were they thankful and happy about it. They cheered every one of us, and they'd meet us and almost lift us out of the cockpit. I have never had a warmer reception in all my life. And I never expect to see a happier gang of tired guys anywhere. All they could say was—"Boy, are we glad to see you" and "Thank God you're here at last" and "Wait 'til Tojo comes over again expecting to meet only eight planes and we go tearin' into them with thirty-two." That was an occasion I'll always remember.

Interviewer: How long were you stationed on Henderson Field, Lieutenant?

March: My squadron was there from September 11 until October 15. That's a pretty long time when you consider that almost every day you go up to fight in the air two or three times—most of the time when you're on the ground you're dodging shells and bombs. And every minute of every day you've got to be on guard against Japanese snipers up in trees—and behind bushes.

Interviewer: I see our time is running a little short, Lieutenant, but how about telling us about some of your other experiences.

March: Well, we had a pretty decent contact on September 12—knocked a number of planes down—and lost only one ourselves. Then the next day we bagged twelve enemy bombers and three Zeros—and only lost one pilot. Then on the 28th, twenty-five enemy bombers came over and we knocked down no less than twenty-three of them.

Interviewer: How many planes did we lose on that meeting?

March: None. Not a single plane or pilot. There's the best proof in the world of the superiority of naval aviation training.

Interviewer: In other words, you think pretty highly of it.

March: I most certainly do. In fact, I'm convinced that even if things were reversed—and we had to fight in Zeros—and the Japs had our Grumman's—we would still have the upper hand in combat—because of our training.

Interviewer: That's a mighty fine tribute. But tell me, Lieutenant, would you actually prefer to fight in a Zero?

March: No, sir. I'll take Grumman protection any day.

Interviewer: Well, thanks a lot for being with us today, Lt. March.

Interviewer: We really do appreciate hearing your story because it gives us all a better understanding of what a courageous group of fighting airmen are actually responsible for the good news we read in our newspapers today—United States in complete control of Guadalcanal.[8]

February also brought "Dirty Eddie" the wonderful news that Elsa was expecting their first child in September 1943.

Chapter 8

Unbearable, We Just Want to Get the Hell Out

By the time the U.S. forces had gained control of and held Guadalcanal, the Allies had defeated the Japanese in Papua New Guinea, which consolidated their position in the area. The next phase of operations, to advance up the Solomon Islands chain, centered on New Georgia and ultimately the key target Rabaul.

"Dirty Eddie's" new squadron, VF-24, was formed on December 1, 1942, at Floyd Bennett Field, New York, as part of Air Group 24 based on the *Belleau Wood*. He reported for duty at the end of December 1942, with the knowledge that he would be going back to the combat area again. For many pilots, the prospect of further combat operations was not something they wished to contemplate, particularly after the horrors of Guadalcanal.

In the early summer of 1943, the *Belleau Wood* embarked on a shakedown cruise in the Gulf of Paria, which lies between the Venezuelan coast and Trinidad.[1] Upon returning in July 1943, VF-24 swapped their FM Wildcats for new F6F Hellcats while based at N.A.S. Willow Grove, Pennsylvania. The Hellcat would go on to be one of the mainstays of the Navy for carrier operations in the Pacific War and was a tremendous success. It was a rugged aircraft, easy to maintain, with a stable gun platform.

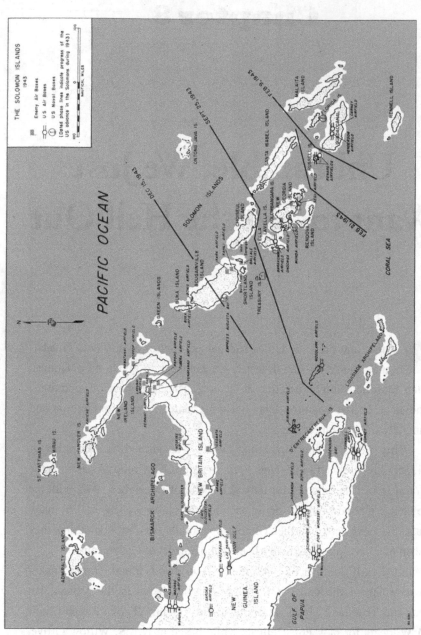

The Solomon Islands in 1943. On June 30, New Georgia was attacked and in August 1943 landings were made at Vella Lavella. Indicated on this map is the progress of the Allied advance towards Rabaul from February 1943 to December 1943. *Source:* United States Marine Corps.

The F6F was powered by the Pratt and Whitney R-200 Double Wasp radial engine, which proved to be one of the finest radial engines ever produced. This engine was used on the robust Republic P-47 Thunderbolt and the awesome and versatile Chance Vought F4U Corsair. For a fighter pilot, this engine was a godsend—it was renowned for taking an extensive amount of punishment and still performing well enough to get a pilot home.[2]

After a couple of weeks at the Philadelphia Navy Yard for modifications, the *Belleau Wood* sailed to join the Pacific Fleet on July 21, 1943. Prior to leaving port, "Dirty Eddie" said farewell to Elsa in Philadelphia. The carrier headed for the Panama Canal and they spent a couple of days in Panama, then proceeded straight to Pearl Harbor. They arrived in Pearl Harbor on August 9, 1943. Flying operations were initially restricted due to the unavailability of parts for the planes, so the squadron had time to relax for a while:

We flew into Kaneohe right away. That's where we were for a while last year—it's the best spot on the island, really pretty. Well, we had a pretty darn good time there. "Stink" and I roomed together and another outfit was next to us. We had several good old-fashioned bitching sessions.

"Stinky" and "Dirty Eddie" had been reunited again in VF-24 and were once again sailing into danger together. They found that some old friends were stationed at Kaneohe. "Sandy" Crews, "Crud" Blair (Lt. (jg) Foster John Blair), "Dick" Loesch, and Alan Fairbanks (Lt. (jg) Henry Alan Fairbanks, Jr.) were with *Fighting Six*. "Ep" Eppler (Lt. (jg) Harold John William Eppler) was also there with the torpedo outfit:

Boy, it sure was good to see all that gang again. "Stink" and I tried to pull some strings to get in their outfit. Maybe when we get back to Pearl, we'll be able to swing it.

The squadron left Kaneohe and went back to the ship on August 22, where "Dirty Eddie" bumped into "Chuck" Ernst, the supply officer on the

Admiral's staff. He was able to ship all of "Dirty Eddie's" extra gear home. Preceding his departure, he was able to play some tennis at Ford Island and had an enjoyable couple of days before leaving port on August 25. A change around in the squadron meant that twenty-four *Fighting Six* pilots (formerly *Fighting Three* under "Butch" O'Hare) were reassigned to the *Independence*. The other twelve planes were transferred to the *Princeton*. VF-22 was then put aboard the *Belleau Wood* and the SBD Douglas Dauntless dive bombers were taken off all the small carriers. VF-22 and VF-24 were to operate as two squadrons, along with nine TBF Grumman Avenger torpedo bombers.

While assigned to VF-24, "Dirty Eddie's" fitness reports (from March 31, 1943 to October 7, 1943) demonstrated how his previous combat experience was a real asset to the squadron:

Lt. (jg) March handles his regular and additional duties in a capable manner. He is neat in person and dress, and his military and personal character is that of an officer and gentleman. In his capacity as Flight Officer, he has disseminated his fleet knowledge and previous combat experience to the junior officers to greatly further their efforts in becoming finished combat pilots. He is recommended for promotion when due.

Lt. March has performed his duties as a Flight Instructor in an excellent manner. He possesses a strong character and a pleasing personality. He is a fine leader and is a person you would like to take with you when the battle is tough.[3]

According to "Dirty Eddie's" logbook he had amassed over 800 hours of flying, with sixty-four carrier landings to his credit by the end of August 1943.[4]

From September 1 to 10, 1943, Air Group 24 were involved in the occupation of Baker Island and later, an attack on Tarawa in the Japanese-held Gilbert Islands.[5] "Dirty Eddie" participated in these actions along with "Stinky," who had recovered from the wounds received a year earlier at Guadalcanal. Baker Island was a tiny atoll just north of the equator, just a dot of land in the vast Pacific Ocean. At the time of this campaign, "Dirty Eddie" made an interesting note in his logbook:

Crossed the equator thirty-two times, plus about ten times every hop.

"Dirty Eddie" and his squadron were part of the carrier group covering Army troops and Seabees building a landing field on Baker Island. "Dirty Eddie" was reminded of the movie *Flight for Freedom* (1943), a fictionalized account of Amelia Earhart:

Remember that picture with Rosalind Russell where she was supposed to land on Howland Island?

Well, that and Baker are right together—just little specks in the ocean. There's nobody there on the island, but the Japs send out P-boats every day and they take those in on their searches from their nearest base about 650 miles away. Well, the Princeton bunch have been over the island on patrol when they get there and shot two of 'em down.

The squadron's part in the operations was flying combat air patrols over the area to protect the forces working there. "Dirty Eddie" completed eight patrols of just under five hours each in ten days.[6] Once the airfield was completed, they would head back to Pearl Harbor, where he and "Stinky" were hoping to be transferred to another unit. They were both unenthusiastic about being in this squadron as there were some personality clashes and they were already looking to get out. He also reactivated his diary:

September 3, 1943. Yesterday, I was going to tell you about "Stink" and I trying to get into VF-6. As soon as we get back, we're going to work on it. These instructors in our outfit make life so damn unbearable that we just want to get the hell out. Boy, it'll be great to be with all that gang— guys who know what the hell all this is about and with no self-styled, big shots and hot pilots telling you how to go about this business of flying. Well baby, from now on I'm going to keep this up like last time.

The combat air patrols over Baker Island became a routine as the Seabees continued construction of the airfield on the atoll:

September 5, 1943. Well, had the hop the Japs usually show up on. They didn't come though, so we just flew round and round for four hours or so. Heard some scuttlebutt that we'll have at least a week more. The Army said it'd take five days for 'em to do the job, so naturally it'll take at least three times that. If we hang around here too long the Japs'll send down some surface craft and then we will be in hot water. Good night for now, honey—I love you.

There was no sign of any Japanese aircraft and the routine combat patrols persisted, with a dawn five-hour sortie for "Dirty Eddie":

Plenty long for the old fanny to get tired!

A most welcome batch of mail caught up with the men and was very well received, while "Stinky" returned from the *Princeton* in the afternoon with a bottle of scotch, which resulted in a few drinks and the accustomed merriment:

Only enjoyment on here—a few drinks and a good old bull session!

The reality of the dangers of flying from a carrier was evident on Monday, September 6, with the loss of a fine pilot:

Hope we leave this place soon—it's costing us more than it's worth. Johnny (Lt. Cdr. John O. Curtis) went over the side today and didn't get out. I didn't see it—we had relieved him over the island. He took off at 0900 and landed at 1300. We took off at 1200 and landed at 1600. He caught the number nine wire, broke it, went right through the barriers, hit two parked planes and went over the port side. It hardly seems possible, but that's the way things are in this game, honey. We broke out a couple of more bottles tonight and drank up—it's the way he would have wanted it.

Johnny Curtis was a well-respected and popular skipper, but his accident brought home the dangers of flying on a carrier and his loss was deeply felt by all of the squadron. As a result of the unfortunate events, the tactical organization was rearranged. Although "Dirty Eddie" and "Stinky" remained together, they were still unhappy with the way things were being run. But for the recent loss of their skipper, they would have applied for transfer earlier:

> *We're going to get out of it if we can, anyway. We'd have done so before if it wasn't for Johnny. Now with Ross* (Lt. Robert Ross) *being the skipper there's nothing to do but get out.*

There was no flying for "Dirty Eddie" the following day (September 7), which turned out a pretty easy day. The scuttlebutt was that the *Belleau Wood* and its air group were going to support the assault on Tarawa in the Gilbert Islands:

> *Gee, I feel that we're too under-manned for that. We need at least some cruisers to even attempt a job like that!*

"Dirty Eddie" took on the responsibility of engineering officer in the squadron, after the loss of Johnny Curtis:

> *What I don't know about that stuff will fill a book!*

There was always the possibility of enemy attack and General Quarters was announced on the afternoon of September 8. The action resulted in the sinking of an enemy patrol boat by the pilots from the *Princeton*. "Dirty Eddie," while on combat patrol for nearly four hours, was sent out on an erroneous contact:

> *I was sent out on what seemed to be a sure bogey. I finally spotted him from 10,000 feet while he was on the water. As I closed though, saw he was a B-24.*

There was still uncertainty as to what would happen next for the squadron, and after the frustrations of bogus enemy aircraft sightings, thoughts would always turn to Elsa:

Don't know how much longer we'll hang around here. A little more dope tonight that we may make a hit-and-run raid on the Gilbert's. Can't see the value of it, though. Honey, your picture sure is cute here on the desk—your eyes twinkle at me all of the time.

The weight of being an expectant father thousands of miles from home led to "Dirty Eddie" waiting anxiously for news of the arrival of his first child:

Just waiting for you to send me the news about the addition to the family. Won't be long will it?

After extensive operations in the area since the start of the month, flying over three hours on the dawn patrol, "Dirty Eddie" had already accumulated more than thirty hours combat flying by Thursday, September 9:

That's a lot of flying for fighters 'specially when it's all operational and with not a let-up in sight. Tonight, we had more dope on Tarawa—looks like we may hit it after all. Had another bull session and a couple of cocktails tonight. Am feeling fine and am in darn good shape.

Aside from the long hours flying, "Dirty Eddie" was set for a restless time in the next few weeks waiting for mail to arrive with news of Elsa and the new baby:

September 10, 1943. Another day and we're still around this damn place. I've flown around in so many left-hand circles that I lean to the left. Imagine a four-hour hop of just making left turns. That's what our hops amount to when we don't get vectored out anywhere. Right now though, honey, I've flown more this month than all of last month. Mail came today—none from you, though. Hope those pictures come soon that you sent and I want you to send a lot of snaps of yourself too, honey. Do you know that I love you?

There was no flying on Saturday, September 11, as it was a day off for "Dirty Eddie," which resulted in him catching up on engineering data. Afterward, he was loafing around and listening to music, so naturally his thoughts turned to Elsa and their time together at home. There was also news of impending action and the return of a pilot thought to be lost:

Another Saturday night, honey. Remember the fun we used to have on Saturday nights!

Got the word at GQ that we're to rendezvous with the Lex (CV-16) on Thursday and then go hit Tarawa. Might have some fun. We got Warren Omark (Lt. (jg) Warren R. Omark) *back from the destroyer tonight, he went over the bow in his TBF about nine days ago—the depth bombs went off and killed his two crewmen, but he wasn't scratched. We opened up a couple more bottles to welcome him home. He sure was glad to get back. Going to close now and hit the sack, honey. I sure do love you—or do you already know that?*

By Sunday, September 12, with the prospect of further combat looming in the next few days, "Dirty Eddie" remembered back to what he was doing the previous year. With no flying scheduled it was more loafing around, evening bull sessions, listening to the music of Johann Strauss, and the inevitable thoughts of Elsa:

Honey, do you know what I was doing one year ago tonight? Burying my head in a big hole while Tojo's cruisers were shelling the hell out of us. "Stink" was shot down a year ago tomorrow, too. Maybe this time next year I'll be home with you and we can celebrate Halloween together.

Think we'll leave here tomorrow. The Army finally moved in, eight days late. That's practically a record for 'em though—only wasting that much time. A beautiful moon's out, honey. Remember those beautiful

one's we used to watch by the rocks at Coronado? It'll be great to have
duty back there again, won't it?

The following day, September 13, again brought back memories of the
suffering and loss that had been the norm on Guadalcanal. This resulted in
a round of drinks to celebrate survival and commemorate the loss of close
friends. The conversation also centered on choosing a name for the forthcoming new baby:

Had a couple of drinks tonight. Sort of special occasion. One year
ago, they tried to get old "Stink" out of the war. Yet, here he is drink-
ing a highball and cussin' the Japs as much as ever. Finally pulled
out of this area tonight—going north to meet the Lex and her escort.
More mail came in today, but still none from you. The boys were
deciding on a name for the kid tonight. They didn't like Frank Joseph
too well. Donald Edward was about the best liked. Then they said he
could be known as D. Eddie—so carry on the "Dirty Eddie" name.
The Donald is "Stink's" name. What do you think of that idea? I love
you, baby—oh so much!

"Dirty Eddie" was obviously proud of his moniker and signed squadron
photos as "Dirty Eddie." He was looking forward to mail call, as a destroyer
had transferred a large number of letters from Pearl Harbor, which arrived on
Tuesday, September 14:

Lots of mail in the last few days—still none from you. Love you though
baby—even if you don't write.

Wednesday, September 15, the *Belleau Wood* made contact with the
Lexington and her escorts, which made up quite a task force, ready for the
anticipated assault on Tarawa in the Gilbert Islands.

Got the word today that we'll be within range of enemy aircraft for
forty-eight hours in the coming raid—and that we should be back at

F6F Hellcats and TBF Avengers of Air Group 24 pictured on the flight deck of the light aircraft carrier *Belleau Wood* during operations off the Gilbert Islands. "Dirty Eddie" served with VF-24 from the end of December 1942 to September 1943. *Courtesy National Museum of Naval Aviation.*

> *Pearl by the end of next week. We'll have to see how close they are to being right.*

The task force steamed closer to the target and the apprehension became more noticeable, the nearer the men came to combat operations:

> *We're going to hit the place the day after tomorrow—real early in the morning. Don't know how tough it'll be, honey—maybe not so bad. Then again, you can never tell. Quiet evening tonight. "Stink" and I went up on deck and walked for a while. Boy, sure is beautiful outside—a big gorgeous moon—just like your eyes! Did I tell you that I love you, my sweet?*

The day before the approaching skirmish, tensions and fears of whether they would come through the battle surfaced and in "Dirty Eddie's" case, no mail or news about Elsa and the baby weighed heavily:

Tomorrow's the day, honey—don't know yet how much we'll meet. We'll just have to hope for the best. Everything's going to turn out okay, just like it did the last time I was writing to you before we went on an attack. Hope I get some mail from you soon, darling—really am anxious to know how you're coming along. I'll quit for now—have to get up mighty early— we take off at 0435. I love you, my sweet—so very much.

The attack on Tarawa duly took place on September 18, with "Dirty Eddie" flying two sorties of combat air patrol covering the task force, amounting to six hours in the air.[7] He was none too happy with his orders, which again highlighted his discontent with his role in the squadron and increased his desire to be re-assigned:

The raid went pretty good today, we (the whole force) only lost a couple of planes and knocked the hell out of the island. Looked like a complete surprise. "Stink" and I were combat air patrol over the ship, our hops never got to go into the island. Ross took care of that—we were junior, so we stayed behind. Hell with 'em! The Captain of the ship sent us down some liquor tonight, so that was the thing we were waiting for—we opened several here at our room and had a real old-fashioned party. About fifteen to twenty of the real boys. We're on our way home (Pearl) now and should be there before long. Let's hope that things break right and we get transferred. Better close now, honey—am going to shower and then hit the sack. I love you though, honey—you know that!

On Sunday, September 19, "Dirty Eddie" had an easy day and after General Quarters snoozed until lunchtime. The flying of the previous day caught up with him as he slept again through General Quarters that evening. He then listened to a little music and was early to bed with the expectation that he would be back at Pearl Harbor in a few days. By Monday, September 20, the traditional "Crossing the Line" ceremony commenced, allowing the men to blow off steam after the actions of the previous few days. Prior to returning to port, "Dirty Eddie" and "Stinky" were still hoping for a new squadron:

> *Had a lot of fun today. Started working on Neptunus Rex and his court to initiate all "Pollywogs." Had a lot of different lookouts posted today looking for Davey Jones—he came aboard and said the King would be here tomorrow. Most everyone on the ship entered into the spirit of the thing. We should be in port in a couple of days. Many changes may be made ...*

Flying was curtailed while the "Pollywogs" were duly initiated on Tuesday, September 21:

> *Had old King Neptune on board this morning—the ceremony went over pretty darn good. Practically everyone took it in good fun. We didn't fly again today—got the word that we fly ashore at 1000, Thursday. Don't know yet where we go or how long we'll be there or anything. Hope we stick around for a while, though. Won about 100 bucks in a crap game tonight. Goodnight now, baby—I sure do love you!*

Wednesday night, September 22, 1943, proved to be the closing chapter on the *Belleau Wood* for "Dirty Eddie," as events would take a new course for him in the next couple of weeks:

> *Last night on this tub for a while. We fly ashore in the morning. Think we'll go to Ford Island. We had a little get together tonight to sort of clean up anything we had to drink. Better stop for now—it's pretty late—sure hope I hear from you soon. I love you honey (sent you $175 today).*

The squadron flew back to shore on Thursday, September 23. Along with a few days of rest and recreation on a large, private estate that had been turned over to the Navy, they renewed old acquaintances and caught up on the news of more buddies missing in action. The word was the ship would go out again along with three large carriers and the scuttlebutt was to hit and take Wake Island. The absence of mail from Elsa was really getting to "Dirty Eddie":

Spending the week at a big mansion on the beach that was given to the Navy for "broken down aviators." Boy, what a place! I'd feel great if it wasn't for the fact that I haven't received a letter from you for a long time. Don't understand why in the world you don't write, honey.

By Sunday, September 26, "Dirty Eddie" had finally received some news, although no word about the baby yet:

Two letters from you. One was dated the 8th and one the 20th—they're still a long way apart. Sure glad to hear from you though, baby. Took it easy today. Drank beer, took pictures, played poker and shot crap! Really a good life. Going to play golf in the morning. I love you, my sweet—very much.

"Dirty Eddie" remained uneasy about his skipper and it seems he was not the only one experiencing conflict with Ross:

September 27, 1943. Played eighteen holes of golf today. I played some tennis with the fellows that run the place there and am going to spend the night here. I hope Ross says something to me about it. Gee, I'd like to pin that guy's ears back. Heard what VF-22 thinks about him today—just the same as all of us do. I love you, honey—boy, how I love you!

The friction between "Dirty Eddie" and his skipper reached a head on Tuesday morning September 28, when "Dirty Eddie" was reassigned to towing targets. For an experienced combat pilot, this could only be described as punishment duty:

Came into the squadron this morning and found out that I had been transferred. Looked fishy to me, so followed it up and found out that

Ross had gotten rid of me. Was transferred to N.A.S. Barber's Point—
which would mean towing targets, etc. Boy, he really gave it to me!
Saw "Chuck" and we went to see some people and it ended up with
my seeing Captain Johnson here. He gave me the whole story (Ross'
side), I gave him my side and he cancelled the orders and said that he'd
probably transfer Ross out of the squadron after this trip. Everyone on
the whole station knows about it and is on my side. They are so damn
mad they don't know what to do. The towing was supposed to be a
disciplinary means and they cancelled 'em. He told me to hang around
here 'til this trip is over.

It was just a matter of waiting to see what transpired in the next few
days after the squadron sailed from Pearl Harbor. Unknown to "Dirty
Eddie," he was now the father of a baby girl, who was born the same
day as his shipmates sailed from port, Wednesday, September 29, 1943.
His daughter would be called Mary Elizabeth March or "Baby Skeex,"
after Mary Elizabeth Shoemaker, widow of his good friend, "Dutch."

The boys left today—sure hated to see 'em go without me. I'll be okay
when they get back though. Can go to any squadron here—or stay with
VF-24 if they get rid of Ross. Should write you tonight but I'm fighting
to stay awake now. I love you, honey!

The next day, "Dirty Eddie" received new orders to report to C.A.S.U. 1
for temporary duty, but he was unsure of what he would be doing. He played
tennis in the afternoon and was still not aware of his newborn baby:

Honey, it won't be long 'til the baby gets here will it—hope I can get the
mail stopped before it goes to the ship so I can get the news in time.

At the time of his promotion to lieutenant on October 1, 1943, there
were a number of things that were up in the air for "Dirty Eddie." He didn't
know that he had a daughter, news of his promotion did not catch up with
him until a few days later, and his future posting was still undetermined.

He played tennis in the afternoon, went to the on-station movie in the evening and thought about his friends and expected new arrival:

Can't help wondering what the boys are doing now. One of these days we'll probably read about it. Won't be long 'til we're proud parents, will it my darling? Played more tennis today and I must be getting old. Wrenched my back on a serve. Hurts like anything. "Chuck" and I really talked over old Coronado times over some beers, too. We both decided that it was wonderful duty there at that time. How'd you like to be back there now honey, with all the gang again? Just looked over a book called "America's Navy in World War II" by Gilbert Cant. It mentions "Dutch" and I in it. Just about the August 24 (1942) battle or the Battle of the Eastern Solomons. Good night for now, my sweet—I love you.

Some good news was received with the arrival in port of the *Bunker Hill*, with two Guadalcanal buddies aboard:

October 3, 1943. "Chuck" and I took the afternoon off today. Took some stuff to eat and some beer and a Jeep ("Chuck" always can get one 'cause he's on the staff) and went for a drive around the island. Really a good ride. The Bunker Hill came in today with VF-17 in F4Us and VF-18 in F6Fs. The F4Us are going south. Johnny Kleinman and Jim Halford are with them.

Honey, our mail is going to get all messed up. Might try and fix it up so I can phone you in a couple of days. Sure would be swell to hear your voice.

By Monday, October 4, he still had no news of the baby, but "Dirty Eddie" managed to catch up with Halford and Kleinman, and also the guys from the *Bunker Hill*:

Stood the watch tonight. Found out "Bud" and Muriel got married two weeks after "Bud" got home—about the middle of August. Sure wish we could have been there to see it—how 'bout you? Fooled around

Ens. John Kleinman in 1941. He and "Dirty Eddie" were close friends and served together at Guadalcanal and later with VF-17. *Courtesy Dale P. Logsdon and Frances Kleinman Rowland.*

today, talking with the boys off the Bunker Hill. Found out Don Runyon and "Bobby" Dibb (Lt. (jg) Robert Allen Murray Dibb) *from old VF-6 are with VF-18. Might try and work in there. Hope that "Stink" and I get a chance to get out of this outfit.*

Within the next ten days, "Dirty Eddie's" life would change forever. He would eventually experience the unbridled joy of becoming a father and receive confirmation of his promotion and extra pay. Lastly, he would report to the premier F4U Corsair squadron in the Navy, VF-17, which was about to embark on what would be a record-breaking tour in the South Pacific Theater.

Chapter 9

Fighting Seventeen

T he Allies were working their way up the Solomon Island chain, had invaded New Georgia, and landed at Vella Lavella. They were heading toward Bougainville and ultimately the crucial target Rabaul. Of great significance to the Navy's primary mission of defeating the Japanese was the introduction into the fleet of the new *Essex*-class carriers and their air groups, equipped with new and more effective combat aircraft. The *Bunker Hill*, built in Bethlehem's Quincy, Massachusetts yard, was launched on the first anniversary of Pearl Harbor and commissioned on May 25, 1943, with Capt. John J. Ballentine commanding. She was the fourth of the new *Essex*-class carriers and her addition to the Pacific Fleet was eagerly awaited. No time was wasted in going through the steps necessary to convert a brand-new ship and crew into a fighting machine.[1]

Carrier Air Group Seventeen (CAG-17) had been commissioned on January 1, 1943, at N.A.S. Norfolk.[2] Its fighter squadron VF-17, led by Tom Blackburn, had nine months to get ready for combat in the then-brand-new Chance Vought F4U Corsair. The Corsair was the first American fighter to house a 2000-horsepower engine and to top 400 mph.[3] The most unusual feature of Vought's design was its inverted gull wing, which allowed a shorter, lighter landing gear. This provided adequate ground clearance for the large, thirteen-feet, four-inch propeller required to absorb the power of what was then the largest engine available for a fighter airplane.[4] After the pilots had become familiar with this powerful new fighter, they had to qualify for carrier landings. This was made all the more difficult due to the long "hose nose" and pronounced bounce on landing. To become carrier-qualified, the pilots had to fly five touchdowns and arrests, not an easy task while still getting to grips with such a new and formidable airplane as the Corsair. Blackburn worked and trained the men hard and instilled a team ethic. He also stressed the importance of gunnery as, after all, the aim of air combat is to shoot down the enemy. Blackburn "worked their tails off" to be proficient in all these areas.[5] Blackburn was best described by VF-17 ace, Lt. (jg) Danny Cunningham:

"I had all the respect and admiration in the world for Blackburn. I think our squadron was good because he trained the hell out of us. We had the best fighter plane and the best skipper in WWII. That's why we were successful. It's like any other business, it starts from the top. The skipper was absolutely great. He was one of those guys that did it, then said 'now do it.' He was an eager-beaver, tough as hell and when he gave an order, you did it. He led by example, which inspired confidence and I respected that. He had the most hours of flying in the whole squadron. Blackburn stressed tremendous amount of gunnery training. Overhead, high side, flat side runs. We got pretty damn good."

On June 28, 1943, flight operations commenced and Air Group 17 started preparing for combat operations in the Pacific. The *Bunker Hill* sailed for its shakedown cruise to Trinidad close to the Gulf of Paria on July 13, 1943. This was designed to mesh the air group as a team and run the bugs out of the ship.[6] This was also the last chance for Blackburn to decide on the team he would take into combat. The *Bunker Hill* returned to Norfolk on August 10, 1943, for Air Group 17 and the ship to make their final preparations to go to war.

Blackburn made a number of changes and at the same time, they took delivery of new F4U-1A Corsairs, which incorporated a number of design modifications resulting from feedback from the pilots during training.

Among a number of changes made was raising the pilot's seat and adding a bubble canopy to improve visibility.[7]

In September, the *Bunker Hill* left via the Panama Canal for Pearl Harbor. When VF-17 arrived at Pearl Harbor, they were detached from the *Bunker Hill*. Ray DeLeva, Chance Vought's Field Service Representative working with the squadron, recalled the event:

"When the Bunker Hill came into Pearl and they were detached, I never saw a more dejected group in my life. They thought they were going to lose the F4U. But owing to the strength of Tom Blackburn and the rest of the squadron who were great enthusiasts of the Corsair, very supportive of Chance Vought, they fought to keep the airplane."[8]

Blackburn had the option of staying on the *Bunker Hill* and flying the Hellcat, but by unanimous vote, the squadron chose to stick with the Corsair. As a consequence, VF-17 would become a land-based squadron when they reached the Solomon Islands.[9] This was a logistical decision, as the Marines had parts for the Corsairs on the islands, whereas the Navy could not support a single carrier-based Corsair squadron at that time.[10]

At Pearl Harbor, Lt. Cdr. Tom Blackburn was still lacking pilots with combat experience and was presented with the opportunity to snag a couple of battle-hardened aviators, "Dirty Eddie" and "Stinky" Innis. "Dirty Eddie" noted his thoughts to Elsa about the eventful day:

October 5, 1943. Big day today, honey. Got into VF-17, made Lt., and won $100 shooting crap! Sending the latter to you. About the squadron, it looks like a pretty good deal. They're flying F4Us and have been together for nine months. Jim Halford and Johnny Kleinman are with 'em—a swell skipper too! It seems he has two brand new Ensigns (Ens. Wilbert Peter "Beads" Popp and Ens. Clyde Dunn) that he doesn't want to take along—no F4U time or experience. So he took me in one of their places 'cause I'm supposed to be experienced. They're going to try to order "Stink" with us too, when they come back in. We'll probably leave before that time, though.

The outfit will be land based honey, so it'll be pretty tough probably. I figure it can't be any tougher than Guadalcanal last year though,

Lt. James A. Halford, Jr., and his F4U Corsair in 1943. "Dirty Eddie" was a good friend of Halford's and served with him at Guadalcanal and later with VF-17. *Courtesy the James A. Halford Collection.*

> *so it'll be okay. Another thing too, we'll have a better chance of getting home sooner than if we were on a carrier.*
>
> *Sleepy as hell now, darling—am going to hit the sack!*

"Dirty Eddie" flew the F4U for the first time on October 6, and the following day he took his physical for promotion, which he passed and then set about letting Elsa know what was happening:

> *Just got through writing you a letter—a fellow will mail it back in the States. He's leaving in the morning. He'll try and phone you, too. Gee, he's lucky—he'll hear your voice pretty soon. Hope he realizes just how lucky he is—to hear my beautiful wife on the phone. I'm the lucky one though, I can love that beautiful wife and have her love me—and nobody else can do that! I love you so much, my dear.*

The next few days for "Dirty Eddie" were spent playing tennis, hearing news that his old squadron, VF-24, had taken part in a raid against Wake Island, and going into town to see a boxing show. He was also looking forward to seeing his pals:

October 10, 1943. "Stink" and the boys should be in tomorrow. Sure hope we can get "Stink" in the outfit.

Once he received the word that his buddies were back in port, "Dirty Eddie," Jim Halford, and Johnny Kleinman flew over to Maui to see the guys. Unfortunately, most of them were still aboard ship after their return from the Wake Island battle:

Our losses were pretty darn much—the fellows were too inexperienced. Finally found "Stink" this afternoon and tomorrow morning we're going to try and get him in the outfit.

He also heard about his former skipper, Ross:

Ross is really in hot water—Capt. Johnson wants Lee Johnson to come up and give him the real dope. Lee is skipper of VF-22 and was with us on the Gilbert island deal. Lee told me today he'd fix me up ok.

After weeks of waiting for information about the baby, "Dirty Eddie" at last received news of his new daughter on October 12, nearly two weeks after she was born. He also had further good news about "Stinky":

Well, baby—the word finally got here today telling me that we are proud parents! Sure am glad that you're over the worry and strain. Are you disappointed that it's a girl—I'm not.

"Stink's" going with us—got out of VF-24 today and will get orders tomorrow. We'll probably shove off then too. Goodnight my only darling—I love you something terrible.

Blackburn gave his word to Halford and Kleinman that once the squadron's first tour was over, they would be detached and sent home. They were still suffering the after-effects of the hell at Guadalcanal. As combat veterans, they agreed to help the young guns of VF-17, but the reality was that they were not in shape for extensive combat operations. "Stinky" was having problems hearing and was in much the same state as the other guys after being shot down and wounded at Guadalcanal. "Dirty Eddie" had suffered too, but despite the ordeal and memories of CACTUS, they would come to play their part in the legend that became "The Skull and Crossbones Squadron."

The *Prince William*, or "Pee Willie," with forty-five officers and sixty-seven enlisted men of VF-17 aboard, got underway at 0730 on Wednesday, October 13, and was scheduled to arrive at Espiritu Santo on October 25, 1943.[11] The daily routine for the voyage was ground training for officers and enlisted men and the usual card games and bull sessions:

Aboard the Prince William tonight, honey—we're shoving-off in the morning. We're passengers—won't fly 'til we get there. Probably go to Buttons again. "Stink" is officially with us now. It's old home week for sure, with him and Jim and Johnny and me. This is a darn good outfit— sure am glad we're in it. Wonder how you and "Skeex" are making out tonight—if she takes after you, she sure is going to be a cute rascal. Good night for now, honey—I sure do love you.

The first day out from port consisted of loafing around, sleeping, and playing cards. "Dirty Eddie" won $50. The following day was much the same and he was pleased to have his good friend, "Stinky" along with him:

October 15, 1943. We're just taking it easy the whole trip. Played Red Dog again this afternoon. Won about $150. I'm going to send you a lot of dough when we hit port. It's really great to have old "Stink" here too. He's happy for the first time since we came back last year. I really am too. This is a damn swell outfit, and I think we're going to do ok.

Sure do think of you a lot, baby. Gee, but it's going to be great to be with you again. I sure am going to be a model husband for you! Sure do love you too, honey!

Prior to "Crossing the Line" on October 18, the men were preparing for the traditional ceremony, with which "Dirty Eddie," as one of the "Shellbacks," was well-versed:

Got ready to meet old King Nep and his party in a couple of days, too. Ought to have lots of fun again. Sort of got things started for "Crossing the Line." Had some of the fellows fooling around and we had a "Kangaroo Court" in the Ward Room to give out subpoenas to all the fellows. We had a lot of fun and had a good program. There's a heck of a lot of talent in this outfit. Found out that the skipper and all the other "Pollywogs" in the outfit had planned a "blitz" against us for tonight. They called it off though—luckily for us.

The *Prince William* crossed "the Line" on October 18, which turned out an eventful day for all the "Pollywogs," but "Dirty Eddie's" luck deserted him in the crap games:

Had a pretty big day today—really worked on all the lowly "Pollywogs" aboard ship. I was the "Royal Barber" and cut about 300+ heads of hair. Boy, I really got tired. Didn't cut 'em all the way—just messed everyone's hair up in general. I've lost about $100 in the last two nights. Have to expect that though—I'm still big winner and am going to send you the dough when we hit Buttons. I love you so much, my darling.

Following the exertions of "the Line" ceremony, the next day was one of rest before the ship docked at Pago Pago for the day on Wednesday, October 20. The squadron went ashore for a few hours while three Grumman J2F Duck seaplanes were unloaded. The guys had a meal at the airfield and some beer at the Officers' Club. The ship then embarked at 1730 heading

"Crossing the Line" ceremony on October 18, 1943, when "Dirty Eddie" was "Royal Barber." Today, this traditional Navy ritual would be considered harsh on the men who had not crossed the Equator. *Courtesy the family of Jean March McAfee.*

for BUTTON. During the cruise to Espiritu Santo there was plenty of time for "Dirty Eddie" to think about Elsa and the future:

> *Passed near the Fiji's today—should be getting there before long. Can't be too soon to suit me—this is getting tiresome. We're going to miss Saturday when they launch our planes. "Stink" and I aren't flying ashore. We have it all figured out, honey. About a week at Buttons just fooling around, then go up the groove and be at some island for three or four months—then back to Pearl for a week or two at the "Rest Home" while awaiting transportation— and then home to you! Sure sounds good on paper, doesn't it?*

The squadron took off, apart from "Dirty Eddie" and "Stinky," who stayed aboard as they were not carrier-qualified in the F4U. The squadron flew off the ship to the airfield on Espiritu Santo. The last night before the *Prince William* docked provided a good excuse for a get-together:

> *Right now, we're having a little party and bull session. Jim, "Stink" and a couple of younger boys here. Pretty good stories floating around.*

Once the "Pee Willie" had docked on October 25, the duty for "Dirty Eddie" and "Stinky" was to see that all the squadron gear was successfully unloaded from the ship:

> *What a time since I last wrote in this! Really had a hell of a time last night getting all of the squadron's equipment and personal gear off the ship and out here to Espiritu Santo. Got a little sleep last night and we're flying up to Guadalcanal at 1130 and going on up north from there. "Stink's" not flying up today but will come up tomorrow and check out in the plane on Combat Air Patrol.*

Memories returned for "Dirty Eddie" once he arrived back on Guadalcanal on Tuesday, October 26, over a year since he left during the darkest days of the campaign. He found the place vastly different from what he remembered:

> *Back on Guadalcanal again, honey. We're spending the night here and then going on up to a field eight miles NW of Munda tomorrow. Gee, this place has sure changed. More damn fields and airplanes than you can shake a stick at. At supper tonight (in a mess hall!) four nurses were there! Gee, this war's getting civilized.*

For "Dirty Eddie," after the primitive conditions of his previous time in this area, the improvement in his surroundings continued to surprise him:

> *Just landed here—landed at Munda first and came over here (Ondonga). Civilization again, honey. We're staying in a Quonset hut with electric lights, cots, mattresses, clean sheets, pillow cases and even a spread.*

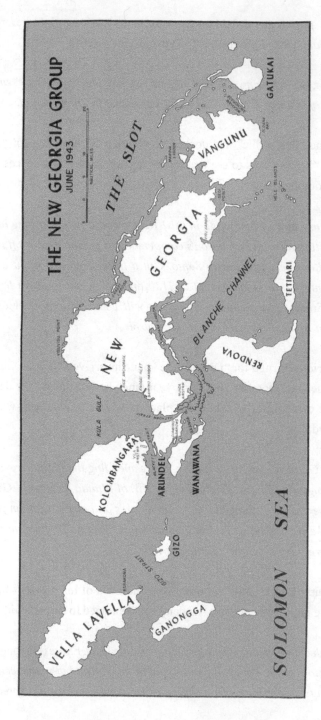

The New Georgia group of islands in June 1943, indicating Munda Airstrip. *Source:* United States Marine Corps.

They even have laundry service here! It sure is a far cry from the Guadalcanal of last year. The more I see, and the further north I go, the more I realize that nothing can ever be as bad as it was last year on Henderson Field.

Although times had changed, there was a familiar sight on the night of Wednesday, October 27:

Well, here we go again! Old "Washing Machine Charlie's" three nephews came over right after chow. They hung around for about two hours. It's now about 2130. Bet he comes back by midnight. Flew a hop up over Bougainville and other Jap bases this afternoon and nothing happened. This time last year, we'd have gotten our butts shot off. Boy, times have changed.

Chapter 10

The Boys Tasted Blood

During 1942 and early 1943, the Allies had originally planned to seize the Japanese bastion of Rabaul. However, by mid-1943, it became apparent that this would consume vital resources and time which they could not spare. It was, therefore, decided to encircle Rabaul, with the aim of cutting off its supply lines, and bomb it into submission. It was officially named Operation CARTWHEEL. The key to achieving their objective was the establishment of airfields on the island of Bougainville in order to put the Allied fighters and light bomber aircraft within range of Rabaul. The Japanese held five airfields in the Rabaul area, supported by 40,000 combat troops and a further 20,000 naval personnel, making the Allied mission a daunting task. The offensive was nicknamed "Operation Shoestring Two."[1]

As part of this campaign, *Fighting Seventeen* flew in to Ondonga, which to the locals meant "Place of Death," on October 27, 1943. This would be the beginning of a tremendously successful period of operations. Their main task was to help support the landings at Empress Augusta Bay (codename CHERRY BLOSSOM) on Bougainville and protect bombers in attacks against the Japanese airfields on the island.[2]

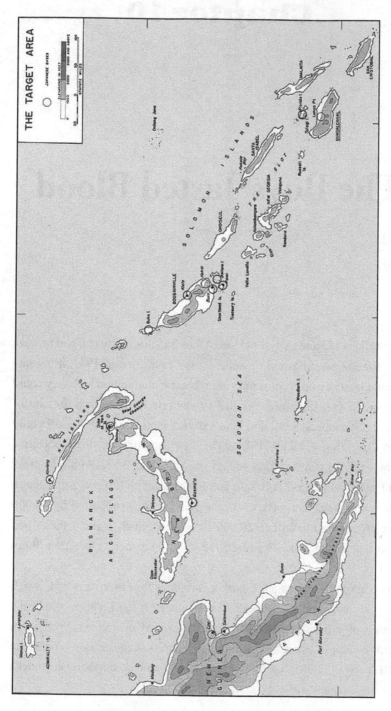

Japanese bases in the Solomon Islands in 1942–1943. After Guadalcanal had been secured the Allies worked their way up the islands with the goal of neutralizing Rabaul, the main Japanese fortress in the area. *Source:* United States Marine Corps.

VF-17 was part of Air Solomons, nicknamed "AirSols," comprised of U.S. Army, Navy, and Marine Corps and the Royal New Zealand Air Force, who worked together to clear the skies of enemy planes.[3] Air Solomons battered the Japanese airfields in and around Bougainville in October, the strategy being to ensure that the five airfields remained unserviceable for enemy operations.

Empress Augusta Bay was chosen for the Allied airfields due to its position far from existing Japanese troop concentrations elsewhere on the island. It was protected by the surrounding mountains and dense jungle, making it less vulnerable to immediate enemy attack. The Japanese had only 2000–3000 troops in the area, and the Allies were able to land successfully on November 1, 1943. The objective was not to capture the existing Japanese airfields or mount a major offensive on the island but to hold enough land to build airstrips adequate to launch attacks on Rabaul. The Allies worked on the assumption that it would take the Japanese weeks or months to hack their way through the mountains, jungles, and swamps to launch a counterattack.[4]

To many of the fresh pilots who flew into Ondonga, it was life in the raw. One of the new boys, "Beads" Popp later recalled:

"One day I made a casual remark to 'Stinky' that our life on Ondonga was somewhat primitive. That was a mistake on my part. He told me the life we were experiencing on Ondonga was idyllic when compared to the life they'd had on Guadalcanal. He said that the memory he carried of the main ingredients of life with the 'Cactus Air Force,' with the bad food, the frightful daily bombings from the Japanese bombers and the shelling from the Japanese battleships, the dysentery, the malaria, the stifling weather, the bugs, the loss of friends, the smell of dead bodies and the stress of continuing unrelenting aerial combat, would live with him forever."[5]

The first day, as far as "Dirty Eddie" was concerned, involved combat air patrol over the Treasury Islands, a short distance south of Bougainville. An interesting note in his logbook indicates that he was one of four pilots who escorted a PBY-5, with the distinguished Adm. William "Bull" Halsey aboard, from Munda to the Russell Islands.[6] Following his induction into the

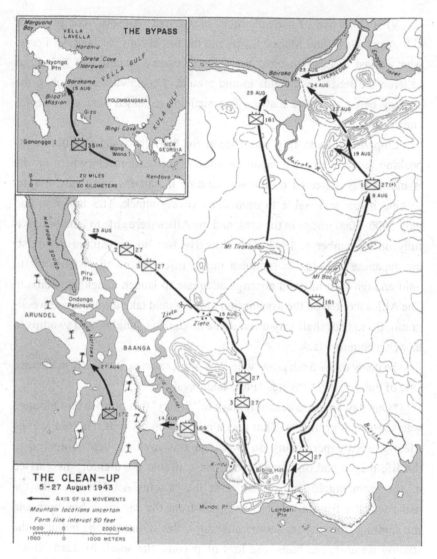

Airfields on the island of New Georgia at Munda Point and Ondonga (Ondongo) in August 1943. "Dirty Eddie" and VF-17 commenced operations from Ondonga on October 27, 1943. *Source:* United States Marine Corps.

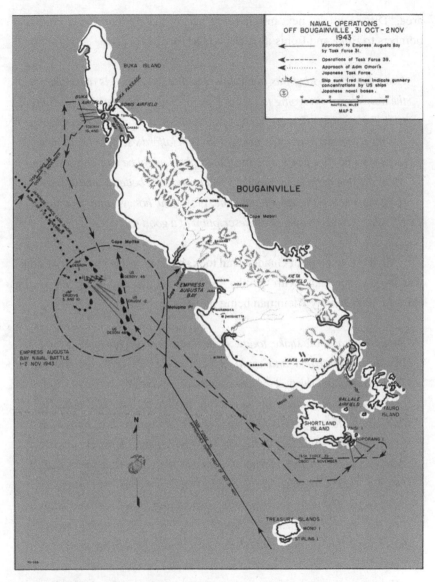

Naval operations off Bougainville from October 31 to November 2, 1943. Landings in Empress Augusta Bay enabled the Allies to build airstrips to bring Rabaul into range for fighters and light bombers. *Source:* United States Marine Corps.

area, "Dirty Eddie's" next mission was part of the medium-cover escorting bombers to Buka and Bonis airfields on October 29:

Hello, honey—writing this about the time that "Charlie" is due. Just got the word that we're going to escort B-25s to Buka Passage on a bombing raid. Twenty-four of us are going up. "Stink" had his first hop today and he's my wingman tomorrow. I think I'm Jim Halford's section leader when skipper wants to use us tomorrow. Looks like it might be fun. The next day, we're starting in on Bougainville. I feel a whole lot better than last year— really have a better airplane this time. I love you, honey—tomorrow night I'll be able to give you a swell description of a good rat race.

All of the veterans of Guadalcanal took part in the mission. "Dirty Eddie" was in good company, with "Stinky" as his wingman and being led by Jim Halford, with Johnny Kleinman being part of the cover too:

Really had a good strike today, honey—and no air opposition either. We hit Buka airfield and another right across the passage (Bonis). There were about thirty B-24s, twelve B-25s, twelve PV-1s, sixteen P-38s and twenty-four of us. Boy, they really plastered those airfields. They threw up quite a bit of AA fire, but it didn't hit anyone. Boy, things have really changed—this time last year, we'd have met at least one hundred Zeros up there. In the afternoon, some of the guys went up in Kahili Harbor—southern part of Bougainville—and shot up a lot of barges and other ships. The Japs are apparently evacuating from Shortland Island. Boy, they're back on their heels now. Honey, I love you so much—wonder how long it'll be before I can tell you that holding you in my arms.

For the next couple of days, the squadron prepared for the landings on Bougainville by softening up the Japanese defenses with a series of strikes and strafing attacks against specified targets:

October 30, 1943. Went on some strikes today—I didn't get in on it but some of the boys shot up the Japs on some of the islands. Tomorrow,

we start protecting our transports coming up the line for Monday's
landing on Bougainville. If the little yellow men don't come out and
play tomorrow or the next day—we really have them where they can't
fight back.

Preparations and briefings for the landings on Empress Augusta Bay
were undertaken on Sunday, October 31, as it was likely the squadron would
encounter their first enemy aircraft. They had learned from veteran
combat pilots the best tactics to shoot down the Zero. When "Dirty Eddie"
returned to the combat area, the Japanese aircraft had become known
by their codenames. This simplified the identification of aircraft such
as the Nakajima B5N2 Type 97 torpedo bomber to Kate. The principal
Japanese fighter, Mitsubishi A6M Zero became known by its codename
Zeke, but Zero was still used by many pilots. By the time VF-17 came up
against the Zero, the Corsair outclassed it in every aspect except maneuverability at low speed. *Fighting Seventeen* pilots believed in the F4U,
as Executive Officer Roger Hedrick (Lt. Cdr. Roger Richards Hedrick)
remembers:

"We were flying something much faster than anything we'd been in prior
to that time. Being an old fighter pilot myself, I knew that speed was the
number one thing I wanted in anything I was going into combat with."[7]

For most of the pilots, it would be the beginning of a long tour of
operations against the Japanese pilots. Veterans like "Dirty Eddie" knew
what to expect, but for many of the pilots, this would be their first experience of air combat.

Today sure didn't seem like Sunday. All the days seem the same here.
Tomorrow will probably be a pretty big day though. Started moving
stuff up the way today. Got the scuttlebutt that we may go back aboard
ship in a week or so. If that's the case, we'll probably get F6Fs. Hope
we don't go aboard though—I'm tired of all that red tape and hooey
that goes on aboard ship. I like this Marine life—wish I was a Marine,
doggone it. That's all for now, honey—will have lot's more to tell you
tomorrow night. I love you, honey.

The U.S. 3rd Marine Division had consolidated the landings on Empress Augusta Bay and building of the airstrips would shortly commence. *Fighting Seventeen* were part of the air cover to ensure that the landings were successful and protected against enemy air attack:[8]

Well, the boys tasted blood today. Knocked down six Zeros. This area knocked down about twenty altogether today. We lost one plane, but don't know about the pilot (Lt. (jg) John Henry Keith). *He was hit by AA on a strafing hop and landed in the water about eighteen miles from Jap territory. It was the only one we lost.*

(I have been interrupted twice by air raids, in fact one's on right now. We're in Condition Red and the planes have dropped their loads but are still hanging around. I still have my clothes on though and am ready for that old foxhole. "Stink" and I put a deck in it the other day and put benches along the sides. It's pretty comfortable!)

The New Zealanders lost one, too. I didn't see anything. Tomorrow some of us are acting as escort for a strike on one of the fields on Bougainville. I love you my darling, so very much.

Keith's aircraft was hit by antiaircraft fire over Kulitunai Harbor, Shortland Island. As a result of the damage he sustained, he was forced to make a water landing at about fifteen miles S.E. of Faisi Island. He was seen getting out of his plane, but without his raft. He was never seen again. Lt. (jg) Johnny Keith from Bourbon County, Kansas, was one of the original members of VF-17 when it was formed and a popular man in the squadron.[9]

Chapter 11

He Exploded Right in My Face

The Allies had landed at Empress Augusta Bay in an area chosen as remote from the main Japanese force on Bougainville and the most weakly-defended part of the island. The plan was to establish forward airfields specifically to target Rabaul. The Allies had established and secured a beachhead and consolidated their position on the island.[1] As part of the air cover protecting the Allied forces, VF-17 proved themselves against the Japanese Zero in their first foray into combat. *Fighting Seventeen* opened their account with a score of six Japanese aircraft confirmed and five damaged. It was a satisfying start to their first tour of combat operations and a sign of things to come.[2] The operations in this area were destined to be long and arduous for the weeks ahead. It would not be unusual for the pilots to fly several sorties each day and encounter regular contact with Japanese fighters.[3] "Dirty Eddie" featured regularly on the squadron roster:

November 2, 1943. Flew a 4½ hour escort hop this morning. Some TBFs were going out to finish off a Jap task force that got crippled in a battle with our cruisers last night. They couldn't find 'em though so we had to turn around and come back home. Nothing much

151

happened today. One of the boys (Lt. (jg) Tom Killefer) *got shot up
a little while he was strafing. Got burned around the ankles. He'll
be able to fly again in a couple of days.*

When Killefer's plane was hit, a 20 mm shell exploded in the cockpit, blowing up the oxygen bottle. Killefer suffered a painful shrapnel wound on the left leg. Both legs and his left forearm suffered first- and second-degree burns.[4]

One thing "Dirty Eddie" was not happy about was the censoring of his letters, but as always, his thoughts were with Elsa and the baby:

*Honey, I haven't had much time to write you—interrupted by air raids
in the evenings and pretty busy during the day time. Another thing too,
in this outfit a guy censors the letters and I just don't like the idea of
anybody reading my personal letters to you.*

*You know how much I love you though, don't you honey? Boy, I'm
really going to show you how I can be a good husband and father.
I hope I've been a good husband, honey—I've tried to be (guess I've
messed it up at times though, haven't I?). Don't know about this father
business though—I'm sort of new at it. Going to stop for now and try
and get a letter off to you. Should write about half dozen more too.*

Blackburn quickly recognized a solid team player in "Dirty Eddie"—the same qualities he had shown on the athletics field. He was a person who could be relied upon to do the job required of him, to carry out a mission as ordered and bring bombers back intact. He was advanced to a division leader and, soon after, to flight leader. "Dirty Eddie" and Blackburn appeared to share a mutual respect; Blackburn brought the best out of "Dirty Eddie," who appreciated the skipper's considerable leadership skills. All the pilots revered their commander, who was always happy to be with his men when the drinks flowed:

*November 3, 1943. Am writing this just as we're ending a sort of party
and get-together in our hut. "Doc"* (Lt. Lyle Herrmann) *got hold of*

three cases of beer and we drank it and one of the boys played the accordion and we all sang. Some of the boys put on specialties. This is really a swell outfit—"Stink" and I, we're plenty lucky to get in it. Skipper and I were just talking and figured that by now you and his wife have probably gotten together. If she's anything like him, she's plenty okay. Nothing much happened today. We were going out on an escort strike mission and had to turn back because of the weather.

The skipper also shuffled up the organization today. He put me leading a division back of Jim. "Stink" is the section leader in my outfit. He'd rather fly there than lead a division. I'd rather have old "Stink" there than anyone. He said he promised you he'd look after me, too. He says he can't hear half the stuff going on in the air—sort of thinks his right ear is shot because of that time he was burned. Love you, honey—feel wonderful all the time now—really am happy and satisfied—this is a really good outfit!

At Ondonga, Harry shared a tent with "Doc" Herrmann, Duke Henning (Lt. (jg) Basil Duke Henning), and "Stinky." Herrmann and Henning, along with Roger Hedrick, were key members of Blackburn's "brains trust." Over time, "Stinky" and "Dirty Eddie" would also become valued members of this group. The grueling pace of the operations continued for the squadron, which was one of the key components in the elimination of the Japanese in the area:

November 4, 1943. Funny thing happened today—we went on an escort mission with two PBYs who were going out to try and rescue three pilots who were shot down today, when we went on an attack on Kahili airfield. This TBF was hit by AA and bailed out about three miles from the Jap airfield. Well, we went up to look for them and doggone if here didn't come a guy sailing down through the sky in his chute. Landed on a little coral reef near Jap territory and we already had the rescue plane there. He really had some quick service.

We're hitting 'em pretty often now—going up to hit another field tomorrow. Bringing in more troops day after tomorrow—going to move in on Rabaul pretty soon, I think. Really carrying the fight to 'em now.

In response to the landings on Bougainville, the Japanese sent a task force to Rabaul with the intention of attacking the Allies. The Americans learned of the Japanese ships and reacted with the bold move of sending in two carriers (*Saratoga* and *Princeton*) to counter the enemy in Simpson Harbor, Rabaul, on November 5. The result of the carrier strike was that six of the seven Japanese cruisers were damaged, four heavily, resulting in the cancellation of the planned counterattack.[5]

Uneventful day today—strikes called off because of the weather. The "Sara" and Princeton went in to hit Rabaul. Haven't heard how they came out. We're all laying around our sacks now having a good old bull session. Really get some good stories when a bunch gets together like this. It's the most fun we have out here. Sure am longing for some

Carrier strike on Rabaul, November 5, 1943. Japanese ships in Simpson Harbor as U.S. carrier planes attack. Several heavy and light cruisers are present. Burning cruiser at left is *Maya*. Cruiser with explosion forward, in center, is probably *Takao*. Photographed from a *Saratoga* TBF. View looks east, with Matupi Island in center and South Daughter crater beyond. *Courtesy National Archives.*

mail from you honey—want to read how much you love me—just like
I love you.

The mission to escort bombers into Buka Harbor on November 6 was carried out by three veterans of Guadalcanal, "Dirty Eddie," Johnny Kleinman, and Jim Halford, who each led sections of four aircraft, in three of the four divisions on this strike. Lt. (jg) William "Country" Landreth was "Dirty Eddie's" wingman.[6] The results were very satisfying:

Had a good day today, honey. Some of us went with some B-25s to hit some ships that were just outside of Buka Harbor. We were only three miles from shore and right within spitting distance of the airfield for fifteen minutes. Between their bombing and our strafing, we sank all three ships. A destroyer escort went down in seven minutes—another smaller one in about twelve and an 8–10,000-ton tanker we left burning—I could see the smoke for eighty miles. Some guys went up there this afternoon and it had sunk—just a big oil slick left. Really felt good to hit 'em like that. On the way home, one of the divisions shot down a Betty bomber. Good day all round.

"Dirty Eddie's" criticism of Army pilots continued while he was at Bougainville:

November 7, 1943. Nothing much today—wrote a few letters and lost some dough playing Red Dog. I'll get it back next time (I hope). Had an escort hop today, but the Army bombers couldn't find the target— finally ended up by bombing and strafing one of our PT boats. Luckily, they missed!

Monday, November 8, 1943, proved to be a memorable day for "Dirty Eddie." On a fighter sweep toward Buka airfield, the flight, led by Tom Blackburn with "Dirty Eddie" and Ens. Whitfield Carlisle Wharton, Jr., observed a transport-type plane, probably a converted Ruth, (Fiat BR.20 Italian-built, twin-engine bomber used by the Japanese Air Force) circling to land. No dorsal turret was observed, and so it was assumed that the plane had been converted to a transport. The three flew right along the Buka strip, strafed a Zeke parked on the SW end and strafed personnel on the edge of the airfield. By this time, Blackburn and "Dirty Eddie" were on the tail of the Ruth, who was halfway up the runway, altitude 10 feet. Both planes had perfect shots (range 200–25 yards), and the Ruth, hit in the wing roots and motors, burst into flames and crashed. The flight then returned to Ondonga.[7] "Dirty Eddie" re-told the action to Elsa in that night's diary entry:

> *Big day today, honey. Supposed to go up as cover for a shipping strike at Buka but the weather was so stinking the bombers didn't come. All the fighters didn't rendezvous and I ended up on the skipper's wing. Well, we go through the most awful weather I've ever seen and go on up the way and come in on Buka from fifty miles out at fifty feet. We went right in the harbor and looked for ships that were supposed to be there. By then we'd broken off in two sections and the skipper and I went right in over Buka airfield at about ten feet and shot a transport plane that was just landing. Broke right in the landing circle. It was about 0710 and shot 'em so quick they didn't know what hit 'em. We both shot the plane—he exploded right in my face!*
>
> *Then we came home right over another Jap field. One of the boys got hit, but he got home okay. The skipper said we'd both take credit for a plane—'specially going in there—a "hot box." Hit 'em so fast they only had time to shoot one AA burst at us. This afternoon we flew another 3½ hours. Had about eight hours today.*

There is some conflicting information regarding "Dirty Eddie's" victory credit on November 8, 1943. His logbook clearly records "one Ruth shot down" on this date and he was later to be awarded the Air Medal for this action, with the citation stating "he flew one of two Corsairs which entered the landing circle over Buka Airfield and shot down a Ruth just as it was about to land." However, the VF-17 War Diary contains contradictory information, giving full credit to Blackburn, while the action report on this date within the War Diary appears to give them both credit for the Ruth. The squadron statistics appear to count the kill twice.[8]

Throughout "Dirty Eddie's" diary, he makes many references to the importance of playing his part in a successful mission rather than individual performance in shooting down enemy planes. In fact, if anything, he under-emphasized his contribution to all his squadrons' successes. For example: *"Planes are where you find 'em. Even though I only have two knocked down, that's just the way it goes. I'll get my chance later on to get some more. Two or twenty-two, it's all the same as long as everyone's doing his part."* It is clear from his journal that he was not inclined to invent a victory or exaggerate. His attitude was *"when I fly through the pieces, I'll claim him."* He had no respect for *"glory-grabbers ... just want*[ing] *to get planes to their credit."* After he shot down the Ruth on November 8, "Dirty Eddie" was later to be awarded two confirmed Japanese fighters destroyed, and from that point on he was universally recognised as an ace by the Navy, with a total of five victories noted in all official records.[9]

After the events of the previous day, "Dirty Eddie" had his first break from flying since he'd arrived at Ondonga. He was still waiting for mail and thinking of Elsa and "Baby Skeex":

A day off today—each division gets one every day now. A little rest doesn't hurt in the least either. Right now, we're having a few drinks and a song session. Boy, this outfit can really sing. We had an air raid a little while ago and we went out by the foxhole with our drinks and continued singing. The skipper's right there, too—right in front in everything. Boy, he's really a swell guy. Can't get over what a good outfit this is. Plenty satisfied with everything. Honey, I sure wish some mail would get through to us—I want to hear from my two girls.

A typical problem was how long it took for mail to catch up with the men serving on the islands. For them, news of home raised morale and, in their darkest times, kept them going. "Dirty Eddie" was assigned a combat air patrol on Wednesday, November 10, prior to one of the most momentous engagements of *Fighting Seventeen*'s time in the Solomon Islands. As they were not carrier qualified in the F4U Corsair, "Dirty Eddie" and "Stinky" were not part of this strike:

> *Big day tomorrow, honey. They're throwing the works at Rabaul.* *"Stink" and I aren't flying 'cause it involves landing aboard a* *carrier and we've never done that in a F4U (or "Hog" as they* *call them in this squadron). We're just going to cover the carri-* *ers as they send in their groups for the attacks. I'll tell you more* *about it tomorrow night. Incidentally honey, I have my own airplane* *and named it (painted on the tail) "Baby Skeex." Do you think the* *baby'll like that?*

After the success of the November 5 carrier raid, a follow-up strike was made on Thursday, November 11, 1943. The squadron's mission was to provide cover for a carrier strike force, consisting of the *Bunker Hill*, *Essex*, and *Independence,* as well as nine destroyers, while their squadrons escorted bombers to Rabaul. VF-17 flew out in early morning darkness through rain squalls to rendezvous with the carrier task force steaming toward the giant base at Rabaul. *Fighting Seventeen* covered the carriers while the strikes were launched; then landed aboard the carriers to refuel and then re-launched. They were there for one reason—to protect this task force from what was expected to be a large raid by the Japanese from Rabaul, who were going to do everything they could to destroy the three carriers. While VF-17 were flying cover, the Japanese attacked the carriers in four waves. The Japanese sent in approximately a hundred aircraft, which followed the returning strike with a dive-bombing and torpedo attack, covered by fighters. The principal opposition to the enemy strike was twenty-four F4Us of VF-17, plus twelve Hellcats. *Fighting Seventeen* pilots shot down eighteen enemy planes and damaged seven. The U.S. carriers were not damaged. The defeat in the Solomons stunned the Japanese. They withdrew their warships from Rabaul, which enabled the Allies to build airstrips on Bougainville.[10]

It was the first time in World War II that F4U Corsairs had operated from carriers in combat. If ever there was a question about the Corsair's suitability for carrier operations, they laid it to rest that morning.[11] William "Country" Landreth would later recall: "We were the first successful carrier-based F4U squadron."[12] Chance Vought Field Service Representative Ray DeLeva stated:

"VF-17 proved the F4U to Chance Vought and they were very much indebted to the squadron because it was through VF-17's efforts that we made it what it is for the Navy. Chance Vought was very much enthused by the way *Fighting Seventeen* handled that airplane. They showed it could be a good fighting airplane and it turned out to be the best fighting airplane in the Pacific. The Japs feared that thing like the devil."[13]

Later in the war, the use of F4Us on carriers would become normal operating procedure in the Pacific area. "Dirty Eddie" was rightfully proud of the squadron's achievement:

Celebrated Armistice Day pretty good today. Knocked down eighteen planes and lost only two planes and they were by water landings. Got the pilots back, though.

I got letters from you today, too. One of the boys brought me a letter from the Bunker Hill—October 24 was the date. Three sacks of mail earlier than that was put ashore at Buttons. Sure should have a lot of mail from you. The letter today sort of worried me when you mention your sore leg sure hope you're okay by now. I love you my sweet—so darn much.

The mail eventually caught up with "Dirty Eddie" on Friday, November 12, which brought Elsa much closer to him:

Happy day! Got a dozen letters from you today! Sure was good to hear from you, darling. Letters sure pep a guy up. Nothing much happening now. "Stink," Johnny, Jim and I went to a movie tonight (what a difference from last year) and then had a beer at the mess hall. We've decided we're all ready to go back home. Things aren't too tough—things are easier, in fact, much better planes, etc.—it's just that we've had enough!

Looking at the full moon just now too, reminding me of our last night together in Coronado last year when we watched the moon from the rocks. Remember—May 31. Love you my darling—so much.

True to his word, Blackburn was making arrangements to send Halford and Kleinman home, as the squadron had been operating at a demanding level of intensity and the two veterans had played their part:

November 13, 1943. Not much happened today. One hop over one of our cruisers that had been hit. She's still okay though. "Stink" and I just came in from the movie and a little party was going on—skipper was a little tight, but he was talking sense. He's going to send Johnny and Jim out on December 1 and wanted to know whether "Stink" and I wanted to go too. He had promised them a long time ago that he'd do that. I don't think he really wants us two to go now, though. We'll wait and see what happens—don't cross any bridges 'til we get to 'em. I love you, baby—or did I tell you that already?

Sunday, November 14, was a "quiet day" according to "Dirty Eddie"—he was one of eight pilots who escorted fifty-four SBDs and eight TBFs through intense antiaircraft fire in a strike against Ballale Island.[14] Following the successful sortie, his thoughts turned to his best pal and to home:

Having it easy for a while. Wrote "Skeex" a letter today—sent her a short snorter bill too. "Stink's" birthday today—he's twenty-nine! Sure doesn't seem that old, does he? Darling, you sure are sweet—how'd it be if I see you in a couple or three months and hold you in my arms again. Do you reckon that would be okay?

The next day (Monday, November 15) involved "Dirty Eddie" leading a flight of eight F4U Corsairs protecting Allied forces in Empress Augusta Bay. At the conclusion of their patrol, they were directed to strafe targets

Fighting Seventeen Ready Room, Ondonga, November 15, 1943. L-R: "Wally" Schub, "Butch" Davenport, Jack Chasnoff, "Dirty Eddie" March, "Ike" Kepford, Tom Blackburn, Whit Wharton (kneeling), Mel Kurlander (kneeling), "Big Jim" Streig and Bob Hogan. *Courtesy Robert Lawson Photograph Collection, National Museum of Naval Aviation/U.S. Navy photo/via Joyce Wharton.*

in the Chabai area in thundery showers and heavy clouds. They strafed Kieta airfield at tree-top level and then set a barge alight before returning to Ondonga for a relaxing evening:[15]

> *Just got back from a movie—this place is really civilized. Was over at Munda for a minute today. Gee, what a hole. That damn place is worse than Norfolk. This place is really paradise compared to there. Nothing much is happening around here at present—the skipper will probably get something cooked up though.*

The following day (Tuesday, November 16) saw "Dirty Eddie" as the flight leader of eight F4Us protecting eighteen SBDs in an attack against the

Jaba River area. Later that day, he was again in the air as part of a "Dumbo" escort.[16] Once the grueling flying was over, it was time to relax and enjoy mail call and the first photos of his new baby:

Put in a good eight-hour day today—and then went to the movie and sat a couple of more hours on a hard bench! The pictures came today— gee, "Skeex" sure is little, isn't she? I don't see how you can tell who she looks like when she's that little. You say that I haven't said anything about "Skeex" not being a boy. Gosh, honey, you know that I'm just tickled to pieces with little "Skeex." I'm just waiting 'til I'll be able to show you and "Skeex" how much I love you!

The intensity of the punishing operational schedule for *Fighting Seventeen* was increasing. Although VF-17 was renowned for its success in shooting down Japanese aircraft, their primary mission was to ensure that the bombers were taken into the target and safely returned home without any losses.[17] This was never more evident than the mission of Wednesday, November 17, 1943:

Another eight-hour day today—really earning our flight pay now. Escorted B-25s to Buka this morning. On our way up there and back there was a lot of stuff going on—but we had to stay with the bombers. One of them was hit and we had to watch him good coming back. Four Zeros showed up near us and "Stink" and his wingman (Ens. Whit Wharton) took a pass at them and they ran. Some of the other fellows knocked some down. We got nine, but lost two pilots. That's not so good.

Skipper told me I did a good job bringing the bombers home. Jim had to come home early—got sick on the way up. I'm still feeling great—must be getting my second wind. I sure do love my little girl (two little girls now, isn't it?). It'll be wonderful when I'll be able to tell you that won't it. A year ago tonight, we were on the Lurline laying off Point Loma, waiting to go in the harbor at San Diego. Wonder how long it'll be 'til we hit there again?

The squadron initiated searches for the two lost pilots (Baker and Anderson) on Thursday, November 18, along with their normal operational schedule.[18] News of Anderson's return was happily received by all in the squadron:

> *Got back one of the pilots we lost yesterday* (Anderson). *Found him in his life raft up near Buka. Have a lead on the other pilot. Really be great if we find him too.*
>
> *The skipper's sending Jim down to Buttons tomorrow. It's best I reckon—he's no good to us or himself the way he is now. Nothing much happened today—slept down at the ready room this morning 'til my hop at 1100. Then I went over to Munda this afternoon for the mail, but there wasn't any! Hope I hear from you tomorrow my darling!*

Ens. Bradford Warren Baker was never seen again. Baker's loss was deeply felt by the squadron as he was always prominent in squadron bull sessions due to his charm, unfailing cheerfulness, and musical talent. It was thought Baker was shot down by the leading Japanese ace of World War II, Tetsuzō Iwamoto. This fearsome opponent was based in the Rabaul area and is believed to have been involved in that engagement. Iwamoto was very impressed with *Fighting Seventeen's* performance that day and had noted in his diary: "These Americans were fine fighters."[19]

The search for Lt. (jg) Robert "Andy" Anderson and his eventual safe rescue was a tale in itself. Anderson had been shot down along with a number of other pilots and they were all presumed to have been lost. Long before dawn the next morning, Lt. Merl "Butch" Davenport was leading a division to intercept a Japanese strafing mission over Bougainville. While on the way, he sighted a light in the water which was held in their direction without blinking. They circled the light but couldn't see anything. After investigating by flying low, the object was eventually found to be small enough to be a pilot afloat in the water. They circled close by and took a bearing a short time before the light blinked out. The following morning, they went out again and eventually section leader, Ens. Ira Cassius "Ike" Kepford, sighted the pilot in his raft. They covered the spot until a PT boat arrived and picked up the pilot and raft. They later found out the pilot was Anderson. A couple of people went over to visit him in the hospital. One of them said, "Andy, you can thank God for that flashlight that you had." Anderson said, "I didn't have a flashlight." Ironically, fate decreed that Anderson's life was saved by one of the other pilots shot down that day.[20]

Chapter 12

I Do Not Know
What Is in Store for Me

The Allies were making headway with the gradual expansion of the beachhead on Bougainville. The Torokina airstrip was progressing and the Seabees had commenced work on the bomber strip Piva Uncle. The Japanese airfields on Bougainville were being regularly bombed and the Allies were rooted on the island.

For the four veteran flyers who joined *Fighting Seventeen* after surviving the living hell that was Guadalcanal in 1942, the stresses of combat flying had caught up with them again. The skipper, Tom Blackburn, had previously agreed to detach Halford and Kleinman who, along with "Dirty Eddie" and "Stinky," had served with distinction in some of the major early battles of the Pacific War. Their experience had proved invaluable to the younger, untested pilots. Blackburn consulted his inner circle of Roger Hedrick (Executive Officer), Duke Henning (Air Combat Intelligence Officer), and "Doc" Herrmann (Flight Surgeon). They had all observed the change in the "old hands" since returning to the combat area and decided that it was time to send them home. "Doc" Herrmann later related his memories of these men:

"When we first went to Ondonga we had some pilots with us that had rendered heroic service in previous combat duty. We began to notice their

165

stress in a fairly early situation. They were unable to concentrate real good on the job that they were to do. They operated with an idea that this was going to be their last day every day. You could see this in them. They were flying defensively, working defensively rather than having that concentration of doing the job they were supposed to do. Every person reaches that point sooner or later. Some people would fly up to a certain point and then go through a terrible harrowing experience that only they could understand and they'd be a changed person after that."[1]

One of the things which is not spoken about much is the importance of the Flight Surgeon's role in combat operations. "Doc's" observations regarding the pilots' mental and physical fatigue and noting how they responded to the stress of flight operations was one of the key factors in the success of the squadron.

November 19, 1943. Skipper sent Jim to Buttons today. Sending Johnny out tomorrow. "Stink's" not in too good shape—he should go soon, too. I think the deal is that the squadron will stay here about two more weeks then go back to Buttons, then down to Australia for about a month and then back up. If "Stink" and I stay 'til we leave here, I think we'll join Johnny and Jim and go before a medical board at Buttons. "Doc" is going to try and get in our orders that we shouldn't be sent back out again—so send us home right from Buttons. May be home with you for Christmas yet, my sweet!

Jim Halford and Johnny Kleinman were detached from VF-17 and, following some leave after arriving home, went on to serve as flight instructors at Naval Auxiliary Air Station, Melbourne, Florida.

Sadly, the courageous Johnny Kleinman was killed in a crash after take-off for a gunnery flight on February 18, 1944. It is believed that shortly after take-off, he ran into a fog bank moving toward the station, which developed a ceiling of 100–150 feet. On investigation, the condition of the wreckage of the airplane indicated that he had tried to fly at very low level below the cloud and had hit the ground at a very shallow, nose-down attitude. The valiant Johnny Kleinman had been married for less than six months at the time of his death. To come through the Guadalcanal Campaign and Bougainville battles and then die in such a tragic accident was one of the unlucky, but not unusual, occurrences of the war. Many men died in training or routine flying accidents, which is one of the least-mentioned aspects of World War II.

After the recent extensive and rigorous combat flying, "Dirty Eddie" was scheduled a rest day on Saturday, November 20, and took the time to relax, catch up on scuttlebutt, and think of home:

Day off again today, honey—it's pretty good just to lay around and loaf all day. Took a lot of pictures—color ones, too. Tried one of the sunset

Bougainville Campaign, 1943–1944. Transports unloading in Empress Augusta Bay, off the Bougainville beachhead, November 20, 1943. Photographed by T/Sgt. J. Sarno, U.S.M.C., from on board a PT boat, one of whose twin .50 caliber machine gun mounts is in the foreground. The landing craft just beyond is from the *President Jackson*. A PT boat, two attack transports (APA) and an LST are in the distance. *Courtesy U.S. Marine Corps Photograph.*

tonight—hope to get a better one, though. Skipper told us tonight that we'll leave here and be in Sydney by December 1. That's pretty good. We'll be there probably a month and then come back up again. Maybe we four will go home—damn if I know. Got a letter from you written November 6—darn I'm sorry to hear you're still in bed. Sure hope you're up and about very soon though, honey.

The mission on Sunday, November 21, was significant for two reasons. The first was that "Dirty Eddie's" division was sent away from the action due to poor fighter direction from base. The second was the disappearance of Lt. Charles Alfred "Chuck" Pillsbury, third in command of *Fighting Seventeen*:[2]

Full day again today—eight hours. My flight hit some Japs this morning. Took off at 0415 and got on station when it was still dark. The fighter director messed my division up and had us vectored out thirty miles when the base was attacked. The other division was right over 'em and knocked down six Zeros. "Stink" only flew one hop today—he's beginning to show signs of wear. Lost "Chuck" Pillsbury this afternoon—missing over Kahili. Must have been shot down while strafing. Boy, he sure was a swell fellow!

"Chuck" Pillsbury was named after his grandfather, who was one of the three founders of what ultimately became The Pillsbury Flour Mills Company (which was purchased by Grand Met in 1989). He graduated from Yale in 1939 and then later decided on a career in the Navy. In one of his last letters home on November 17, 1943, "Chuck" detailed the intensity of the combat operations:

"We are doing a lot of flying, but have a hard time finding the Japs. I've only seen them once so far and then did not get close enough for a shot. Two days ago, some AA gunner put two pretty big holes in my left wing, but the plane flew okay. We are lucky in having the best fighter in this area so have not much to worry about and are eager to find some Zeros. We are quartered and fed pretty well, but seem to be getting up between

0300 and 0400 in the morning and fly often 8½ hours per day. On two days, I flew over 10 hours which is a little tiring in a single seat fighter. I do not know what is in store for me, but I would just as soon stay out here until the Japs give up."

After the war, in 1949, a team searched in an effort to locate Lieutenant Pillsbury and his aircraft. Despite their best efforts they were unable to locate him or his Corsair. Nothing further happened until May 7, 1968, when the Royal Australian Air Force visited the Buin area and located the wreckage of a Corsair which was identified as Pillsbury's. It was concluded that his death probably occurred upon impact of the aircraft or as a result of antiaircraft fire prior to impact. His remains were returned to his family and he is buried in the Pillsbury family plot in Minneapolis.[3]

The loss of "Chuck" Pillsbury hit the squadron hard. As the senior lieutenant and operations officer, he was highly regarded and an integral part of the team. All of the younger pilots looked up to him. What had happened to him was a possibility for any of the pilots. The hazards of low-level flying and being shot at from the ground were dangers that they all faced. The lengthy, laborious missions and burden of combat flying started to tell on the squadron toward the end of their first tour in the combat area. For worldly old-timers like "Dirty Eddie" and "Stinky," the extensive period of operations had to catch up with them. But for the thrilling news of his new daughter, which left him on cloud nine, "Dirty Eddie" would have been in worse shape. For Blackburn, the loss of his pilots weighed heavily, as he regarded them as his family. In the cases of Keith, Baker, and Pillsbury, they had been with the squadron since the early days.

For "Dirty Eddie," the missions continued and it is clear in his diary that the grueling number of flying hours was taking its toll:

November 22, 1943. Would have had another big day today but my engine crapped out on a hop and I came back early. Only ended up with five hours total then! Old "Stink" was fooling around with his gun today and shot himself in his left hand. Just in the fleshy part—really not serious. Nothing much else happening except that I've been so busy lately I haven't had time to write any letters even. Lots of the fellows

*are showing signs of the wear and tear (skipper too, now) so I have to
fly a lot. Still feel great. Little headache yesterday was all I had. Good
night my darling, I sure love you!*

It was becoming clear by November 23 that another tour was likely
for "Dirty Eddie" and "Stinky." The question was, could they both endure
another arduous duty of operations:

*Only have one hop today—things were lax all day. Just brought "Stink"
home from the dispensary—mighty drunk. He feels bad as hell about
his accident yesterday 'cause he feels that the fellows think he did it on
purpose to keep from flying. Looks like we'll both go on down to Sydney
and come back up for one more fling. I can take it okay and I think with
a month's rest that "Stink" can too. I love you, my darling. Can't wait
'til I see you again.*

As a result of the attrition which *Fighting Seventeen* and other units
had inflicted on the Japanese in the Bougainville area, the air opposition
dwindled. The Bougainville campaign was a success, and VF-17 had
played their part.[4] The next phase of operations was soon to be upon them,
and the squadron was looking forward to a period of rest away from the
combat area:

*November 24, 1943. Day before Thanksgiving, honey—different
than last year, isn't it? We're just tapering off around here now—
only one hop a day. Looks like they're going to take us out of here
before the first of the month as they planned. Everyone's pretty
tired, so the big shots don't want to take any chances with the outfit.
Want 'em to be ready when we come back. They do say that our
squadron is the best one that's ever been out here in this area. That's
a plenty good compliment, honey. Mail came in today—didn't get
any from you though, baby—tomorrow will be different—I bet I'll
get lots of letters from you! Good night, my darling—I love you so
damn much.*

The squadron celebrated Thanksgiving on Thursday, November 25, 1943, with thoughts of a change of scenery and of home:

Today was a pretty darn good Thanksgiving Day, honey—as good as it could be out here. We had a wonderful turkey dinner with all the trimmings and pumpkin pie and ice cream. Over at Munda, the poor guys had cheese sandwiches and coffee. Had an easy day today. Went on strike escort, but came back 'cause of stinking weather. All the boys are feeling pretty good now—a couple of easy days and knowing that we'll soon be down in Sydney helps a lot. Got the early hop again tomorrow—maybe we'll have another clambake. Baby, I sure miss you and love you so doggone much.

The Thanksgiving events helped lessen the burden of another long day in the air for "Dirty Eddie" on November 26, plus the time was soon approaching when the squadron would leave the forward area:

Another full day today—about nine hours in the air. Went to the movies tonight and then went down to the dispensary to get something to eat. Dropped over to the ready hut and found your picture that I couldn't find on the ship. Got a letter from you today too—dated November 12. I'm a little worried 'cause you're still in bed.

We're getting relieved December 1—that became definite today. Better hit the sack now—really feel like a good sleep.

The last few days of their time at Ondonga would involve winding-down operations. Just one mission for the squadron on November 27, and a rest day for "Dirty Eddie":

No flying today for me—what an easy day the squadron had too. One hop this morning for twenty-four fellows and then no more work all day. Made some ice-cream down at the dispensary today—boy, it sure was good, really hit the spot. Have a pretty full day tomorrow, though—lots of flying scheduled. Few more days and we'll be heading for Australia.

Gee, I love you my darling—every night I pray for you and "Skeex" and for the time when we're all going to be together again.

Operations continued and mail started to catch up with the men more regularly, which helped raise the morale of the squadron after a period of intense operations. They would soon be leaving the front line and were looking forward to some downtime in Australia:

November 28, 1943. A normal day, today—only one hop. Had some champagne during the cocktail hour this afternoon. Got a V-mail letter from you today—written November 17. You still seem to think that I'm not getting your letters. Gee, honey, I'm hearing from you pretty darn regularly. Got the early hop in the morning today so I'd better sign off for now. I love you my precious—so damn much.

After over a month in the combat area and an exhausting period of operations, *Fighting Seventeen* had to wait to be relieved by another squadron. Most of the thoughts were now centered on Australia and the inevitable blowing off steam and enjoyment that would bring:

November 29, 1943. About five hours today—and a day off tomorrow! Think we're leaving the next day, too. Got three more letters from you today. Gee, but it's swell to hear from you, honey! I bought me a Christmas present from you today. A pair of those fur-lined English flying boots. Always have wanted a pair—don't know how much I'll get to use 'em back home there, but I like 'em anyway. Nothing much to say tonight— 'cept I love you so very, very much my darling!

"Dirty Eddie's" combat flying hours in November 1943 totalled more than 109 hours, which gives an indication of the intensity of the operations on Bougainville.

November 30, 1943. Day off today—and I'd thought it would be my last day of flying here. We have a hop tomorrow and leave the next day.

Those boots I got yesterday were too small so I sold 'em to the skipper
and I got another pair tonight that fit me much better. Baby, I sure want
to see you so darn bad. Darn, I love you so much!

By the time "Dirty Eddie" and the squadron were due to leave the combat area, the Allies were firmly entrenched on Bougainville and the beachhead perimeter was strongly defended. The Torokina airstrip was almost complete and the Seabees had started construction on the bomber strip Piva Uncle. *Fighting Seventeen* had endured a concentrated period of combat operations and supported the successful landings on Bougainville. Their score for the tour, according to "Dirty Eddie's" logbook, was 47.5 enemy aircraft destroyed. Considering their primary mission was to escort and protect the bombers, this was an outstanding achievement.

Chapter 13

Beards Don't Go So Well Down in Sydney!

While the Seabees constructed new airfields on Bougainville, the squadron received nine days much needed rest and recreation in Australia. By Wednesday, December 1, 1943, the squadron was preparing to leave Ondonga for its hard-earned furlough in Sydney:

> *Getting ready to leave here, honey—all packed ready to take off tomorrow at 0800 for Buttons and from there to Sydney. Got me a pair of those flying boots that fit me today. Also think I'll trade two quarts of whiskey for a carbine—a .30-caliber semi-automatic short rifle. Boy, we'll really have fun with it when we go off together. I have two sleeping bags I'm going to bring home. If we get any leave when I get home, we'll go off by ourselves up in the mountains somewhere. You'll have to look things over and get a place all picked out for us. Gee, baby, I can't wait 'til we're together again and having fun together.*

The squadron flew to Guadalcanal as the first part of the journey, which gave "Dirty Eddie" the opportunity to pay his respects to his fallen comrades:

December 2, 1943. Back at Guadalcanal again, honey. We're staying here tonight and then going to Santos in the morning. Went to Bill's grave today. Gee, it's pretty. Took some pictures. Duke Alexander's grave was near his. I used to high jump against him. This place has certainly changed, honey. I love you though—that'll never change.

The following day, the squadron flew to Espiritu Santo, and there was the opportunity to catch up with some old friends in the Officers' Club:

December 3, 1943. Back in Espiritu Santo—or Buttons, today. Had some cold beers at the O' Club! Boy—this place has changed too! Think I'll shave tomorrow—they say beards don't go so well down in Sydney!

The skipper, Blackburn, always demanded strict discipline and performance in the air while on combat operations and training. However, on the ground, he was relaxed about what the men wore and how they looked (shaved or not), and he was always in amongst the guys during bull sessions. Once the squadron had arrived at BUTTON, it was just a matter of drinking, relaxing, and letting off steam while they waited to be transported to Australia:

December 4, 1943. Really having a good time just loafing around. They have a good O' Club and we had some good cold beer. "Stink" came in today. Some guys are leaving tomorrow for Sydney and he and I and the skipper and several others are leaving Monday morning. I shaved today—the guys hardly recognized me!

By Sunday night, December 5, the men heard at last that they would be leaving for Australia early in the morning:

All ready to head for Australia, honey! We take off at 0300 tomorrow. Got three letters from you today. Got a Christmas package from Dad and the fudge you made me got here. It was moldy though, honey—it *took too long to get here. Got paid today—I have over $300. Sure is funny to have money again. Hope I don't spend too much so I can send you some. I love you my darling—so much!*

The squadron had nine days to relax and let off steam, and the Australians gave them a warm welcome. After flying from BUTTON to Tontouta in New Caledonia and then a prolonged flight to Sydney, they finally arrived:

Well, here we are in Sydney, honey. Gee, who thought I'd ever be here! We flew down today—about a ten-hour trip. "Stink" and I must have walked ten miles tonight. Made us plenty tired—should sleep good. Going to shop in the morning—if we get up in time!

After catching up on sleep over the next few days, they just took it easy. They were billeted close to town in a nice area of Sydney:

Bought some clothes—a pair of green pants and a beautiful wool gabardine shirt. Had to get something to keep from freezing to death. This is a pretty nice town here—lots of good food and plenty of milk. It rains a heck of a lot though—that's one drawback. Can't have everything though, I guess. I have you—reckon that's more than I'm entitled to!

Cold as hell down here. Rains all day and even looked like snow. This is supposed to be summer down here too! Slept late today—then went to the theater and did some window shopping. I got three beautiful leather wallets. One for your dad, my dad and "Bud." I really think they'll like 'em a lot.

The shopping trips proved successful and with Christmas approaching, the aim was to post the gifts as soon as possible, as they would take some time to get back to the States:

December 10, 1943. Did a lot of shopping today, honey—got 'em all off in the mail too. I got beautiful wool sweaters for your mother,

Jean, JoAnn, Dora, Marion; a little toy koala bear for Jean (Marion's daughter) and got you two beautiful sweater sets, a real stuffed koala bear—this is the only place in the world they live—and two beautiful white sheepskin rugs to use in the bedroom—or any place else you want 'em. Got "Skeex" a little toy bear but hope to get hold of a little suit for her. Sure hope you all like the stuff.

Moved in our apartment today—still keeping our other rooms too, though—closer to town. Tonight "Mom Fishnick," the landlady, cooked us a wonderful fried chicken dinner. The darn place is too nice to leave. You'd love it darling—we're on a big hill about 75 yards from the ocean!

As well as shopping for presents to send home, another feature of "Dirty Eddie's" stay in Sydney was time at the beach:

December 12, 1943. Went to the beach today—really seems funny to be there this time of the year. The sun was nice though—got a little "pink." Came back about 1700 and I went to sleep on the floor in the front room listening to the radio—still had my trunks on. "Stink" went to sleep too—didn't wake up 'til about 1900.

On the final day in Sydney, "Dirty Eddie" made preparations to leave after making the most of his last few days there with plenty of parties. The squadron left early on Wednesday, December 14, and headed back to BUTTON:

December 18, 1943. Am writing this on Saturday night, honey—sort of got behind a little so will make this one do for all of 'em and try to include some of the dope during that time. We looked around in Sydney 'til Wednesday morning when we left pretty early. We checked out of the apartment and spent the last night at one of the Officers' Clubs so we could make the plane easier. The last few nights we had several parties either at our place or someone else's. Don't worry though, honey—our landlady was at our place 'til all hours of the night so we were plenty chaperoned. "Doc" and "Stink" and I were together all the time when we went out.

The hungover squadron left Sydney and spent the night at Tontouta in New Caledonia. They departed there on the 1300 plane the next day and got to BUTTON late on Thursday afternoon. Lem Cooke (Lt. Lemuel Doty Cooke), "Stinky," and "Dirty Eddie" stopped at the Officers' Club for a few beers and ran into Chief Balenti from the *Bunker Hill*, which had its whole air group in the area:

Yesterday we fooled around the squadron in the morning, took a nap and then went to the Club. The Bunker Hill gave a party and we all went. Gee, honey—what a rat race it was. Ran into Don Runyon and Bob Dibb from old VF-6 and we all really put away a lot of the free liquor. In fact, darling your little Harry got really stinko! Boy, it's the first time I've ever been that way—it'll be the last too. I finally got home (I wasn't too bad while I was there—acted okay) and the effects hit me later. I got a little sick when I got home and didn't feel any too chipper today. Most of the guys were in the same boat. Didn't fly today but some of 'em did. I'll probably fly some tomorrow. "Stink" and I went to a movie here tonight and now I'm writing this. That about covers everything up to date, honey. I love you my sweet—you know that, don't you?

After surviving the perils of combat, the men of *Fighting Seventeen* had made sure their time in Sydney was memorable, with nonstop drinking and revelry. After unwinding in Australia, the pilots now had to get back into the swing of things:

December 19, 1943. Got in the air again today—flew about forty-five minutes today to get the feel of things and then flew tonight. Boy, it sure was dark up there tonight too! Got two letters from you today—the last one was dated December 7. You say you'd just received my cablegram. Sure glad you got it so soon, honey—wish I could get one from you.

I love you darling—but wish you didn't cut your hair like you said you would—I like it long the way it was in your last picture.

On December 19, 1943, as a result of his dedicated service during his first tour with *Fighting Seventeen*, "Dirty Eddie" was put forward by Tom Blackburn for an award with the following recommendation:[1]

Between October 27 and December 1, 1943, Lt. March flew 41 sorties, 122 hours of combat flying. He participated in five strafing missions, three of which were in the face of intense anti-aircraft fire. On November 8, he (with Lt. Cdr. Blackburn) hit Buka Airfield just as a Ruth was about to land, destroyed the Ruth, and strafed a parked Zeke and personnel.

Suggested Citation:

For meritorious achievement while participating in aerial flights against the enemy in the Solomon Islands area. On November 8, 1943, he flew one of two Corsairs which entered the landing circle over Buka Airfield and shot down a Ruth just as it was about to land. On this occasion he also strafed a parked Zeke and troops along the runway. In addition to the above engagement, he has participated in numerous patrols, escort missions and strafing missions, meeting heavy concentrations of enemy AA on several occasions. His devotion to duty, his successful audacity, and his skillful marksmanship were in keeping with the highest traditions of the U.S. Naval Service.

Chapter 14

The Rains Came

While the VF-17 pilots were living it up in Sydney, the Torokina airstrip on Bougainville had become operational, and this brought Rabaul within 210 miles of the Allied Air Force. The Seabees were working flat-out on two new airfields close by, Piva Yoke (fighters) and Piva Uncle (bombers). Preparations for the bombing campaign against Rabaul gathered pace, and in December 1943 Air Solomons intensified the bombardment of Rabaul. Once the new airfields became operational, VF-17 would join the campaign to neutralize the Japanese bastion.[1]

Following their return from Australia, Blackburn made a few personnel changes, with some pilots being reassigned and replacements coming in. The few weeks they had before returning to combat were used for indoctrinating new pilots, refresher training, and tactics.[2] An indication of the stresses involved with combat flying is clear from what "Dirty Eddie" recorded about "Stinky's" mindset:

December 20, 1943. Lem's trying to talk me into deserting with him, honey. He wouldn't have much trouble either! Those letters we got from you all are too darn sweet! We moved down to C.A.S.U. 10, this

Bougainville, Solomon Islands. Seabees laying steel mats during the construction of a new bomber airfield on Bougainville, December 15–19, 1943. *Courtesy National Archives.*

afternoon. We have a nice hut right on the ocean. The waves are breaking about thirty yards from the door—and I'm right by the door. Gee, the surf should really make me sleep. The skipper mentioned today that we may not leave here 'til about January 8. Still don't know exactly where we'll go. "Stink's" about all through flying. I think he'll stay with the outfit, but no more combat flying. "Doc" seems to think—and I agree with him—that he's deathly afraid of fire and I don't blame him in the least. Not only because of him getting burned, but there was a terrible fire on the Belleau Wood during the Wake Island fight when a fighter crashed and burned seven men to death. He saw all that happen. It's too bad 'cause he was a wonderful flyer. Goodnight my sweet—I love you!

"Stinky" had served his time as a combat flier and would now support the squadron on the ground, where his experience would be invaluable. "Stinky" seldom spoke about his experiences of flying the Wildcat against hordes of superior Japanese Zeros, or about the time he was shot down by a Zero only to be rescued by a PBY.[3] One of the squadron pilots, "Beads" Popp, later recalled:

"Blackburn made a very wise decision with Innis. He kept 'Stinky' on a non-flying status. He assumed many tasks all of which he performed exceedingly well. He worked with Blackburn, Hedrick, Henning et al on interpreting intelligence and imparting to us specifics as to the best tactics we should use. He would help Blackburn in briefing us before a flight and would work with Duke Henning in debriefing us after a flight. Probably the greatest contribution he gave us was as a morale officer. He could recognize flight fatigue and would work with 'Doc' Herrmann and apply the right amount of talk and booze to calm you down. After all, due to Guadalcanal, he had been there, seen that and done it all. 'Stinky,' because of his experiences, became a natural in helping us conquer our daily stress."[4]

"Dirty Eddie" was now the only Guadalcanal veteran left on combat operations, as Halford and Kleinman had been shipped home and "Stinky" was through flying:

December 21, 1943. Another day, darling—pretty good day though. Ran into a fellow here that used to hurdle at Georgia Tech. We knew each other back in those good old days. It was lots of fun to talk over old times. Did a little flying—took up a couple of the new boys on a tactics hop—it went pretty good. Did bounce drill too—doesn't feel as good in this as in the old "6" (F6F). It's ok though.

It's nice around here—went right outside the door here this noon and lay on the beach for about thirty minutes just before lunch. If I keep this up, I may even have a nice sun tan when I come home to you—I don't get brown very easy either do I? Remember this time last year, honey—we were certainly having a wonderful time, weren't we? Gee, just wait 'til I get home next time though, honey—I'll be so sweet to you and love you so darn much!

Considering what he'd been through in the last eighteen months, *Dirty Eddie* had coped with everything that had been thrown at him and come through. So many of his friends had died or suffered from the stresses of combat flying, but he was still in there fighting and serving his country:

December 22, 1943. About ready to hit the hay tonight, honey. It's just a little after 2000—I've been in the sack here reading one of Thorne Smith's books. All the other guys are flying or seeing the movie. Got a letter from "Bud" today. He said that he had been to see you and "Skeex." He said the same thing as all the boys here—that he sure was glad the baby looked like you instead of me! My darling, I want to come home to you so much. I can't just go and say that I can't stand it anymore out here, though and ask to go home. I wouldn't be able to live with myself if I did that. I'm in good physical shape—and good mental shape too right now—and all the fellows more or less take it for granted that it's only natural for me to keep on after Jim and Johnny left and now "Stink" isn't flying.

In the long run I think it'll turn out that this is the best way, honey. When we finally do get together, we'll both know that I feel better and I'm sure you'll like it better, too. And we'll really have fun while I have my tour of shore duty, won't we?

Two days before Christmas and "Dirty Eddie" was studying, flying, and thinking of Elsa:

Hello, honey—I love you. Didn't do much today—played some ball this afternoon and this morning I finished an instrument course. Ran into Al Dietrich this afternoon—an old VF-38 and 22 pilot. Knew him during training. Did have to get up for a 0300 hop—don't have enough planes for all of us.

Although most of the time since Elsa and "Dirty Eddie" had been together had been spent apart, this year turned out to be the first Christmas Day they had been absent from each other:

Let's hope and pray that it's our last one. It sure was a funny Christmas, honey—hard to get in the spirit of it. Had a day off all day. Had a good dinner and then some of us went over to the Club where everything was on-the-house. Came back in time for supper and then went to the movies here. Saw Bette Davis in "The Letter." After the show some mail came in and I got a letter from Johnny Morriss. He's at Iowa pre-flight school now. Gee, it was good to hear from him. He certainly does write a good letter—lots of news in it. Good night my darling—I love you!

"Dirty Eddie" was evidently corresponding friends and former comrades, including his former U.N.C. hurdles coach Johnny Morriss. Keeping in touch with people who had been through similar experiences enabled servicemen to share thoughts which they couldn't share with their wives and gave them an important outlet for the difficult feelings they must have encountered in combat. The squadron's preparations to return to the combat zone continued on the day after Christmas:

Got a really early hop in the morning and it's late as hell right now. Haven't had time to bathe even tonight—had to run around all afternoon after ordnance gear. Good night my pet—I love you!

"Dirty Eddie" took the time to go to the Officers' Club and catch up with some old buddies:

December 27, 1943. Went over to fighter strip tonight—"Timmy" (Lt. Clement Dexter Gile) *and I went over to the O'Club there. Gee, it's just like a big Country Club back home. Really a wonderful set up. I lost a little dough shooting crap—can't win all the time, though. The place is really different from last year when I was there. Got six letters from you tonight, my sweet!*

"Dirty Eddie" was tasked for the next few days to find some material for a makeshift bomb rack which Blackburn wanted to develop:

December 28, 1943. No flying again today. I'm trying to run down some gear to make up a bomb rack the skipper wants. I've been all over this damn island and still can't find what I want.

In 1943, the Navy did not believe that the F4U Corsair was suitable for carrier operations, until *Fighting Seventeen* proved its capabilities. The airframe was capable of carrying a large bomb load as well, and on their second tour of operations in the combat area, Blackburn and the squadron started to investigate how the Corsair could deliver bombs to a specified target. With help from Chance Vought Field Service representatives, such as Ray DeLeva, VF-17 instigated many design modifications which later became standard.[5] As was proved later in the Pacific War, the F4U became a versatile fighter-bomber and one of the longest-serving propeller aircraft in history. *Fighting Seventeen* started to develop an improvised bomb rack early in 1944 and used it successfully.

A feature throughout "Dirty Eddie's" journal had been his frustration with the Army pilots, and this continued:

Got the word today that a S.C.A.T. plane was lost yesterday between Tontouta and here. John Little and five of his pilots and twelve rear-seat men were on it. As usual, an Army guy was flying and had an Army navigator. That makes four planes lost—and all of 'em with Army crews! They should take all Army pilots and navigators, put 'em all in one barrel, and shove 'em over Niagara Falls!

The Army aircraft which was confirmed lost on Wednesday, December 29, more than likely had mail aboard which never reached its destination. Mail often took a while to catch up with guys in the combat area, and one of the frustrations for service personnel was the infrequency of news from home. Planes carrying mail were sometimes shot down, just as ships carrying mail were sunk.

Hello my sweet—how are you tonight—on little "Skeex's" birthday! Three months old today. Ran around the island a lot today again picking up bomb gear. If it's as good as we think it is, they want to get the stuff from the States and make it regular squadron equipment. They found the wreckage of that S.C.A.T. plane today. Some natives saw it crash in the water. No telling what really happened.

New Year's Eve, 1943, provided time for "Dirty Eddie" to reminisce about the previous year, along with spending time at the Officers' Clubs. Time was running out before he would return to combat:

New Year's Eve on Espiritu Santo! Gee, sure is different from last year, isn't it? Remember that great big mob we battled on Times Square? Wonder where we'll be next New Years? If we're lucky, we'll be down in Florida somewhere at an advance fighter training base. Went to the Navy Club this afternoon and evening and then went to the Marine Club at night. It was a pretty fair night—but not so good as if I'd been at home!

An easy day followed after celebrating the start of the New Year, with some welcome letters from home and even a roast dinner:

Well, here we start a new year, honey—wonder where we'll be when we start next New Year? Had the day off today (trained most of the time, too) and after breakfast we went back to bed and shot the bull 'til time for the turkey dinner. After dinner, "Doc" and I drove out to the Navy Club, had two beers and then drove to the Marine Club had one more and read some old papers (new to us, though!) and then came home and saw "This is the Army." Had one letter from you (December 20th just received the $100 money order) a Christmas card and a letter from Grandma.

For the next couple of weeks, the squadron spent the time working on their aircraft, training new pilots, and preparing to move into Bougainville, where the Seabees were still busy building the two new airstrips.[6] "Dirty Eddie" was continuing work on the bomb rack and the rest of the time was spent playing poker and enduring the continual rain:

January 2, 1944. Nothing special happened today. Duke got back from Noumea so we went over to the Club to sort of celebrate his return. After we came home for dinner "Tim", Duke and I went over to the fighter strip. Really got sore for the first time in a long time. They won't allow anyone in there without an invitation. And to think I lived there last year! We finally got in—even though it did take us about an hour.

With the torrential rain, days rolled into one another as plans were initiated to get the squadron aircraft and pilots back to combat readiness:

January 3, 1944. Nothing much today either, honey. We fly some in the morning and try to get the planes ready to go. Rained like hell for a while today, too. Went to the Club and then headed for home.

Blackburn left no stone unturned in formulating his tactics for what would be a grueling tour of operations. One of the well-thought-out ideas was to have the squadron advised by a survival expert in case they were shot down:

January 4, 1944. Went on a hike through the woods this morning with someone giving us the dope on things that would help us if we were forced down in the jungle. Pretty darn interesting. Took a hop this after-noon. Still nothing much else going on. Haven't heard much from you lately. Lots of mail came in today and all I got was a Times-Herald. That makes the 4th I've received now. I love you my darling.

Mail arrival had been erratic, which was normal in the Islands. The prospect of dinner at a large local plantation was something that "Dirty Eddie" was looking forward to:

January 5, 1944. Flew a little today. No mail from home today, though it hasn't been coming through so well lately. Went to the Club this afternoon. Going to a big squadron dinner at "The Frenchman's" tomorrow.

Part of the experienced pilots' duties was to ensure the replacement pilots, who joined the squadron at the end of December 1943 and early January 1944, were fully integrated into the squadron. Where Blackburn was concerned, this meant gunnery, gunnery, and more gunnery, which would later prove to pay off handsomely:

January 6, 1944. Hello baby—me again. Had a couple of gunnery hops today. Took the new pilots out and led 'em on the hops. It's the first time I've made any runs on the sleeve with this plane. We went up to "The Frenchman's" for dinner tonight. Boy, it's a beautiful plantation right on the water. A heck of a pretty place. We had lots of food and it was all very good. There was plenty of good, French red wine, too.

The construction of the airfields on Bougainville was progressing but would not be completed until late January 1944. Once the airfields were ready, fighters and light bombers could join the operations to hammer the Japanese stronghold at Rabaul.[7] This was where *Fighting Seventeen* would really make their name:

January 7, 1944. Mail came in today, honey—but none from you. Boy, my mail sure is messed up a lot lately. Got the word today that we'll be here 'til the 25th. We're moving over to the fighter strip on Sunday. That'll be nice 'cause it's really a nice place. Don't know why we're going to wait so long, unless they're holding us out for a big push about the first of the month. Baby, I love you and miss you so much.

"Dirty Eddie" was due to return to familiar territory, the fighter strip on Espiritu Santo. There were still problems with the mail:

Hello darling—got one letter from you today. It was written December 9—late getting here. The mail is still messed up—sure hope it'll get straightened out. Moving to the fighter strip tomorrow—it should be pretty darn good over there.

After relocating to the fighter strip, the battle with the elements continued and mail was still in short supply:

*January 9, 1944. Writing this in my hut at the fighter strip—same place
I was with all the boys last year. By the way, I found out today that all
the boys are Majors. Oh, for the life of a Marine!*

*It's raining like hell right now. Did all morning, too. Looks like
we really hit the rainy season for sure this time, honey. Your Christmas
package came today—maybe your mail will start getting here now.*

"Dirty Eddie" visited some old haunts and managed to get some gear
shipped home:

*January 10, 1944. Went over to the old place today—had some things
to do over there. As usual, it rained all day. Tonight, I ran into a fellow
on the Barnes—used to be Fighter Director on the "Sara." He said
he'd take our gear home for us so "Stink" and I got our crew's boxes
and sent 'em with him. Boy, that's really a break.*

Being overseas for so many months played on "Dirty Eddie's" mind
and not getting letters from Elsa was difficult to bear. Then, at long last,
he received some news:

*January 11, 1944. Finally got a letter from you today, honey—I was
worried as the devil. It's the one you wrote on December 29. Gee, I'd
have given anything to have been there for Christmas with you and our
"Skeex." That letter made me want you and miss you more than any
I've ever gotten from you. I love you so much it hurts, my darling.*

The tiresome rains lingered on and the only pleasure was news from his
former squadron, VF-24:

*January 12, 1944. Not much doing today. We had our usual rain, which
always seems to knock hell out of every day. Got a letter from "Arky"*

today. He went in the drink again on a landing and "Tuffy" went in twice on take-offs. The boys had a big party to celebrate the first birthday of the squadron. Really must have been a humdinger!

Another important feature of Blackburn's training program was extensive practice of night and early morning flying, which thoroughly drilled the pilots for their forthcoming missions:

January 13, 1944. Night flying tonight. Boy, it was terrible weather. Two hops were scheduled, but we only had one. Too much cloud and rain. Awfully tired tonight—don't know why, but I'm sure hitting the sack now.

Despite the unrelenting rain, the squadron's pilots persevered with their preparations, as the time would soon draw near when they would yet again be immersed in the ravages of combat. News filtered through that they were in for a tough time:

January 14, 1944. Nothing much today. Rain as usual and some poker tonight. Really some rough games. Didn't do too well this time. "Stink" and I sort of borrowed an Army jeep and got it painted up. We're taking it over. One of the fellows on the Barnes "borrowed" it off the Navy O' Club and brought it out here and left it here while they went home. It'll come in mighty handy! VF-33 came back from up the line. From what they say, things are getting a little rougher than they were.

Operations were curtailed due to the bad weather, and it provided the excuse for the usual poker and breaking out the drinks:

January 15, 1944. Rained like hell all day today. In fact, we secured the squadron early this morning because of it. Duke, "Stink" and I went over to the bomber strip for a while and then back here. Played some poker and then had a couple of drinks in the hut. A sort of wetting down party for Duke—he made Lt. today. Your box of cookies came today—they're really fine, honey—they came through in good shape. The fellows all like 'em!

Word came through that the squadron would soon be leaving Espiritu Santo and moving into the new airfields at Bougainville:

January 16, 1944. A day off today, honey—and same old story— "The Rains Came." Damn, we're really hitting the rainy season here now. Went over to C.A.S.U. today and then to the Navy Club and met Chief Balenti again. It's good to see the old boys and shoot the bull with 'em. We're leaving here the 24th, honey. In fact, a lot of outfits are shoving up north at that same time. We must be going to spearhead a big push or something. I love you my darling—goodnight!

For the next few days, nothing much changed:

Rain and poker today—usual day. Sent you 200 more dollars today and made some more this evening. Will have more in the mail for you, my darling. Saw "Claudia" tonight. Gee, the girl in it really reminds me of you. You look alike and some of your actions are alike. You're still the best of the two, though honey. You're the best of anyone to be exact!

The 1943 movie *Claudia* featured Dorothy McGuire as the female lead in her first feature film. She was cast in the part after appearing in the successful stage show *Claudia* for two years.[8] On January 19, "Dirty Eddie" had a windfall:

Rain again today—nothing much else doing all day. "Doc" and I ran over to C.A.S.U. for lunch and a little business. Played forty minutes of poker after supper and won a lot of money. Got $200 money order for you yesterday and payed off $222 in debts. Right now, I have $375 owed me. I love you my sweetheart!
January 20, 1944. Same sort of day today. Rain. Went to the Club in the afternoon and after supper. There's no more cash poker now 'cause I won it all—lent it out to guys in the squadron and they lost it to fellows out of the squadron!

Between the downpours, "Dirty Eddie" was still spending time developing the bomb rack, which was nearing its completion:

January 21, 1944. Supposed to be a day off today, but I had to be down at the squadron to fool around with ordnance. Ate supper at C.A.S.U. and came back to the show. Got a letter from you late last night—January 6 it was written.

The next couple of days proved to be busy in preparation for leaving for Bougainville, and many last-minute details needed tidying up:

January 22, 1944. Busy day today getting all the gunnery gear ready to go. The bomb rack finally got finished and the tests proved okay. Went to C.A.S.U. for supper and then came back to the Club here and had a couple of beers. Ran into some luck on the crap table and won $220 in a few minutes. No way to send you the money for a while—can't get anywhere now to get a money order. The one here will be closed tomorrow.

The pilots were presented with a dilemma before leaving Espiritu Santo. They had managed to secure a large cache of beer and other liquor but couldn't work out how to get it safely to Bougainville. This caused some consternation until Lt. (jg) Robert Hal Jackson had a brainwave:

January 23, 1944. Spent most of today getting things all ready to leave. Packed my plane with my gear. We're taking 150 cases of beer and about 60 cases of fruit juice and fruit cocktail up in the ammunition cans. In each plane we have four cans of ammo and eight of beer, etc! Wish some mail would come from you 'cause it'll take lots of time for it to catch up to us up there. My flight's leaving first in the morning—0900.

The stash was successfully transported without incident, and upon completion of the long flight from BUTTON to the new Piva Yoke airfield on Bougainville, the squadron was rewarded with refreshingly chilled beer.

Chapter 15

The Hunters
Became the Hunted

T he Piva Uncle bomber airfield on Bougainville was completed on December 30, 1943, and on January 22, 1944, the fighter strip, Piva Yoke, was ready for combat operations.

The Japanese had up to 100,000 troops in Rabaul and the surrounding islands and would put up a valiant defense of their bastion in the South Pacific. Long-range heavy bombers had already been bombing Rabaul, but once the Allied airfields became operational on Bougainville, the lighter bomber aircraft were within range to intensify the bombing campaign. They could now rely on good fighter cover all the way there and back. Almost 3000 sorties were made over Rabaul in the first nineteen days of February 1944.[1]

VF-17 was part of the major air offensive against Rabaul and the five airfields that were nearby. When *Fighting Seventeen* returned to combat on January 26, 1944, they faced an entirely different challenge. The Allies had taken only a small part of the island of Bougainville, the rest being held by the Japanese. This meant that when the aircraft took off, the Japanese could radio their base at Rabaul and tell them how many aircraft were coming, from which direction and when to expect them. The enemy would then be waiting for the Allied aircraft to arrive, and instead of being the hunters, they became

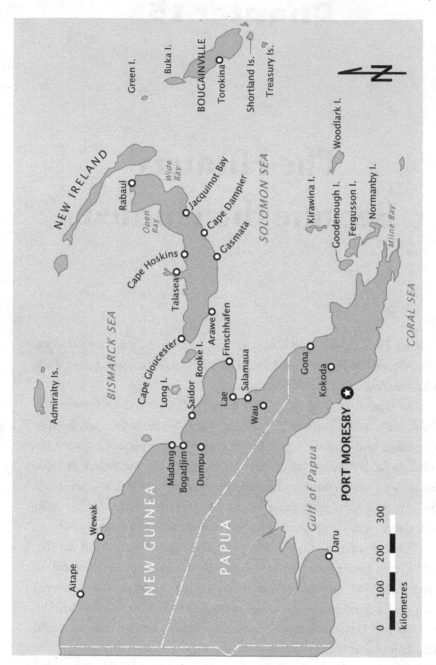

The strategic importance of Bougainville. This map shows the close proximity of the airstrips in the Torokina area, enabling the Allied fighters to escort light bombers to strike Rabaul and return to Bougainville. *Source: Own work Coastlines and locations: Open Street Map.*

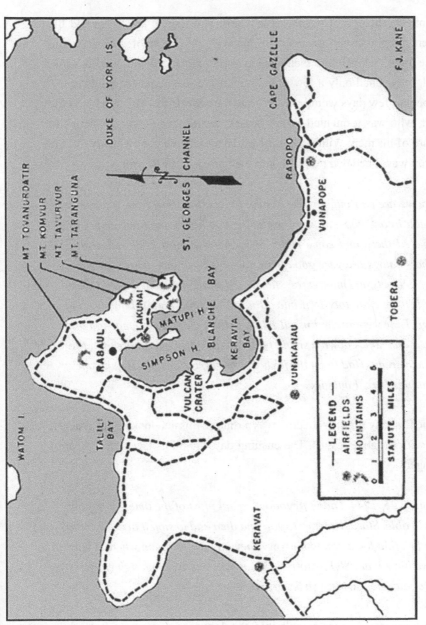

The five key Japanese airfields defending Rabaul. This map indicates Lakunai, Vunakanau, Rapopo, Tobera, and Keravat airstrips and clearly shows Simpson Harbor, one of the best natural harbors in the South Pacific. *Source:* United States Marine Corps.

the hunted.[2] The test of whether Blackburn had trained and integrated the replacement pilots well enough to cope with the rigors of combat would soon be upon them. Before their second tour commenced with missions into Rabaul, they'd had only a few weeks to get the inexperienced pilots ready. The opening few days would demonstrate the ordeals that lay ahead, and the skipper, who was tormented by any losses, would face the big challenge to take care of his men. Within a couple of days of arriving, on January 24, the squadron was scheduled missions into the "hot box" of Rabaul:

Here we are on Bougainville, honey! Flew all the way from Espiritu to Munda in one hop—we were in the air five hours and fifteen minutes. Refueled there and came right on up here. Almost 1000 miles alto-gether. Things are very good here, too. We have nine tents with wood floors. Sheets and mattresses, showers, a swell mess and the food looks like it'll be okay too. Ran into "Bucky" Ireland here (Major Ireland now). They were at the Russell Islands while we were at Ondonga and they didn't knock down a single plane. So far, they have more than fifty to their credit. Had to hit the foxhole tonight, too. We'll get quite a few bombings here, I imagine.

The first day for the squadron was a routine mission looking for downed pilots, with negative results. The ensuing day, the pilots faced their greatest challenge:

January 25, 1944. Didn't fly today—spent most of the time getting our tent livable. Started a letter to you and then had to stop it in order to go to a briefing for a hop tomorrow. They messed us up on where it was, so we have it at 0800 tomorrow. Think we're going on a fighter sweep to Rabaul—following a strike group in!

The squadron's first assault into the Japanese fortress of Rabaul on January 26, 1944, proved to be a daunting encounter. After receiving infor-mation on the impending strike from their sources on Bougainville, the Japanese scrambled from fifty to one hundred fighters, and by the time the formation arrived the Zeros had an altitude advantage.[3] *Fighting Seventeen's* primary task was to escort and protect the bombers safely to and from the target, which for the first mission was Lakunai Airfield:

First trip over Rabaul today. A plenty hot time in the old town, too. We covered forty-eight SBDs and eighteen TBFs. Brought all of 'em home ok, but took a beating. Lots of guys came home all shot up and we lost two pilots (Lt. (jg) James Warren Farley and Lt. (jg) Robert Roy Hogan). *Going up again tomorrow morning on a B-25 strike. This is going to be a pretty rough trip, darling—the Japs seem to have plenty of planes they're willing to lose.*

Goodnight, my sweet—I love you so much and miss you so doggone much. I hope and pray every night that it won't be too long before I'll be home to you again.

Fighting Seventeen scored eight confirmed Japanese aircraft with the loss of two pilots. Hogan had been with the squadron all through training and had completed the first tour. It was Farley's first and last combat mission with the squadron. Neither pilot was seen again.[4]

"Dirty Eddie" was an experienced fighter pilot, but flying into the "hot box" of Rabaul, and being outnumbered by hordes of waiting Japanese fighters, was a new challenge. There was to be no respite from the daily anguish, trials, and onslaughts that would come. "Dirty Eddie" had successfully negotiated the first mission, and he was scheduled to fly the following day, Thursday, January 27:

Another run to Rabaul today, honey—it was plenty rough too. We knocked down fifteen but lost "Jug" Bell (Lt. Thaddeus Richard Bell). *We're giving the bombers good cover, but we're laying ourselves wide open. They were waiting for us today over the target and came down on us. I didn't get many shots today, but was in hot water plenty of the time. My wingman got separated and left me alone. They were all over me 'til I joined the skipper. Going up again in the morning—SBDs and TBFs are hitting them this time. Baby, I love you so much and miss you so much.*

The Japanese, with sixty to seventy fighters waiting for the formation, had attacked aggressively, and Bell was shot down. Lt. Thaddeus Richard "Jug" Bell had been with VF-17 since the early days of training. He was never seen again. Despite the loss of Bell, *Fighting Seventeen* scored fifteen confirmed enemy aircraft, but it was apparent that if the rate of attrition continued, there would not be many pilots left by the end of the tour.[5]

Blackburn was having a hard time coping with the losses of his pilots, so he conceived an innovative tactic to break up the Japanese fighters before they had time to attack the bombers and escort. He called it "roving high cover."[6] As not every pilot or aircraft was scheduled to take part in each mission, he devised a plan where a spare division of planes flew in advance of the main attack at a high altitude. Then, with no other duty than to attack the Japanese fighters, they swooped down on the waiting enemy aircraft and broke up their formations. This resulted in the dual benefit to the squadron of protecting the bombers while also shooting down numerous Japanese aircraft. In his usual leadership style, Blackburn made sure every pilot had a chance to do what was called the "gravy train." The top Zero ace of the time, Lt. Tetsuzō Iwamoto, wrote of them as "wolves who pounce on the unsuspecting Zeros."[7]

"Dirty Eddie" was scheduled for his third consecutive mission to Rabaul on Friday, January 28, and it would prove his most eventful:

> Made the Rabaul run again today. The yellow boys didn't get through us to the bombers today either. I finally got the chance to do a little shooting and got two Zeros. It felt good to knock the bastards down, honey—the more we can do, the quicker we can get this thing over with. Had our usual air-raid early this morning. One or two always come down right at 0400. The AA gets one about every other night.

The official combat report for "Dirty Eddie's" part in this mission read as follows:

Twenty F4Us were assigned as partial cover on the TBFs in a joint SBD-TBF strike on Tobera Airfield, New Britain. A roving high cover of six F4Us came in at 32,000 ft. About forty or fifty Zekes and Hamps intercepted the strike as they were about ten miles SE of the target, but none of the Japs got through to the bombers. The high cover disorganized at least part of the enemy's attack, and the low and medium cover was strong enough to turn back all fighters who got through to them, accounting for at least nine. Lt. March shot down a Zeke in what was apparently his first attack on the TBF cover—March was at about 15,000 ft. over Kabanga Bay in the approach, weaving over the bombers with another division. About eight Zekes came down in a dive on the second division. March turned in and up and got a good burst into a Zeke who was recovering in a wingover. The Zeke was seen to crash in flames. Lt. (jg) Carl Wilson Gilbert, March's wingman, got in a snap shot at another Zeke and saw pieces fly from his tail. Almost immediately afterwards, a Zeke began a run on March, but pulled away and over on his back. March pulled up his nose, fired and set the Zeke afire. At this point the bombers went down in their dive, with March and his division over them. Zekes made several attacks on the formation during the retirement, but disengaged when the fighters turned towards them.[8]

"Dirty Eddie" engaged the Japanese fighters with total disregard for the odds against him, and his strike was so well-timed that the attack on the bombers was repulsed. With skillful marksmanship, he succeeded in shooting down two of the enemy. His score of two Zekes that day qualified him as an ace with a total of five confirmed Japanese aircraft to his credit.[9]

After his heroic actions the previous day, "Dirty Eddie" had an easy time with no flying and another scheduled day off. The timetable for the pilots was one strike a day and a day off every fifth day. The most hazardous part of the missions to the Japanese fortress was the time going into the Rabaul area and out again, lasting only about thirty minutes, but the toughest to take:

We got ten more today. That makes 48½ for four days and 96 for one trip and four days. The best ever done is 104 for three trips made by a Marine Squadron. Heck, we'll break that record all to pieces at this pace. Hope we continue to get everyone home every

L-R: Lt. Harry "Dirty Eddie" March and Lt. (jg) William "Country" Landreth at Bougainville, February 1944. March and Landreth had flown their first missions into Rabaul on January 26, 1944. *Courtesy U.S. Naval Historical Center/M. W. "Butch" Davenport Collection.*

day though—that's what really counts. Yesterday and today we did get everyone home safely. You know, honey—last time we figured it out, there were only seven or eight aces in the entire Navy (five planes or more). Right now, in this squadron we have eight, that's really something to write down in your books. Going to close now and drop you a few lines. I love you, my sweet.

January 29, 1944, was a productive day for the roving high cover executed by just two pilots, Lt. (jg) Ira Cassius "Ike" Kepford and Lt. (jg) Howard McClain "Mac" Burriss. Working together, the two aggressive ace pilots shot down four Japanese aircraft each, resulting in the Navy Cross for Kepford and Silver Star for Burriss.[10]

Although January 30 was a non-flying day for "Dirty Eddie," missions continued, and while the VF-17 pilots were shooting down the Japanese like flies, the losses were also unceasing:

> *Quite a day today, honey. My day off today, so I spent most of the time building a table for the tent and fooling around in general. The boys got two more planes on the strike this morning and then all hell broke loose this afternoon. Word came through that there was a carrier in the harbor at Rabaul, so a strike was sent out. Well, since the Army reported it, we should have known it was bum dope. As it was, it turned out to be a big cargo ship. Our boys went up as escort and knocked ten planes down but it was plenty tough going. They came back after dark and it was really a rat race. The artillery is just opening up now and they're certainly raising hell. Lots of machine guns, too. Must be a good fight going on.*
>
> *Well, to get back to the other thing, some of the kids lost their heads coming in to land and messed up the runways with wrecks and two of our fellows (Lt. (jg) Douglas Hugo Charles Gutenkunst and a Marine pilot) ran into each other just as they were landing. Burned pretty badly.*
>
> *Today's total makes sixty in five days or a total of 108½ for one trip and five days. That's a record unequalled by any other outfit I've ever heard of. Don't know how much longer our planes can last though—we've already lost twelve out of thirty-six. We'll have to get more before long. Lots of mail came in today and everyone got some but me! Hope your letters catch up with me soon. Gee, from the sound of the shooting the Nips must be trying to break through. Good night my darling, I love you!*

Lt. (jg) Douglas "Gute" Gutenkunst was killed when he collided with a seriously wounded Marine pilot coming in to land. For Blackburn, the loss of Gutenkunst was hard to take as he had been his wingman and was like a younger brother. Gutenkunst was awarded the Distinguished Flying Cross posthumously for "heroism and extraordinary achievement." His body was returned to the United States on June 3, 1948, as requested by his family, and he was buried at Forest Home Cemetery, Milwaukee.[11]

Gutenkunst and the Marine pilot were not the only ones to pay the ultimate price for this debacle. Also involved in VF-17's response to the erroneous report was Tom Kropf, who did not return from this mission and was listed missing in action. Lt. (jg) Thomas Frederick Kropf from Wamego, Kansas, had been with *Fighting Seventeen* since March 1943. He was described by Tom Blackburn as a "fine, courageous officer." He was never seen again.[12]

"Beads" Popp called the mission "a fiasco."[13] Unbeknownst to Popp, he'd taken some hits to the lower part of his aircraft and one of his tires was blown, causing his plane to cartwheel down the runway and land on its back. Lt. Shelton Ray Beacham was forced to ditch his aircraft into the water due to damage to his hydraulics. He made a perfect water landing but still broke his nose in the process. Lt. (jg) Ira "Ike" Kepford was badly hit in the right wing and the ammunition cases exploded. He could not get his right wheel down but still managed to make a one-wheel landing, although the plane was destroyed.

The next day (Monday, January 31), "Dirty Eddie" was leading a division as part of the medium cover in a strike against shipping in Keravia Harbor, when his second section was attacked by Japanese Fighters:

Raining again now. Seems maybe that lousy weather we had down in Buttons has caught up to us. The weather was pretty bad on the strike today. Rabaul was just about to be closed in. I think it has moved down to here. We went up on an SBD and TBF strike at the same time as B-24s hit the general area. It was rough again as usual, but we didn't knock down any planes. I think that the Marines got about five as a total.

The yellow boys got off easy today. Burriss got shot down up there—I saw him smoking just after he was hit. He landed in the water just outside of Cape Gazelle. The "Dumbo" didn't get him today.

*Hope they have better luck tomorrow. He was my 2ⁿᵈ section leader
and I feel sort of responsible for him. The skipper saw him get it though
and he said I couldn't help him in any way. He and his wingman were
straggling too doggone far behind me and I couldn't see him and
couldn't turn anyway to help him. That's the way it goes though.*

*Old "Stink" was hit pretty bad last night by "Gute's" crash. He saw
his body when they brought him in and he was pretty badly messed up.
The "Doc" said "Stink" was really shaken up. Old "Stink" has had
pretty darn much during this war. Goodnight my sweetheart—I love
you so much.*

The aggressive and high-spirited Burriss had proved himself an exceptional fighter pilot, an ace with seven and a half Japanese aircraft to his
credit. Lieutenant "Timmy" Gile, *Fighting Seventeen* ace with eight victories, described Burriss as "so bright and resourceful, one of the best, a quick
thinker and courageous."[14] Burriss had previously been shot down and rescued
on January 27, and in a letter to his girlfriend the next day wrote: "I'm living
right now on a little borrowed time, I figure."[15] These words proved to be
prophetic as Burriss was never seen again. He was twenty-two years old.

There was some respite for a couple of days for "Dirty Eddie" due to poor
weather and flight scheduling, and he was hoping for some news from Elsa:

*February 1, 1944. No strike today—the weather was too bad up the
way. A couple of local hops went out, but I didn't go. Don't fly tomorrow
either—I've been up four times and some flights only three. Hope I get
more letters written tomorrow. Mail today, but still none from you. Gee,
hope you're not mad at me, honey! I love you—do you know that?*

For the first couple of days in February 1944, the adverse weather
curtailed operations to Rabaul. This downtime allowed "Dirty Eddie" to
reminisce and think of his times with Elsa:

*February 2, 1944. It rained all day today. No flying at all. My flight
had to stand-by in the afternoon and I spent the time playing a little*

Fighting Seventeen pilots in front of the rapidly growing scoreboard, January 1944. Back row, L-R: "Dirty Eddie" March, Carl Gilbert and "Wally" Schub. Front row, L-R: Whit Wharton, "Andy" Jagger, and Harold Bitzegaio. *Courtesy Robert Lawson Photograph Collection, National Museum of Naval Aviation/U.S. Navy photo.*

bridge. After supper, I sat through the drizzle to see "Air Force" again. Remember when you and I saw it together up in New York? Gee, it's going to be great to go to places with you again. I just want to go any place you want to go when I get back. My whole objective will be to make you happy. Just being with you is going to make me happy,

my darling. I wonder how long it's going to be before that time will
come? Regardless of how long it is sweetheart, I love you more than
anything else in the whole world!

The film *Air Force* (1943), directed by the eminent Howard Hawks
and starring John Garfield, was a prominent movie of the time. It was
one of many "flag-waver" movies made to raise morale during World
War II.[16]

An indication of the intensity of the air operations was the erosion of
aircraft numbers since the squadron returned to combat. The complement of
F4Us was dwindling rapidly due to losses, crashes, and water landings.
Nevertheless, *Fighting Seventeen* had safely escorted the bombers and was
also shooting down Japanese aircraft in record numbers:

February 3, 1944. Didn't do much today, honey. Fooled around the
hut some and stood-by for a little while in the afternoon. We're short
of planes now—lost twelve—so in order to keep the hops distributed
pretty well, we're not flying much. Have the day off tomorrow, so won't
fly for another day. Lots of the guys hung around the hut and drank
beer tonight. They said it was a pre-birthday for me. Sid Delaney,
Gus Shearer and Mickey McClennlen from VB-98 (old VC-24) came
over too. Mickey was with us at the Latin Quarter that night, a bunch
of us were there—remember? They all are tickled with the way we're
covering them on their strikes. We've brought 'em all home so far—
knock on wood.

"Dirty Eddie" celebrated his twenty-fifth birthday on Friday, February 4,
1944, and was still anxiously waiting to hear from Elsa:

Another year older, honey—boy on my next one you and I will really
celebrate, won't we? Gee, it'd be great if I could be home with you on
your birthday, wouldn't it? Stranger things have happened, my sweet!
Had the day off today. Really enjoyed just loafing around. Puttered
around the tent a little and took it easy in general.

L-R: "Dirty Eddie" March, "Wally" Schub, "Country" Landreth, "Ike" Kepford, Don McQueen and Dan Cunningham relaxing with a beer between missions. Taken at Bougainville shortly after McQueen joined the squadron as a replacement pilot in January 1944. Note "Dirty Eddie" wearing the sought-after boots. *Courtesy Alexandra Bowers.*

However, February 4, 1944, proved to be another tragic day for *Fighting Seventeen* with further losses:

Lost two pilots today—only got one Jap. Not so good. Still no mail—sure hope it comes soon—I'm really longing to hear from you! Good-night my darling—I love you!

Ens. Percy Eugene Divenney and Lt. (jg) Donald Thomas Malone were listed as missing in action. Divenney was a replacement pilot, who had only joined the squadron on January 11, 1944. On his first combat mission on January 28, he had proved his worth and shot down two Zekes. On February 4, 1944, while escorting B-24s on a strike to Tobera, Divenney was jumped by eight Zekes and shot down. He was twenty years old.[17] Malone, twenty-three years old, had been with the squadron all through training and was an accomplished musician on the violin, clarinet, and saxophone and led a dance band before becoming hooked on flying. He was shot down by a Zeke and forced to bail out.[18] Neither pilot was seen again.

"Dirty Eddie" returned to combat operations on Saturday, February 5, when he led the flight of twelve F4Us escorting SBDs on a strike to Lakunai Airfield:

Flew again today. Went up to Rabaul again. There were plenty of the yellow boys around but none bothered my boys any. Felt real good after the hop today, honey 'cause it was one hop I didn't want to go on. Had a funny feeling all last night and this morning about it. Now, though I feel great! Had a few more false alarm air raids tonight. All it did was interrupt our sleep a little.

Further losses and damage to aircraft caused the groundcrews immense problems, and crew chiefs like George Mauhar had their work cut out to keep the aircraft in flying condition.[19] The implications of this were that pilots had more downtime, as there were not enough aircraft available. Even though they were lacking planes, the squadron still continued to rack up a record score. "Dirty Eddie" was not scheduled to fly, but did at last hear from Elsa:

February 6, 1944. This sure didn't seem like a Sunday today. In fact, I didn't realize it was Sunday 'til this afternoon. Didn't fly today but the boys who did knocked down nine more planes. Gives us 73 for this trip, or a total of 122 so far. We've broken all existing records and by the

Lt. (jg) William "Country" Landreth with his assigned Corsair #39, which he flew on the second tour at Bougainville. Landreth scored his first aerial victory on February 5, 1944. *Courtesy Vought.*

time we leave here we'll really leave a record to shoot at. The skipper got four more today. Got a letter from you today, honey—sure was swell to hear from you!

When "Dirty Eddie" was scheduled for the "gravy train" on February 7, his usual assigned aircraft was having mechanical problems and he had to return to base, curtailing the mission:

Played a little bridge tonight—enjoyed it for a change. Went to Rabaul today and was heading for a darn good set-up. My flight was roving high cover—supposed to go in just ahead of the bombers and split up the Japs. We were to be about 30–35,000 feet and would really have knocked 'em on their ear. At 27,000 feet the "old girl" started acting-up and I had to bring her home—thought for a while she wouldn't make the grade. Knocked down four more today—we're going to hit 100 this trip yet!

After the mechanical problems of the previous day, "Dirty Eddie's" only flying—despite poor weather—was a test flight to check if the repairs to the aircraft had fixed the problem:

February 8, 1944. Rain and low ceilings again today—no strikes went out. Doggone it, just when we have the yellow boys groggy the weather comes and helps 'em along. Today it was planned for sixty SBDs, twenty-four TBFs, three squadrons of B-25s and two of B-24s to hit 'em, one right after the other. We have to do that in order to knock out the fields by the 15th when we move in to Green Island and set up fields there.

Enjoyable evening tonight. As usual, all the guys hung around our hut to shoot the bull. The skipper was writing a letter and "Stink" was cutting my hair. I can't see the back of it but it must really be something from the way the guys were laughing.

Gee, the boys from VMF-215 are raising hell, right now. They have a right to though, honey. They finished up a trip today—heading back home. They're not doing anything like we'll be doing when we start for home though—we'll put 'em to shame! Day off today (February 9)— wrote you two letters today, honey—one this morning and one just now. I love you lots and lots in both of them too!

Amateur barbers prevented *Fighting Seventeen* pilots from becoming
long-haired whilst stationed on Bougainville. The client apparently about
to lose an ear is Lt. B. D. Henning, a Yale professor before he became an
Intelligence Officer. Lt. D. A. Innis clips, while Lt. (jg) Earle C. Peterson
cocks a critical eye over his can of fruit juice. Lt. H. A. March is definitely
not interested in the performance. Bougainville, February 1944.
Courtesy the Tom Blackburn Collection/National Archives.

The day of "Dirty Eddie's" second wedding anniversary was marked by
two flights, one a scouting mission over Bougainville and another to Rabaul.
However, Thursday, February 10, 1944, was still a day to remember the
special occasion:

*Two years ago tonight, my darling! Remember! Gee, that was a
wonderful day in my life. Do you know that we've been together*

approximately ten months out of the twenty-four? Let's hope we do better in the next year.

Went to Rabaul again today. Brought the bombers home and didn't even get a shot in again. I'm beginning to think that if you do your job right and stay where you belong, you'll very seldom get into trouble. Had a two hour early-morning hop too—feel pretty tired tonight for a change. I love you though, my darling—so much. I pray that this night next year we'll be together.

A quiet day for "Dirty Eddie," with just a short flight as combat air patrol on February 11, but still no letters from Elsa:

All the boys are around as usual tonight, honey. I got a letter off to you but it was a job with all the guys shooting the bull so much. Have roving high cover tomorrow, honey—that'll be the first time I've ever had the advantage on 'em (if it works out okay). No mail from you yet, honey—damn but I wish I could hear from you—about ten letters from you would fix me up okay. I love you my sweet, so much.

"Dirty Eddie" was one of twenty-two pilots scheduled to escort B-25 bombers in a strike against Tobera Airfield on February 12, although it turned out anticlimactic:

Nothing came out of that high cover hop today. Didn't even see a Zero— not one! I wish we had 'cause we were in good shape for 'em. Maybe it's a good sign, though—maybe they're beginning to feel the beating we've been giving them. Got a letter from you today. Also got the Presidential Unit Citation from the Navy Department today for VF-6. Now that'll make two of 'em if and when VF-5's ever comes through. Don't fly tomorrow but the next day, they're going to hit the town of Rabaul with everything we have. They want to destroy the communication system so the following day—15th when we go into Green Island, they'll be totally bewildered.

Marine PBJ bombers. Raid on Rabaul, circa 1943–44. Note flak bursts.
Courtesy Naval History and Heritage Command.

The only flying assigned to "Dirty Eddie" on February 13 was to checkout three new replacement pilots who had just reported for duty with *Fighting Seventeen*. Still no news from Elsa, which was a source of irritation:

> *Took up three new boys for a little hop this afternoon—they were pretty darn good.[20] Just fresh from the States. Nothing much else happened, except mail came in and as usual none came from you. I was going to write another pretty nasty letter to you tonight, but decided to wait 'til tomorrow and maybe I'd cool off. Maybe I'm wrong honey, but when some guys get two or three letters from their girls and wives every mail and I get one letter from you every 2nd or 3rd mail—well, I can't blame it on the mail system all the time 'cause other people's mail gets through!*

The "new boys" (Ens. Jack Evans Diteman, Ens. Richard Martin "Dick" Einar, Jr., and Ens. Harvey "Matty" Matthews) went on to serve in various squadrons, distinguishing themselves in action against the Japanese, and all survived the war.[21]

"Dirty Eddie's" humor improved when he bumped into some old squadron buddies, leading to another bull session:

February 14, 1944. Ran into a couple of old guys from the Belleau Wood today. Lt. Cdr. Finnegan, who roomed next to us, is now on some amphibious force (on the staff) and is Liaison Officer. Tomorrow he's observing the landing on Green Island from a TBF. Then there was "Buster" Fitzpatrick who was Intelligence Officer of VF-22, who was with us on a cruise aboard ship. He's to be around here now. We all got together tonight with some drinks and lots of bull. Mail again today—with the usual result for me—none!

The continued days of no mail were a cause of consternation to "Dirty Eddie." He had been away for many months and his only link to Elsa and "Baby Skeex" was by letter. He was part of the cover for the Green Island operations, but no enemy aircraft were sighted:

February 15, 1944. Another day with no mail—I'm getting used to it by now though. We (our forces) moved into Green Island today. We cover 'em while they start to set up an airfield. Some dive bombers came over unescorted and all got knocked down. Only ten of 'em. None of our bunch even saw 'em though. All the guys are here doing card tricks. Very fascinating.

The squadron had not seen enemy aircraft for a few days, leading them to believe that air opposition was fading in the area:

February 16, 1944. The usual bull session is going on here in the tent tonight. Old "Stink's" in rare form. Nothing much happened today. No contact with the yellow boys anywhere. Tomorrow my bunch goes

*to Green Island for a patrol. Pretty easy day if the schedule goes off as
it's supposed to. Mail today—same story though, none from you. That
makes a heck of a lot of mail that's come and none for me!*

By Thursday night, February 17, "Dirty Eddie's" mood was lousy—
tiredness, flying in poor weather and the loss of another two pilots weighed
heavily upon him. His morale was low and he was desperate for some news
from home:

*Too tired to write you a letter tonight—about all I'd do in it would
gripe at you for not writing, 'cause today, as usual, I got no mail from
you. Had two hops today—and stinking weather all the time. Gee, it
really got me down. I'm tired as hell right now. Lost two boys over
Rabaul today (Ens. Clyde Howard Dunn and Lt. (jg) James Miller).
One nobody saw and the other had his wing shot off by AA and had to
bail out right over the town. Gosh, I hope he's okay now. It's hard to tell
what they're doing to him now. Darling, if I don't get some mail from
you soon, I don't know what I'm going to do.*

In his short time with *Fighting Seventeen* as a replacement pilot, James
Miller scored two confirmed and two probable Japanese aircraft shot down.
Antiaircraft fire shot off five feet of his right wing and he was seen to bail
out and land safely. He was the sole *Fighting Seventeen* pilot shot down who
survived to be captured by the Japanese, only to face the living hell of being
a prisoner of war at Rabaul. He died in captivity of beriberi, dysentery, and
starvation on May 7, 1945. Out of approximately 75–80 POWs at Rabaul,
only six survived.[22]

Clyde Dunn was originally not scheduled to fly, but he had volunteered
to take the place of a malingering pilot. He was listed as missing in action
and was never seen again.[23] His close friend, "Beads" Popp, was devastated
by his disappearance. After being informed of Dunn's loss, he attacked the
shirking pilot with a knife and had to be forcibly dragged off him. The pilot
was detached from the squadron and sent home.[24] Miller and Dunn were the
last *Fighting Seventeen* pilots listed missing in action.[25]

An example of Vought F4U-1A Corsair fighters flying in formation during a mission in the Solomon Islands area in early 1944. "Dirty Eddie" became an ace flying this type of aircraft. *Courtesy National Archives.*

On February 18, "Dirty Eddie" was scheduled on another mission to Rabaul. The squadron kept scoring, and the air opposition was further weakened:

> *Another strike today—the B-24s did a fine job for a change. About the only damn time I can say that about the Army though. Not much else happened today. Some of the boys hit Rabaul about thirty minutes before the bombers hit. They knocked down seven, which gives us 138 for an official new record. We've paid a big price for it though.*
>
> *Still no mail though—it sure better come soon though, I'm really getting desperate for some word from you. A day off tomorrow—hope I get caught up on some letters so I may get a chance to get more letters—or should I say get some letters! I love you my darling.*

Word started to spread about *Fighting Seventeen*'s achievements, which led to press men descending on the squadron. This resulted in numerous articles published in the newspapers back home, which appeared all over the country. During the war VF-17 was known as "The Skull and Crossbones Squadron," "Blackburn's Irregulars," and "The Bearded Pirates."[26] It was not until the publication in 1989 of Tom Blackburn's book, *The Jolly Rogers*, that they became known by this name.

Ironically, now that their success was being recognized more widely, February 19, 1944 was the last time VF-17 encountered enemy aircraft:

> *Day off today and the boys really ran into something. Knocked down sixteen and everyone came back. "Ike" got jumped on the water by about twenty Zeros while he was by himself. He went from about 160 knots to 305 indicated by using water injection. Since we've broken all records by a long way, we've had photographers and newspapermen all around us all the time. They were even here at the tent tonight for the usual party. Still no mail from you, honey.*

The aggressive and fearless Lt. (jg) Ira Cassius "Ike" Kepford was the "Top Gun" of the squadron and finished his tour with *Fighting Seventeen* as the Navy's top ace with sixteen confirmed victories.[27]

Chapter 16

Where Are They?

The nonstop bombing of Rabaul during January and February 1944 finally resulted in the Japanese withdrawing most of their aircraft to Truk on February 20, 1944.[1] Applying the valuable lesson gained from the Guadalcanal Campaign, the Allies knew that once the skies had been cleared over Rabaul, there was no need to invade New Britain. From then on it was bypassed by the Allies who moved on up the island chain. The Japanese were unable to supply and support the island, and it was left to wither on the vine.[2] Unaware that the enemy aircraft had pulled out, *Fighting Seventeen* was puzzled by the lack of aerial opposition over the target area.[3]

> *Went up to Rabaul and didn't see any of the yellow boys—that's two days in a row where they haven't shown up. Two of the boys went to Guadalcanal and came back with beer, some fresh oranges and even a 15lb turkey! Nothing much else to report today, honey—'cept that I love you very much—or do you already know that?*

At long last, mail arrived from Elsa, much to the relief of "Dirty Eddie." The letters were a huge comfort to him, along with the possibility that finally he would be going home:

February 20, 1944. Didn't know it was Sunday again 'til I started to write this. Got four letters from you today—three V-mails and one regular one. Gee, it's good to hear from you again and to know that everything is okay with you. Honey, I'm not telling you this in your letters yet, but there seems to be a small chance that we won't make a third trip up here, but will go home after this one. We base that on our good record and the amount of flying we do. The Marines here fly only every other day, while we fly four and rest one. Also, the fact that we've lost so many pilots enters into the story. So maybe I'll be home for your birthday after all!

According to the *Fighting Seventeen* War Diary, prior to his second tour with VF-17, "Dirty Eddie" had flown 322 combat hours which, other than Lt. (jg) Tom Killefer, was the most in the squadron. On his second tour up to February 21, 1944, in the twelve days he flew he had fifteen combat sorties, with eleven of those missions to the "hot box" of Rabaul and with 45.3 combat hours flown.[4]

The skies were quiet, apart from the inevitable antiaircraft fire, and after the intensive and stressful missions to Rabaul with constant aerial opposition, the squadron settled into thoughts of going home:

February 22, 1944. Writing this at the Club while some of the boys are playing bridge. Went to Rabaul today—no interception again. Went to see "Arsenic and Old Lace" tonight. Gee, we'll have to see that play if it's still running in NY. Just got through with a long chat with the Captain. We were talking about our chances of going home after this trip. I sort of feel that the chances are pretty good, honey! No mail from you today and a lot came in!

Considering *Fighting Seventeen*'s primary mission was to escort bombers, they shot down record numbers of Japanese aircraft and ensured none of the bombers were lost to enemy air attack while under their protection. VF-17 was part of the major air offensive against Rabaul, which dramatically reduced the number of enemy planes.[5] With the relief of not having to worry about attacks from Japanese fighters, thoughts of going home were prevalent:

> *February 23, 1944. Things are pretty quiet lately. No Zeros around today either. We can't figure out whether they're through—or just building up to something big. Day off tomorrow—I'll spend it writing letters and sunning myself. Saw "Tennessee Johnson" at a movie tonight—very good. Got back home and then talk was getting around to what we'll do when we leave here. May try and keep the squadron together—go home for some leave, and then go over to Burma. All I know now, honey, is that I want to see you as soon as possible and be with you and hold you in my arms!*

The timely arrival of letters from home was welcome and, as "Dirty Eddie" was scheduled for a day off, he could catch up on all the news:

> *February 24, 1944. Day off again today—and I got lots of letters from you. Got V-mail letters dated January 29, 30, 31 and February 5 and 6, I think. Regular letters February 4 and 14 and a Valentine, February 11. Gee, but it was wonderful to hear from you my darling. It's beginning to really make me feel homesick when I get some of your letters, though. We both miss each other so damn much, it's not good. When I read what you said I know exactly how you feel and what you mean 'cause I feel the same doggone way. Gee, it's wonderful that we love each other so darn much, my sweet—we're always so happy when we're together!*

The tedium of meeting no opposition led to constant talk about going home. The squadron had endured grievous losses, which had taken its toll on the pilots, and they were ready to go home:

> *February 25, 1944. Just a few lines tonight, honey and then I'm going to hit the sack. Tired as the devil today, honey, I'll have to admit. I'm getting tired much easier lately—all the other fellows are feeling it more, too. Flew from 0630–1130 today and was so tired when I got*

back that I almost hurt. I don't think this outfit can stand another trip—
they're pretty near through right now. Let's hope and pray that I'll be
home with you within two months at the most!

Speculation was rife about the possibility of another arduous combat
tour. "Dirty Eddie" had come through every battle he had faced, from
Guadalcanal to Rabaul, and just wanted to be with Elsa at long last:

February 26, 1944. Nothing much today, honey. One hop—patrol
over Green Island. The boys didn't see anything at Rabaul today. I go
tomorrow morning. All the talk among us is debating as to when we'll
get out of here and whether or not we'll go home without another trip.
Let's hope so honey!

The scuttlebutt continued, but there was no official news on what was
going to happen to the squadron:

February 27, 1944. Went to church tonight, honey—"Stink" and I went
right after chow. It was nice to be in that atmosphere again. Tomorrow
is the beginning of our sixth week here. Hope by this time next week
we're out of this place. I don't know honey, but I've had just about
enough of this stuff. I need some sort of change. We still haven't had any
word as to when we're going to be relieved, let alone what we're going
to do after we leave here. I want to come home to you, my darling—
want to more than anything else in the world. Gee, how I hope that it
won't be long before I'll be able to tell you in this letter that the word is
for us to come home. Goodnight, my darling, I love you.

The work "Dirty Eddie" had undertaken with the improvised bomb rack
came to fruition when F4Us, equipped with 500 lb. general purpose bombs
(with delay fuses) searched the coastal area for shipping or suitable bombing targets. The pilots carrying the bombs made practice runs on a beached
hulk and a deserted building. Following this first try-out, the squadron started
bombing missions until the end of their tour.[6] *Fighting Seventeen* held the

distinction of being the first Corsair fighters to drop bombs. The crude rigs they had fabricated were later modified, and by the end of the war F4Us were routinely used as fighter-bombers.[7]

Confirmation finally came that the squadron would be leaving the area, but there was no information as to whether the pilots would be going home:

> *February 28, 1944. Just another day today, honey—a patrol over Green Island and that was all. The skipper went down to Guadalcanal today and got some word, but he can't tell us for another week. He did tell us though that by next Monday, we'll be at Santos with our planes. No telling what we'll do after that though. I sure wish I knew what we're going to do. The way I figure it, we won't go back aboard ship and by the time we're ready to come back up here, there won't be anything for us to do. We'll simply have to wait for a few days 'til we get the word. I'll let you know as soon as I hear my sweet—I love you honey!*

Speculation about whether they would be assigned further combat was the talk of the squadron:

> *February 29, 1944. Day off again—and it rained most of the day! We got rumor today that VF-34 will be in tomorrow. Hope it's true honey, it'd mean we'd be out of here in a couple of days. It's none too soon, honey 'cause some of the fellows who seemed as if they'd never crack, are beginning to show signs of having enough. Hope that in about six days, I'll be able to tell you I'm coming home to you my sweet!*

The stress, the losses, and the fear of whether they would make it through to the end of the tour all played on the pilots' minds. The flight surgeon, Lt. Lyle "Doc" Herrmann, detailed in his medical report the effects of constant combat on the pilots:

"The results of the daily combat showed rapidly. From the first day until the close of the fourth week, contacts with the enemy were a daily routine and the enemy was always above. The first ten days cost us eight pilots, the majority of whom were seasoned men. The whole outfit became tense and worried. This tenseness was evident in everything they did. It was very notice-able even in the approach to the field and in the traffic circle. At camp in the evenings the pilots were irritable, looked very tired and slept poorly. Sedation was used in some of these cases, but on the whole was unsatisfactory. Liquor proved to be the only solution. Sedation produced sleep, but the channel of thought remained and dreams robbed them of the rest and relaxation that undis-turbed sleep should bring. However, when they gathered around and had a few beers the morbid channel of thought was discarded, they became 'happy,' sang a few songs and when they turned in, they usually slept 'like babies.' This type of living, while expedient, cannot be continued forever. After four weeks of this type of stress, and after losing two more pilots in one day, the situation became serious. It seemed advisable to terminate the tour at that point, however from that day on nearly all enemy air resistance disappeared and the situation was relieved. It has been an important psychological factor now that they have continued, for they, while tired, have regained their confidence and this is important if they are to return to combat flying again."[8]

"Dirty Eddie's" spirits were raised by welcome letters from Elsa, along with the news that he had received some recognition:

March 1, 1944. Heard from you again today. You wrote the letter February 19. Gee, there's still a heck of a bunch of mail of yours on the way to me. Think we'll leave here about the 4th and go on down to Buttons. Wish I knew what we're going to do after that! Got the Air Medal awarded to me today. I'd like to get the D.F.C. or Navy Cross now for you and I'd be happy. Don't think I'm asking for too much after two years of flying in this war 'specially since I know guys who have 'em for about one day's combat and one plane to their credit!

Morale was enhanced by the word that operational flying was nearly over for *Fighting Seventeen*:

March 2, 1944. Writing this sitting on the bed in our tent. The usual party is going on. There are sixteen of us in here now—including two American reporters and one Australian reporter. Went to see

Ira "Ike" Kepford leading a division of Fighting Seventeen Corsairs near Bougainville in March 1944. This is one of the best-known photographs from World War II.

#29 "Ike" Kepford.

#8 Hal Jackson.

#3 "Big Jim" Streig has an old Star & Bar insignia, perhaps with the red outline that was replaced with blue the previous summer.

#28 Wilbert Peter "Beads" Popp.

Courtesy Robert Lawson Photograph Collection, National Museum of Naval Aviation/U.S. Navy photo.

"The Keeper of the Flame" tonight. Saw it at Norfolk, but it was swell the second time, too. Tomorrow is our last day of operational flying—we leave the day after that. Should be in Buttons on Saturday or Sunday and in Sydney a week from tonight. Gee, honey, it'll be great to be in civilization again! Got a letter with two pictures in it—one of the baby and one of you and her. She sure has grown, honey—I'll bet she's bigger now, too than she was then. I love you, my sweet—so very much. Let's pray that it'll be only a month or a little more before we're back together again.

The questions surrounding the future plans for the squadron were finally cleared up in the usual bull sessions and drinks on Friday night, March 3. The relief was palpable and the squadron could at last relax in the knowledge they would be going home:

Well honey, the news leaked out tonight. We had Colonel Brice over for drinks tonight and during the conversation he mentioned the fact that we were mighty lucky to be going back to "Uncle Sugar"— U.S.! The skipper had wanted to surprise us with it himself. Found out, too that we expect to leave Santos within a week after we get there. We'll either go home on a ship or fly by N.A.T.S. to Pearl Harbor and go home by ship from there. Gee, it's a wonderful feeling darling— sort of feel relaxed as hell to have the word now. All of a sudden, I feel tired as the devil—and I love you more than ever. I'll be home for your birthday if things go right. How'd you like that?

Until VF-17 was relieved, it was a matter of waiting for the new squadron to come in and thinking of home:

Our relief hasn't shown up yet, honey—the bums are messing us up somewhere along the line. I have the day off tomorrow though, so I'm going to take it easy and hope we leave on Monday. I wrote you today but didn't tell you the news. Skipper says to hold the dope from you. Got a February 17 V-mail from you today—I love you, honey.

The frustration of waiting to fly out of the combat area was growing by the day, which is evident from "Dirty Eddie's" thoughts on the matter:

Another day without even a smell of our relief. Don't even know where the hell they are by now—they should've been here a couple of days ago. Boy, all of us are really getting sore at this new outfit—they're certainly getting a bad name with us! Whenever an outfit is late in relieving like this outfit is, it's really a heck of a kick in the pants. Had the day off and spent the morning in the sack and got so disgusted in the afternoon, I started drinking again.

The relief squadron finally arrived on March 6, 1944, although that was not the end of the action:

Relief finally came in today—and already we're at odds with 'em. The damn guys won't fly tomorrow—say their planes aren't ready. So we have a full day tomorrow. Skipper's plenty sore about it and is going to see the Colonel tomorrow and try and get us out of here by noon. To make the cheese more binding 'cause the Japs are supposed to make a big push starting at midnight tonight. Right now, the doggone artillery is raising hell. We might just have one last, big battle.

Fighting Seventeen prepared to finally depart the island, and after many delays "Dirty Eddie" was all-set to leave:

March 7, 1944. Well honey, we're all packed ready to go. Take off 0645 in the morning—should be in Santo tomorrow night!

March 8, 1944. It's a little after 0500 Wednesday morning, honey and we're just getting things ready to leave. Ran out of ink last night or I'd have written more than I did. Gee, but it's a wonderful feeling to be leaving here! With any luck we should be on our way home from Buttons within a week. I'll be home for your birthday yet! Darling, I've gotten so I love you more and more every single day! Oh, it's going to be so wonderful to hold you in my arms once more!

"Dirty Eddie" in flying gear at Bougainville in 1944. *Courtesy National Archives.*

However, VF-17's exit from the island was not to be the straightforward departure they envisaged, as "Dirty Eddie" was to find out:

Well, honey—a lot has happened since I wrote this morning. The Japs started shelling us about 0630 and we all got off just in time. One of our men got hurt pretty badly—hope "Stink" and all the rest get out okay. Stopped off at Cactus and eleven of us got stuck here.

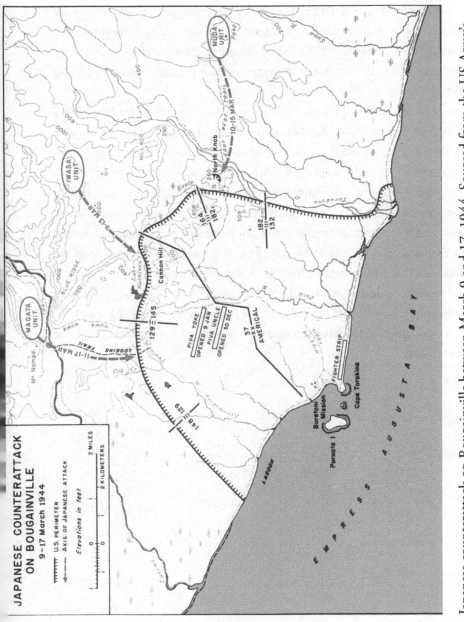

Japanese counterattack on Bougainville between March 9 and 17, 1944. Sourced from the US Army's official history of the campaign *CARTWHEEL—The Reduction of Rabaul* by John Miller, Jr.

Once the Japanese realized the Allies were not going to take the whole island, they started planning a counterattack, but unfortunately for them, they underestimated the size of the forces defending the airfields. Anticipating a Japanese attack, the Allies had strengthened their perimeter and prepared for the onslaught.[9]

The Japanese artillery opened fire on the airstrip around the time VF-17 was departing on March 8, 1944. Fortunately, all of the squadron were able to fly out safely, although two of their groundcrew, Robert Whitley and Hugo Engler, were severely wounded by shrapnel and taken to the hospital.[10]

The fighting on Bougainville would continue until the very end of the war. Japanese forces did finally cross through the mountains, swamps, and jungle to mount a counterattack on the Allied beachhead and airfield at Empress Augusta Bay in March 1944. The result was a massacre of the Japanese (for which gunfire from U.S. Navy destroyers was given significant credit). Following the failed Japanese attack, Australian troops took over responsibility for occupying the island of Bougainville and conducted offensive operations on the island against the remaining Japanese forces until the war ended.[11]

Chapter 17

Coming Home— I Want to Surprise You!

When record-breaking *Fighting Seventeen* was to leave the combat area, their fame would follow them. Their extraordinary achievements were reported all over the United States.[1] From January 26 to January 30, 1944, they shot down 60.5 Japanese aircraft in the "hot box" of Rabaul.[2] Among *Fighting Seventeen*'s heroic exploits was the record shooting down of 152 Japanese aircraft in aerial combat in only seventy-six days. No bomber escorted by them was lost to enemy air action and no ship, for which they provided cover, was hit by enemy bombs or aerial torpedoes. VF-17 flew more combat hours and sorties than any other fighter squadron in the Pacific up to that time. The squadron had thirteen aces, with Lt. (jg) Ira Cassius "Ike" Kepford the leading Navy ace at that time. One of the outstanding contributions made by "The Skull and Crossbones Squadron" was being the first, under combat conditions, to demonstrate the suitability of the F4U in carrier operations.[3] Their record in the Pacific and the later success of other Navy squadrons proved that they were right to persevere with this aircraft. The pilots of the gull-wing Corsairs were the toughest foe faced by enemy aviators. Under interrogation at the end of the war, the Japanese high command disclosed the fact that they considered the Corsair the top fighter in use by any opposing service in the Pacific. In the course of shooting down 2140 enemy aircraft, only 189 Corsairs were lost in combat, a ratio of better than eleven to one.[4]

The final tally for *Fighting Seventeen* was 152 confirmed Japanese aircraft shot down, which meant they outscored the "Black Sheep" Squadron (VMF-214) in the same theater of operations by a considerable margin.[5] Tom Blackburn had always stressed teamwork and led the squadron to a Navy Unit Commendation, earning "The Skull and Crossbones Squadron" a reputation as one of the most successful squadrons in the annals of air warfare.[6]

Once "Dirty Eddie" had arrived safely on Espiritu Santo on March 9, he was mightily relieved, and the most pressing thing on his mind now would be Elsa, "Baby Skeex," and at long last, going home:

Well honey, back at Santos once more. Really felt good to get that old "Hog" down for the last time for a while. We left Guadalcanal with a S.C.A.T. leading us this morning. Nice weather all the way down. Last night we had drinks and dinner with Admiral Fitch and his staff and spent the night in one of the guys' huts. Gee, they're treating us like kings. It's been a swell experience and I'm sure all the fellows had a swell time! Had breakfast with the Admiral before we left.

Gee, it's going to be wonderful here—no flying, no getting up early, no big guns going off in your ears! Still don't know about the rest of the fellows—hope they got out of there okay. Had about five letters to post to you when I got here. It tickles me that I'm coming home to you—and you don't know anything about it. Boy, are you going to be surprised!

There was no news about when the squadron was due to leave BUTTON, but there was a surprise in store, when some of the pilots got to meet movie star Ray Milland:

March 10, 1944. Had a good evening today, honey. It seems that on the way down, "Timmy" and I flew on the plane that had three U.S.O. girls on it who are out here with Ray Milland. We got to meet 'em and were

out with 'em last night. Gee, he's a heck of a swell guy. He has about 700
hours and gets a big kick out of talking flying with us. Still no dope as to
when we leave. The skipper got here yesterday but the other fellows are
still up the way. They may have to come out by boat.

A day of relaxation, beer, and bull sessions followed, as "Dirty Eddie"
and the rest of the squadron waited for news of their departure:

March 11, 1944. Had a swell day today, honey. Went over to the Marine
Club and had a picnic out on an island near there—"Buck" and another
Marine, "Timmy," "Oc" (Lt. Oscar Ivan Chenoweth, Jr.) and I and Ray
Milland and the three girls with him. It was really swell, we had beer
and sandwiches and a lot of sunshine. I'm sure the girls enjoyed them-
selves 'cause it's the first real relaxation they've had since they left the
States. This Milland is a regular fellow too—very nice. Duke got down
today—"Stink's" still up there. He should be here tomorrow.

"Stinky" duly arrived, but the news he brought with him was disap-
pointing for "Dirty Eddie":

March 12, 1944. "Stink" got down today and brought some bad news.
He was bringing my parachute bag down and it turned up missing in
Guadalcanal. I had lots of stuff in it but the main thing is all of the
undeveloped rolls of film I had. About six rolls of 35mm and 200' of
movie film. Darn, if those don't turn up, it'll make me sick. The Bunker
Hill pulled in today. "Stink" got away early and is aboard tonight—I'm
going to see all the boys tomorrow.

It was a day to catch up with old comrades when the *Bunker Hill* arrived,
and they were able to enjoy the facilities on board:

March 13, 1944. Another day of fooling around today, honey.
Seen all the boys. Went aboard ship this morning and had a hot
shower! Pro (Lt. Olivier Provosty) and all the others seemed really

glad to see me. Gee, they're really giving Ross a bad time though.
Oveland's (Lt. (jg) Collin Oveland) finally come around and admits
how wrong he was. He's turned out to be a pretty darn good boy.
Went over to the Club and the air group gave a little party. "Stink"
and the skipper and I went.

While waiting for word of their departure, the squadron continued to
enjoy time out of the combat area and on the ship:

March 14, 1944. Went aboard the Bunker Hill for lunch today with
"Timmy." Captain Pride ate with us in the wardroom (first time he's
eaten there in five to six months). Ray would like to have gone but he
was too darn tired. Gee, he's really a swell egg.

It wouldn't be long before "Dirty Eddie" would be going home and it
was a time to relax, enjoy the rest, and think of home:

March 15, 1944. "Timmy" pulled out early this morning. My bunch
leaves in the morning with "Stink's" bunch a day later and the skipper's
bunch bringing up the rear. Nobody can say we haven't been having a
wonderful change since we last flew over Rabaul. Gosh, nobody does a
darn thing! Saw where the skipper recommended me for the Navy Cross
today. Hope it goes through 'cause it'll make you proud of me.

On Thursday, March 16, "Dirty Eddie" departed Espiritu Santo for the
long trip to Pearl Harbor:

Am writing this on the Pan American Clipper way up in the sky over
the Pacific. It's really a relief to be flying with some guys who know
what they're doing rather than with those Army guys in S.C.A.T. Should
arrive in Canton tonight and then go on to Pearl tomorrow. We'll prob-
ably stay there a few days and then go home by ship. I hope I can
surprise you—I will if somebody hasn't spilled the beans and you get
hold of the dope from them!

The difference between living in the combat area and the relative luxury of the trip home hit "Dirty Eddie," and he was struggling to sleep:

This may still be Thursday—I think we lost a day somewhere along "the Line" today. Spent last night on Canton and left there at 0300 this morning. We stayed at Pan American quarters and the quarters were something we're not used to. In fact, "Wally" Schub (Lt. Walter Schub) and I roomed together and went to bed at 2115. We lay awake for almost two hours. It was too quiet to sleep—didn't have the guns to put us to sleep. Mattress was also too much—couldn't get comfortable on it. Finally, we got up and hit the snake-bite remedy and when that didn't put me to sleep, I read a couple of stories out of a magazine. Back on the plane here I've gotten some sleep. We stopped at Palmyra and are now only a little more than an hour out of Pearl. It's been a very nice hop. Hope you don't get any word about me coming home—I want to surprise you!

Upon his arrival in Pearl Harbor, "Dirty Eddie" was ear-marked for public relations duties, much as he had done previously after returning from Guadalcanal:

March 18, 1944. Fooled around most of the day today. Duke told me I'm to be at a press conference on Wednesday after-noon. The skipper, "Rog" (Hedrick), "Ike" (Kepford) and myself still don't know when we're leaving. Nothing to do 'til we leave though—what a life!

"Dirty Eddie" settled into his new accommodation and awaited news of when he would be leaving for home:

March 19, 1944. Sort of moved into the "rest home" today. I wasn't one of the ten to go out—let some of the others go in my place—but I'm going to hang around as a "guest." It's not the same place as we were at last time—this is another home opened up in conjunction with the

Holmes place. It's a little smaller, but really nice. The food is wonder-
ful here—may get back some of my weight. I'm down to about 163 lb.
Feel great though.

News arrived that in two days he would be on his way home on the
Prince William and the expectation was mounting as to when he would be
with Elsa again:

Found out we're going aboard the "Pee Willie" on Wednesday night
and leaving for 'Frisco Thursday morning. About the 28–29th you'll
really get a surprise call from me. Gee, my darling, I can't wait to see
you! Won't it be wonderful to be together again though!

Some last-minute shopping was on the agenda for Tuesday, March 21,
as time was running out before he was due to embark:

Stayed in at the Moana tonight. Fooled around out at the "Rest Home"
for the most part of the day and did a little shopping. Wish I could get
things for everybody but not only would I probably leave someone out
but then too, I probably wouldn't be able to carry everything. Got you
a lot of birthday presents.

"Dirty Eddie," along with some other aces of *Fighting Seventeen*, was
presented to the press, as their fame had grown after their illustrious deeds in
the Solomon Islands:

March 22, 1944. Last night in town today. The skipper, "Rog", "Ike"
and I went to Admiral Pannel's for a big press conference. There
were two Admirals, about three Captains and about twenty corre-
spondents there. Even had a Reuters man there. It was all pretty
interesting. We went back into town and had a little get together at
the home and then I spent the night at the hotel again. The skipper
got word that Rose (Blackburn's wife) was sick and is flying home
tomorrow.

RAdm. J. J. Ballentine is shown with four of the thirteen aces of *Fighting Seventeen*. L-R: Lt. Harry March, (5 victories); Lt. Cdr. Roger Hedrick (9 victories); RAdm. Ballentine, Chief of Staff, Air Force, Pacific Fleet; Lt. Cdr. J. T. Blackburn, (11 victories) and the No. 1 U.S. Navy ace, at that time, Lt. (jg) Ira C. Kepford, (16 victories). *Courtesy Robert Lawson Photograph Collection, National Museum of Naval Aviation/U.S. Navy photo.*

"Dirty Eddie" had wanted to surprise Elsa about his return home, but it appeared that this was in vain, as word would get there before him:

March 23, 1944. Am writing this aboard the Prince William tonight, and it's a funny thing, honey but doggone if I don't have the same room now as I did when we left here to go down to Espiritu Santo back in October! That's really a strange coincidence. Darling, I hope that you don't have the scarlet fever the same as Rose, it's pretty astonishing isn't it? Now that the skipper is flying home, you'll get the word that

I'm coming home and all the surprise will be gone. I wanted so much to really surprise you—that's the reason I haven't written lately—wanted you to think that I was still down in Sydney.

Until they arrived in port, "Dirty Eddie's" life was one of relaxation and taking in some sun where he could, along with the usual bull sessions:

March 24, 1944. Just a nice day of loafing around today. Got a little sun today up on the flight deck. Doggone it, honey—I get as much sun as most fellows and only get half as brown. You'll have to be satisfied with your old man the way he is I reckon—brown just enough to look dirty. This is going to be a nice trip. Had a movie after supper and then went in the ward room and played records 'til about 2300. Really living the life of Riley!

It was just a case of passing away the time before getting home:

March 25, 1944. Just spent about 4½ hours putting a jigsaw puzzle together in the ward room after the movie! Nice quiet day today—got more sun during the day too. Spent about thirty minutes watching the seagulls— about thirty of 'em were following the ship. Gee, but they're graceful!

Just a final few days on board, and soon he would be reunited with Elsa again:

March 26, 1944. Lot of sun today—and then went to movies tonight— played poker during the day and then after the movies—came out $91 ahead. I'm going to make enough so I can fly right home to you! Gee, but it's going to be wonderful to be home again with you my dearest!

As the *Prince William* headed home the weather gradually got colder, and after the heat of the South Pacific it was really noticeable:

March 27, 1944. Boy, we sure must be getting close to California—it's colder than the devil! No sun out all day, so I slept 'til lunchtime and

just loafed the rest of the day. We got the report that it was 17° (Celsius)
above zero in 'Frisco—and all I have are my khaki pants and shirt.
I don't even have a leather jacket, it was among the things I had in
the parachute bag. Honey, if everything goes right, we'll be together
one week from today. I figure that with luck, we won't be in 'Frisco
more than two days and then I'll fly home to you!

The nearer they came to port, the idea of being home with Elsa and "Baby Skeex" filled his every waking thought:

March 29, 1944. Baby's six months old tonight, honey. Didn't write
anything last night 'cause I stayed up 'til 0400 reading and then stayed
awake for two more hours thinking of you. Gee, every night I long
more to see you. Don't know how we'll make out tonight—we put in
tomorrow morning and I'll call you right away. Played some basketball
yesterday and volleyball today. It's too cold outside—getting near that
California weather.

Thursday night, March 30, 1944, was the last night on board. He had come through all the fierce battles unscathed and was soon to be with his love Elsa and their new baby:

Last night aboard my darling and last night to write this letter to
you. It's been wonderful being with you every night like this, hasn't
it? Bye for now my sweet, see you soon.

All officers and enlisted men disembarked at N.A.S. Alameda, California. On April 10, 1944, Fighting Squadron Seventeen was decommissioned and the men received a well-earned leave before being re-assigned.[7]

One of the pilots assigned new orders was the dependable "Stinky." Following a deserved leave, he reported to N.A.S. San Diego for duty which involved flying in the Aircraft Ordnance Development Unit at Inyokern, California. Having survived being shot down by the Japanese at Guadalcanal and lasting through two further combat tours, "Stinky" was killed in a crash

Lt. Donald "Stinky" Innis at Bougainville. His nickname was believed to have originated at Guadalcanal, where he served in 1942. "Stinky" Innis and "Dirty Eddie" were best friends and served together in squadrons VF-5, VF-24, and VF-17. *Courtesy Alexandra Bowers.*

in an F6F Hellcat on June 20, 1944. He was over the Salton Sea in Southern California when a rocket exploded prematurely on his starboard wing and his aircraft crashed into the sea.

Following his tragic accident, the Commander of the U.S. Naval Ordnance Test Station, Inyokern, California, wrote to his mother with the sad news, on June 21, 1944:

Dear Mrs. Innis,

It is with the deepest sympathy that I write you regarding your son, Donald, who was instantly killed in an airplane crash yesterday. Donald was assigned to duty with the Aviation Ordnance Development Unit attached to this station. His time has been devoted to test flights in connection with the development of a new weapon for aircraft. He has been of material assistance to this most important work.

I feel a deep personal loss in the death of this fine young man. I found Donald to be at all times extremely capable, intelligent, and most thorough in the performance of his duties. His behavior was always above reproach, indicating that his home surroundings and general upbringing were of the very best. He was well-liked and respected by officers and men alike.

All hands on this station join me in expressing our sympathy for you in this great sorrow. These are sad days for a great many Americans who have lost their loved ones in the service of our country. We must all remember that these costly sacrifices are the price of freedom, and continue to bend our every effort to shortening this war.

Sincerely yours

S. E. Burroughs, Jr.

Captain U.S. Navy.[8]

The steadfast "Stinky" joined Bill, "Dutch," Johnny, and so many other close friends of "Dirty Eddie" who did not survive the war.

Chapter 18

Instructing the "Nuggets"

n early 1944, the Pacific War was progressing with the successful American raid on Truk Lagoon. By this time the United States had built up a vast task force of ships, protected by the *Essex*-class aircraft carriers. This laid the foundations for landings on Saipan, Peleliu, and the invasion of the Philippines in the months ahead.[1]

"Dirty Eddie," after many months away from his beloved Elsa and never having seen "Baby Skeex," was finally reunited with his family. They had so much to catch up on while he was on leave. After the uncertainty of whether he would be one of the lucky ones to make it back, it was a time of trying to rehabilitate himself back to life at home.

"Dirty Eddie" was officially detached from the Pacific Fleet on April 3, 1944, and after his leave, was ordered to N.A.S. Jacksonville to report on May 4, 1944. Prior to reporting there however, "Dirty Eddie" received orders on April 17, 1944, from the Chief of Naval Personnel stating: "On or about April 18, 1944, you will proceed to the Brewster Aeronautical Corporation, Long Island City, New York, thence to the Brewster Aeronautical Corporation, Johnsville, Pennsylvania, and thence to the Goodyear Aircraft Corporation, Akron Ohio, in connection with incentive activities."[2]

Lt. Harry "Dirty Eddie" March, fighter ace with five victories. *Courtesy the March Family.*

Being experienced in public relations, "Dirty Eddie" was one of many *Fighting Seventeen* aces who were called upon to raise morale by visiting factories and promoting the F4U Corsair. Chance Vought, the manufacturer of the Corsair, was thrilled with the record of *Fighting Seventeen*, as they were the first successful carrier-based F4U squadron in the Navy:

Chance Vought Aircraft takes pleasure in sending you the enclosed snapshots of personnel of VF-17 in the combat areas. The men and women who build the Corsair are proud of the top-notch record which "The Skull and Crossbones Squadron" set while flying the F4U.[3]

On May 6, 1944, "Dirty Eddie" reported to N.A.A.S. Green Cove Springs, Florida, as a flight instructor.[4] In World War II, Florida was the perfect place to build airfields for training bases and other military installations due to the mild weather. There were forty airfields in the state used to train budding young aviators and many VF-17 pilots had passed through Naval Air Stations such as Jacksonville, Pensacola, and Miami prior to combat.[5] It was inevitable that experienced pilots returning from overseas tours would become instructors there. This was where they would pass on their extensive knowledge of combat operations to the "Nuggets," naval slang for "New Useless Guys."

There were over a dozen former *Fighting Seventeen* pilots based at Green Cove Springs. Here, they had the opportunity to relax and enjoy the beaches along the coast, such as at St. Augustine. Only forty minutes away, this was a popular destination for pilots to live and visit in the evenings to unwind. "Hap" Bowers was one of the VF-17 veterans based there, and an interesting note appeared in his letter to his girlfriend Alice on September 11, 1944:

"Damn near forgot—I got a D.F.C. today. Got my citation anyhow. Will probably have to wait for an inspection and an Admiral to pin it on. Anyhow I got the D.F.C. What a hot rock. 'Dirty Eddie' has only an Air Medal and earned twice what I did—I can do nothing but feel sorry for him."[6]

Over the course of the next seven months, while serving as a flight instructor at N.A.A.S. Green Cove Springs, "Dirty Eddie's" fitness reports gave an enlightening picture of this veteran of the Pacific War:

October 14, 1944: Lt. March is an extremely capable pilot and performs all duties of a Flight Instructor in a very efficient manner. He is most good-natured and performs all extra assigned duties cheerfully. By his nature he has the ability to obtain the best from officers and men while maintaining high standards of morale. He is well-liked by all his associates and is recommended for promotion when due. Good military bearing and appearance.

March 28, 1945: This officer possesses great moral courage and has always handled his official duties with satisfaction. He has a very pleasing personality which qualifies him to work with others.

May 24, 1945: Lt. March has a very pleasing personality and is well liked by the officers and men that work under him. He has a good combat record and possesses a strong competitive spirit. He is recommended for promotion when due and for a commission in the line of the regular Navy.[7]

"Dirty Eddie's" extensive experience in combat from 1942 to 1944 was invaluable to new pilots, many of whom would soon be reporting to the Pacific Theater. The U.S. forces' tactic of island-hopping toward Japan continued and the capture of the Mariana Islands put Japan within operating distance of long-range B-29 bombers. The Americans landed on the island of Iwo Jima in February 1945 as it provided an important landing field for crippled bombers unable to get back to the Marianas. The six-week battle saw the fiercest fighting so far in the Pacific War. Once the island had been secured it became a base for fighters to escort bombers to Japan. The U.S. invasion of Okinawa was the next phase of the campaign and resulted in the Japanese resorting to kamikaze attacks on the American ships. The losses incurred by the U.S. Navy were the heaviest casualties inflicted by the Japanese Navy in any battle of the entire war.[8]

"Dirty Eddie" was detached from Green Cove Springs on May 15, 1945, and reported to Commander Air Force Atlantic Fleet. He was then detached and assigned to VBF-74 at Otis Field, Camp Edwards, Massachusetts, as executive officer. "Dirty Eddie" was one of a number of former VF-17 pilots assigned to Air Group 74, whose Commander was Tom Blackburn. Other "old hands" were Lem Cooke, Tom Killefer, "Hap" Bowers, and "Andy" Anderson.

"Dirty Eddie" had resumed his athletics training and despite the intensive preparations for returning to combat, he was able to start competing again. On June 30, 1945, he achieved sixth position in his favored event, the 400 m hurdles, at the A.A.U. National Championships in New York.[9]

"Dirty Eddie" (6th from left) with VBF-74 shortly before the war ended. He is pictured with former *Fighting Seventeen* veterans, Tom Blackburn (5th from left) and Lem Cooke (2nd from left). *Courtesy U.S. Navy Photo.*

It appears that Harry was also trying out the decathlon, which was an Olympic event, unlike his former event, the pentathlon. Just over a week later, he finished in a creditable sixth place at the A.A.U. National Decathlon Championships.[10] Despite a four-year break, he was back competing at the top level, and his goal was to be a contender at the 1948 Olympics.[11]

On May 8, 1945, the war in Europe had ended and finally, in August 1945, the war in the Pacific was over, when the Americans dropped atomic bombs on Hiroshima and Nagasaki. From the evidence of the Iwo Jima and Okinawa battles, the Japanese fought ferociously and would have defended their homeland to the last. Although contentious to this day, the momentous decision to employ the new atom bomb against Japan probably saved hundreds of thousands of Japanese and American lives.[12]

Air Group 74 was assigned to the new aircraft carrier, *Midway*. The *Midway*, named after the famous battle in 1942, was built in only seventeen months. From the time "Dirty Eddie" had joined VBF-74, the squadron was training to resume an operational role in preparation for a planned American invasion of Japan. However, the *Midway*, described as the largest ship in the world, missed out on World War II as it was not commissioned until September 10, 1945.[13] On October 3, 1945, "Dirty Eddie" was promoted to lieutenant commander, and along with the other "plank owners" sailed to the Caribbean in the winter of 1945 on the *Midway* to undertake her shakedown cruise.[14] The *Midway* became the longest serving aircraft carrier in the twentieth century and was the first in a three-ship class of large carriers that featured an armored flight deck and a powerful air group of 120 planes. It was decommissioned on April 11, 1992, and ultimately opened as a museum in San Diego in 2004.[15]

While serving with VBF-74, "Dirty Eddie's" fitness report, dated October 1945, stated:

Lt. March as Flight Officer and Operations Officer, during the period of this report, has performed all of his assigned duties in an excellent manner. He has taken an unusual interest in the squadron and its progress to a successful completion of training. An excellent pilot and leader, he insists on good work from those with him. Foresight and good judgement are present in all of his work. Lt. March has a most pleasing and affable personality, which has lent much to the morale of the squadron. His personal and military character are of the best and he is qualified for promotion when due.[16]

Following the cessation of hostilities, "Dirty Eddie" had to make the decision whether to apply to stay in the Navy or start a new career outside of the services. This was a big decision for him and after much thought, he applied to join the regular Navy. He submitted his application on November 12, 1945, which was well received:

The applicant made an excellent impression on the board by means of his pleasing appearance and good presence. His candid and

Harry and Elsa with Mary in the summer of 1945. *Courtesy the family of Jean March McAfee.*

well-considered answers to interrogation showed firm motivation and fine qualifications for transfer to the regular service. It is further noted that the applicant was selected for the 1940 Olympic team in the 400 m hurdles, and that he is a former National Pentathlon Champion. As Executive Officer of the VBF squadron attached to this vessel, Lt. Cdr. March has performed all of his assigned duties in an excellent manner. He undertakes all tasks with a cheerful, light hearted disposition and open mind. His work shows intelligent and logical thought. He is an excellent pilot and leader and requires the best of those with him. His extremely friendly and likeable nature makes him an asset to any unit. With a good solid background and excellent officer-like qualities, Lt. Cdr. March is strongly recommended for transfer to the regular Navy.[17]

"Dirty Eddie" passed his medical on November 16, 1945. He was 6'½" tall, weighed 175 pounds, and was in prime condition. The Board of Medical Examiners in the Navy Department, Washington, D.C., later considered the report of "Dirty Eddie's" physical examination and found that he had met the standards required for the regular Navy. On January 30, 1946, "Dirty Eddie's" application was approved, graded "very highly recommended". It was recorded that he possessed all the physical and educational requirements.[18]

For the first time since Harry and Elsa had been together, they were able to make plans for the future. Harry had a devoted wife and a young family. He was held in the highest esteem by the Navy and was assured of a secure career in the service. He finally had the opportunity to fulfil his potential as a top athlete, with the dream of representing his country at the 1948 Olympics in London. At twenty-six, he had his whole life ahead of him.

Epilogue

I n late February 1946, shortly after his twenty-seventh birthday, Harry went to Chapel Hill, N.C., to participate in the University of North Carolina indoor track meet, as part of his training for the 1948 London Olympics.[1] The *Daily Tar Heel*, the U.N.C. newspaper, reported the event as follows:

Strong Field Slated to Run in Track Meet
It is the largest field the big meet has attracted since it was opened to service as well as college stars four years ago. Among the entries received for the Southern Invitation Indoor Track Championships is one from Harry March, former Carolina track star, who will compete in the hurdles and high jump.

He's a much-decorated air ace and a full-fledged Lieutenant Commander now, but to his many friends here, Harry March is still the "one-man track team" from Carolina. Commander March, will be carrying the colors of the Norfolk Naval Air Station, but the Carolina coaches and boys he was in college with will be pulling for the Washington, D.C., flier to star just as they did in his days here in 1936–40.

March will try the ironman here Saturday, entering both the hurdle races and both the jumps, and his ex-coaches at Carolina say the spectators at the annual indoor classic are in for a one-man show, as March is one of the greatest competitors they have ever tutored. He'll have plenty of competition to spur him on to his best, too, for the record field of 39 teams and 286 contestants is headed by such strong teams as Carolina, Duke, Georgia Tech, Cherry Point, and the Little Creek Amphibious Base.[2]

On February 23, 1946, while at the meet, Harry suddenly became acutely ill, with chills and a very high fever. He was admitted to the University of North Carolina Infirmary, Chapel Hill, N.C., where a diagnosis of viral pneumonia was given. Despite large doses of penicillin being administered, Harry's illness grew rapidly worse. He was in need of specialist care; however, the nearest Naval Hospital was the U.S. Naval Hospital, Portsmouth, Va., which was more than two hundred miles away. Harry was far too ill to transfer to the Naval Hospital, so he was sent by private ambulance to Watts Hospital, Durham, N.C., a civilian hospital about twelve miles away.[3] Further x-rays revealed a very rapid spread of an atypical pneumonia, from the right lung where the infection began, to an extremely extensive involvement of both lungs. Friedlander's Bacillus or staphylococcus was suspected, although laboratory work failed to identify the exact causative organism. At 0400 on March 2, 1946, despite intensive care, Harry succumbed to pneumonia.[4] Notwithstanding his superb physical condition, this robust, ace pilot with indomitable spirit, who had overcome a mountain of adversity in the Pacific Theater, had lost his life to a rare disease within a week. The Olympic dream died with him.

The *Daily Tar Heel* reported his death:

Harry March, Star Trackman in 1940, Dies of Pneumonia

Chapel Hill, March 2——Lt. Cdr. Harry March, 27, Navy air ace and former track star for the University of North Carolina, who won the National Pentathlon for Carolina in 1940, died of pneumonia in a Durham hospital early this morning.

Commander March, who was stationed at Norfolk Naval Air Station came to Chapel Hill last weekend to participate in the annual

Southern Indoor Games and was taken sick while here. Despite his protest that he wanted to participate even though he was running a fever, athletic officials refused to allow him to enter the contests. That night he was taken to a Durham hospital in an ambulance.

A native of East Liverpool, Ohio, Commander March was living with his family in Washington, D.C., when he entered the University in 1936. During his four years here he starred in track, specializing in the high and low hurdles and the broad and high jumps.

In addition to winning the National Pentathlon in 1940, he averaged 16 points a meet all the season and was undefeated in the hurdles. He won three first places in the Southern Conference Outdoor Championships that same year and scored 20 points against the Navy in a dual meet.

Commander March was a much-decorated Navy ace in the Pacific theater and was one of the 13 aces in the Navy's famed "Skull and Crossbones Squadron" which was cited for downing 152 enemy planes in 76 days.

Commander March married the former Miss Elsa Winters of Raleigh, who was a member of the University class of 1941. There is one child, Mary Elizabeth, two years old. Mrs. March was with him when he died.[5]

The resolute Harry March, who had rendered heroic service to his country over a prolonged period of duty, was buried at Arlington National Cemetery.

Decorations:

Distinguished Flying Cross
Air Medal with one Gold Star
Presidential Unit Citation with two Stars (USS *Enterprise*, 1st Marine
    Division)
Navy Unit Commendation
American Defense Service Medal
Asiatic–Pacific Area Campaign Medal with one Bronze Star
World War II Victory Medal.[6]

Following a review of awards by the Navy, on October 10, 1947, Harry was finally awarded permanent citations for the Distinguished Flying Cross and Gold Star in lieu of Second Air Medal.[7] As recorded in his diary, the D.F.C. and Navy Cross were awards that Harry dearly wanted for his devoted wife, Elsa. He did achieve one of these, albeit after his death. Considering his length of service in the combat area and where he served in two of the most brutal campaigns of the Pacific War, it was remarkable that Harry survived. When his record is compared to many other men who were awarded the Navy Cross, it is surprising that he did not receive this honor.

Harry Andrew March, Jr.
February 4, 1919—March 2, 1946

....

A.A.U. National Championships, 1940–400 m Hurdle Competitors

Harry March remains largely unknown for his athletic achievements. It was always Harry's dream to appear in the Olympic Games, and despite running the third best time in the world in the 400 m Hurdles at the A.A.U. National Championships in 1940, Harry was denied this opportunity. The same was true for the other athletes in this race, however, McBain, Cochran, and Borican were all later honored as Hall of Fame athletes:

Carl McBain (1st) never raced again after posting the best time in the world in 1940 and being at the top of his form. Carl was devastated to not be able to run in the Olympics. "That was the big shock of my life." Like all other athletes at the time, their destiny was changed by world events. Carl said, "I've been sorry about that my whole life." Like Harry, Carl became a naval officer during World War II and later a successful businessman. He died on September 22, 2015, aged ninety-seven.[8]

LeRoy Braxton "Roy" Cochran (2nd) would have been one of the favorites for the 1940 Olympic 400 m hurdles. Like Harry, he served as an officer in the Navy in the Pacific in World War II and retired a commander.

He believed his athletic career was over, but when running in his leisure time, he discovered he had retained his speed. He started to train more seriously and won the 400 m Hurdles Olympic Gold medal in 1948 at the London Games. He also won Gold in the 400 m relay. At what was considered an advanced age (29) for runners of that time, he proved persistence was the key. Roy Cochran died on September 26, 1981, aged sixty-two.[9]

John Borican (4th) like the others in the race, was denied the chance to appear in Olympic competition. He went on to win the 1941 A.A.U. National Pentathlon title, repeating his triumphs of 1938 and 1939. He also became the first athlete to achieve the double, also winning the Decathlon in 1941. At the time, he was described as "America's greatest track and field athlete." In 1942, John set three world records before becoming seriously ill with pernicious anemia. He died on December 22, 1942, aged twenty-nine.[10]

....

Guadalcanal Veterans

There were many among "Dirty Eddie's" Navy comrades who did not survive the war. Among them were his close friends Bill Wileman, "Dutch" Shoemaker, "Stinky" Innis, and Johnny Kleinman, who are venerated in Appendix 2, along with Jim Halford, one of the lucky ones. The stories of some of the other pilots who served with "Dirty Eddie" are outlined below:

Julius Albert "Joe" Achten after being shot down and wounded on August 7, 1942, returned home. After his recovery, he served as an instructor at Green Cove Springs Florida. He died on April 4, 2006.[11]

Louis Hallowell Bauer, Commanding Officer of *Fighting Six*, was awarded the Navy Cross for his stellar leadership of the squadron. He continued in the Navy after the war and served in the Korean conflict before retiring in 1965 as a captain after distinguished service. He died on April 26, 2008.[12]

Mark Bright was awarded the Navy Cross for his actions at Guadalcanal and was an ace with nine victories. He was killed in action on June 17, 1944, while flying with VF-16.[13]

Howard W. "Sandy" Crews survived the war and was highly regarded as a combat pilot. After twenty-seven years of service, he retired as a captain and died on January 28, 1992.[14]

Benjamin Franklin "Benny" Currie, after his distinguished service in the Guadalcanal Campaign, survived the war and died on June 28, 1988.[15]

Robert Allen Murray "Bobby" Dibb won the Navy Cross at Midway and became an ace with seven victories. He died on August 29, 1944, in a flying accident at the Naval Ordnance Test Station, Inyokern.[16]

Robert E. Galer was awarded the Medal of Honor for his service as commander of VMF-224. He was credited with shooting down eleven Japanese aircraft in twenty-nine days. After distinguished service, he retired in 1957 as a brigadier general and died on June 27, 2005.[17]

Henry Edward "Bud" Hartmann continued in the Navy after WWII, was promoted to commander, and died on December 2, 1954.[18]

Richards Llewellyn "Dick" Loesch, Jr., recovered from his wounds at Guadalcanal, continued in the Navy and survived the war. He became a test pilot for Boeing and later Chief of Test Flight. He died on August 8, 2007.[19]

Francis Roland "Cash" Register, fighter ace with seven confirmed Japanese aircraft, died on May 16, 1943, in Attu in the Aleutian Islands while serving with VC-11.[20]

Melvin C. Roach was awarded a Distinguished Flying Cross for his deeds at Guadalcanal. He died shortly after taking off from the *Essex* in the Pacific on June 12, 1944.[21]

Donald E. Runyon became an ace with eleven confirmed victories and had an illustrious naval career. He retired on June 30, 1963, as a commander. He died on December 25, 1984, and is buried at Arlington National Cemetery.[22]

LeRoy Coard Simpler led Fighting Squadron Five at Guadalcanal and was awarded the Navy Cross in this campaign. He continued in the Navy and retired as a rear admiral in 1959 after meritorious service. He died on November 6, 1988.[23]

Albert Ogden "Scoop" Vorse, Jr., an ace pilot who scored ten and a half victories and had a distinguished naval career, being awarded the Navy Cross for gallantry on January 15, 1945. He retired a rear admiral and died on October 27, 1979.[24]

William Howard "Bill" Warden, after being shot down on August 7, 1942, survived the war and died on February 18, 1992, in San Diego, California.[25]

Fighting Seventeen Veterans

Robert "Andy" Anderson took a long time to recuperate after he was shot down in November 1943. After the war, he bought a parts company and became a businessman until he retired in 1968 at the age of fifty. He died on his forty-third wedding anniversary, during his second heart bypass surgery, on May 14, 1985.[26]

Tom Blackburn, an ace with eleven victories, was awarded two Navy Crosses and recognized as one of the finest skippers of a fighter squadron in the Navy. He retired after an illustrious career, with active service of thirty-three years, on July 31, 1962. He died on March 21, 1994, aged eighty-one. He is interred in Arlington National Cemetery.[27]

Lemuel Doty Cooke assumed command of Bombing Fighting Squadron 74 on May 24, 1945, with "Dirty Eddie" as his executive officer. Cdr. Cooke had passed his physical in April 1950 to be a test pilot. While waiting to report for his new role, he was practicing for the armed forces parade when his jet aircraft lost power and crashed on May 17, 1950, in Atlantic City, New Jersey. He is buried at Arlington National Cemetery.[28]

Clement Dexter "Timmy" Gile returned home an ace with eight victories after his service with *Fighting Seventeen*. He continued in the Navy until September 1945. He was awarded three Distinguished Flying Crosses, three Air Medals, and a Purple Heart for wounds received on March 18, 1945. After the war, he was the Vice President of Panagra, a seaplane and helicopter commuter airline and spent three years in Lima, Peru. He then went to work at Morgan Guarantee Trust Company and was Vice

President at the time he took early retirement in 1976. "Timmy" Gile died on November 21, 1978.[29]

Roger Hedrick finished the war an ace with twelve victories. He continued in the Navy after WWII. In October 1958, after a distinguished twenty-two-year naval career, he retired from the service as a rear admiral. Roger went to work for a construction company and retired in 1975 at the age of sixty-two. He died on January 15, 2006, aged ninety-one.[30]

Basil Duke Henning devoted his life to Yale University for forty-three years between 1935 and his retirement in 1978. This was only interrupted by the war years and his service in the Navy. The 1933 BA student rose to become Professor of History at Yale. For a record twenty-nine years, from 1946 to 1975, Duke Henning was Master of Saybrook College. He died on January 15, 1990.[31]

Lyle "Doc" Herrmann served as the Flight Surgeon with *Fighting Seventeen*. He served in the Navy for fourteen years, plus seven years in the Navy Reserve, and retired with the rank of captain. After the Navy, he practiced medicine in the Atlanta, Georgia, area until he retired in 1985. Lyle Herrmann died on October 12, 1994, in Seminole County, Florida.[32]

Ira Cassius "Ike" Kepford returned to the States in April 1944 as the top ace of the U.S. Navy and received a hero's welcome. He spent a lot of time on public relations tours for the Navy all around the country and conducted many speaking engagements. Following the war, Kepford worked his way up the ladder and later retired as President of Liggett–Rexall Drug Co. in 1971. He retired to Harbor Springs at age fifty-one as he "had lived a hard life" and went on to enjoy his retirement as "an outdoors man." "Ike" Kepford died in Michigan on January 19, 1987.[33]

Tom Killefer later served with "Dirty Eddie" in VBF-74 on the *Midway* shortly before the end of World War II. Tom then practiced law and had a distinguished career as a financial executive. During the late 1970s, he became the chairman and chief executive of the United States Trust Corporation. He died on June 16, 1996, at his Portola Valley home in California.[34]

William "Country" Landreth was the youngest original pilot of *Fighting Seventeen* and went on to serve with VF/VBF-10 before being captured by the Japanese in March 1945 and incarcerated for six months as a prisoner of war. "Country" was one of the lucky ones who survived as a prisoner of the Japanese. "Country" served in the Navy for twenty-seven years in various assignments before retiring as a commander in 1969. He died on Memorial Day, May 28, 2012.[35]

George Mauhar was requested by Roger Hedrick to join VF-84 as crew chief after his service with VF-17. George served in the Navy for twenty-two years and retired to work in the civil service and engineering. He died in 2012.[36]

Wilbert Peter "Beads" Popp served with VF-84 and was on the *Bunker Hill* on May 11, 1945, when it was struck by two kamikaze planes. After the war he graduated from the University of Washington in 1947 and became an insurance agent.[37] He died on February 25, 2006.[38]

Whitfield Carlisle Wharton, Jr., stayed in the Navy on active service until June 1947, then remained in the Navy Reserve and retired in October 1956. He died of a heart attack in September 1983. He was sixty-two years old.[39]

....

Elsa and Mary March

At the time of Harry's death, the faithful Elsa was approaching her twenty-eighth birthday and Mary was two years old. Both had to face life without their devoted husband and father, although Elsa had the continuing support from her father-in-law, Harry March, Sr., and other members of the family. Harry's father died in 1979, having survived his wife by nearly thirty-eight years, and he was buried with her at Fort Lincoln Cemetery, Brentwood, Maryland. Harry's eldest sister Jean died in 1994 aged 73, and JoAnn passed away in 2019, aged 95.[40]

Harry's sister-in-law, Dora, now in her nineties, has shared her fond memories of what happened to her spirited niece, Mary and sister Elsa:

Mary

"Mary was a lovely, bright, young girl as fun-loving as her parents—and in many ways was Harry's daughter in looks and personality. She led a very normal life, although I believe at times there was a deep sense of sadness over the loss of her father. She spent a lot of time creating a shadow box for his medals and keeping scrapbooks. In later years, some of the poetry she wrote echoed that sadness.

"After her first year of college, she made her debut in Raleigh and said that at some of the dances that she felt as though she might lose her equilibrium. By Thanksgiving of her sophomore year, she knew something was wrong and Elsa took her to a neuro-surgeon. He was concerned and sent her to Duke University Hospital, Durham, N.C. At first, she was wrongly diagnosed with an inoperable brain tumor and was given radiation treatment. She lost her hair and had to resort to wigs, but still the radiation did nothing to reduce the deteriorating effects the disease was having on her body and her eyes. After many more tests, she was diagnosed with Syringomyelia. This is a rare condition caused by a cyst in the spinal cord which causes slow disintegration of brain function, eventually affecting all parts of the body.

"Mary fought it all the way, refusing to resort to a wheel chair, struggling to walk and finally using leg braces. Through it all, she persevered to continue her college work, with a lot of help from Elsa, and finally graduated as a day student at U.N.C. State College in Raleigh. Her grandfather March (Harry's father) travelled from California and escorted her to the podium to receive her diploma. She persevered for many years, never losing her faith—always praying for healing."

Despite immense courage and tenacity, Mary died on January 1, 1976, in Raleigh, North Carolina, aged thirty-two after battling the disease for thirteen years.

Mary Elizabeth March
September 29, 1943—January 1, 1976

....

Elsa

After Harry's sudden death, Elsa was faced with starting her life over again. During this difficult time, she received several notifications of citations and awards given to Harry posthumously. Elsa set about approaching the task of raising Mary with devotion, patience, and love. Her sister Dora described her life after Harry:

"She loved Harry dearly—I believe he was her one and only true love. When he died so suddenly, she never ranted and raved against God or played the part of the pitiful, young widow. Of course, all our family gathered around to support and comfort her. But she wanted to make a new life for Mary and herself and for a while she thought it meant moving to California where she and Harry had been so happy and where his father and a sister lived.

"Unfortunately, it wasn't long before Elsa realized that California without Harry was not the place she wanted to raise Mary and she decided to return home. Before this, Elsa stopped in Utah and stayed with Mary Shoemaker for several months and took a business course at the University. Elsa had graduated at U.N.C. with an A.B. degree in History, but she did not want to teach.

"By this time, I had finished college and planned to move back to our old home town, Raleigh, N.C. Elsa decided that she would like to take Mary there too. We knew that Mama and Daddy would be returning there when he retired and we had many relatives there, so it was a good place for Mary to grow up. Elsa got a good job as a secretary with the Agricultural Extension service at North Carolina State University in Raleigh, and she worked there until she retired. She was active in the work of the Ladies Auxiliary of the Good Shepherd Church and found time for service with the Junior League. She never remarried, as she didn't think anyone measured up to Harry.

"Elsa was a very special person to me, to all our extended family and to many friends. We could all depend on her—she cared very deeply about people in general but family in particular and was always generous with her time and assets; and though for many years she worked hard as a secretary, in no way was she weighed down with excess cash. However, she was one of those blessed people who knew how to manage her money and was never in debt. She knew how to budget her daily expenses but also knew how to save in order to take a nice trip or plan for a special occasion, but she was always ready to share generously with others and to enjoy a good time. In her later years she was a loving care-giver to many friends and took many needy people under her wing. She was the mainstay of our parents in their later years, perhaps the most unselfish person (along with my dad) I have ever known.

"Truly, Elsa and Mary were 'over-comers' and an inspiration to many. After retiring, Elsa was looking forward to travelling and really having a life of her own, but in her later years she had health problems and that was not to be. However, she never lost her faith and good humor and always rejoiced in the blessings that others experienced."

Elsa was finally reunited with Harry and Mary on May 1, 2003, at the age of 85. She was buried in the Memorial Garden at the Episcopal Retirement Village in Southern Pines, N.C. Dora recalled:

"She could have been buried beside Harry at Arlington Cemetery, but she believed that Arlington should be reserved for the brave men and women who served in the armed services."[41]

Elsa Smedes March
April 5, 1918—May 1, 2003

Appendix 1

Harry March Victory Credits and Citations

Harry March was officially credited with five confirmed Japanese aircraft shot down. This tallies with his Flight Logbook, which also states five victories.[1]

Flight Logbook

August 7, 1942:

Attack on Tulagi and Guadalcanal. One dive bomber (Aichi D3A1 Type 99) shot down, three sorties that day with 7.1 hours flying time.

August 24, 1942:

Battle of the Eastern Solomons or Battle of the Stewart Islands, one Type 97 torpedo bomber (Nakajima B5N2) shot down, one sortie with three hours flying time.

November 8, 1943:

One Ruth (Fiat BR.20 Italian-built, twin-engine bomber) shot down on a fighter sweep over Buka airfield. Two sorties with 6.9 hours flying time.

January 28, 1944:

Two Zeros (Mitsubishi A6M) shot down during a strike on Lakunai Airfield. One sortie with 3.8 hours flying time.

Citations

On December 19, 1943, following his first tour with *Fighting Seventeen*, Harry March was put forward by Tom Blackburn for an award with the following recommendation:

> Between October 27 and December 1, 1943, Lt. March flew 41 sorties, 122 hours of combat flying. He participated in five strafing missions, three of which were in the face of intense anti-aircraft fire. On November 8 he (with Lt. Cdr. Blackburn) hit Buka Airfield just as a Ruth was about to land, destroyed the Ruth, and strafed a parked Zeke and personnel.

Suggested Citation:

> For meritorious achievement while participating in aerial flights against the enemy in the Solomon Islands area. On November 8, 1943, he flew one of two Corsairs which entered the landing circle over Buka Airfield and shot down a Ruth just as it was about to land. On this occasion he also strafed a parked Zeke and troops along the runway. In addition to the above engagement he has participated in numerous patrols, escort missions and strafing missions, meeting heavy concentrations of enemy AA on several occasions. His devotion to duty, his successful audacity, and his skilful marksmanship were in keeping with the highest traditions of the U.S. Naval Service.

On March 14, 1944, Harry March was recommended for the Navy Cross by Tom Blackburn, with the following report:

> Lt. March was a member of VF-6 from June 10, through August 25, 1942, of VF-5 from August 25, through November 22, 1942,

and of VF-24 from December 22, 1942, through September 15, 1943. He flew twenty-five combat sorties off the USS *Enterprise* between July 15 and August 25, 1942, four off the USS *Saratoga* between August 25 and September 2, 1942, and forty-three while based on Guadalcanal between September 10 and October 7, 1942, during which last period his squadron was in almost daily contact with the enemy. On August 7, 1942, while covering our landing on Guadalcanal his flight engaged a large force of enemy bombers attacking our transports. During the ensuing action his flight of six F4Fs shot down six Vals, of which he shot down one. On August 24, 1942, in the Battle of Stewart Island he was one of only five fighter pilots available to defend the USS *Enterprise* against a dive-bombing and torpedo plane attack. The attack was successfully repulsed, and Lt. March destroyed one Kate. On the next day, he was transferred aboard the USS *Saratoga* off which ship he operated until she was torpedoed on August 31, 1942, flying to Efate on September 2. On September 10, he flew to Guadalcanal, operating there under the most hazardous conditions until October 7. While operating with VF-24 off the USS *Belleau Wood* he covered the landing on Baker Island from September 1, through September 10, 1943, and participated in the attack on Tarawa on September 18. On his second tour of duty in the combat zone with VF-17, during which tour the squadron was based at Piva Yoke, Bougainville, from January 25, through March 7, Lt. March, as a flight leader, flew twenty-four combat sorties, of which eighteen were escort missions or fighter sweeps over the Rabaul Area. He encountered enemy aircraft on eight occasions: on January 26, 27, 28 and 31, and on February 5, 10, 17 and 18. On January 28, the TBFs which he was escorting on a strike against Tobera Airfield were vigorously intercepted by fifty or sixty enemy fighters. With utter disregard for the odds against him, Lt. March attacked a group of eight Zekes as they were making their runs on our bombers. By skillful marksmanship he succeeded in shooting down two of the enemy before they could reach the TBFs.

Suggested Citation:

For extraordinary heroism while participating in aerial combat. Lt. March as a member of four squadrons which have operated in the South Pacific under frequently difficult and occasionally hazardous conditions, has seen action intermittently since June 10, 1942, in a series of campaigns ranging from Guadalcanal to New Britain, from aircraft carriers until bases were established and then from the bases themselves. In the early stages of the severe Guadalcanal campaign his flight of six F4Fs attacked a force of enemy bombers which attacked our transports. During this action, he shot down one of the six Vals destroyed. Again, on August 24, 1942, he was one of the five fighters who repulsed a determined enemy attack on the USS *Enterprise* and in this action, he shot down one Jap torpedo plane. Following this, he operated from the USS *Saratoga* and Guadalcanal, where his squadron was in almost daily contact with the enemy. Then, after participating in three more actions while in VF-24, Lt. March began his second tour of combat as a member of VF-17. As a flight leader, during the squadron's second tour of combat, Lt. March flew twenty-four combat sorties, of which eighteen were escort missions or fighter sweeps over the Rabaul Area, and on eight of which he encountered enemy aircraft. On January 28, the bombers he was escorting in a Rabaul strike were intercepted by a swarm of enemy fighters which Lt. March attacked without regard for the odds against him. The attack was so well-timed and executed that the enemy attack was repulsed. During the melee Lt. March shot down two Zekes. His untiring devotion to duty, his heroic conduct in a long series of action which mark the progress of the whole Solomons Campaign, his steady and experienced leadership, and his intelligent airmanship were in keeping with the highest traditions of the U.S. Naval Service.[2]

In the event, Harry March was not awarded the Navy Cross, but instead was posthumously awarded a D.F.C. with the following citation:

For heroism and extraordinary achievement in aerial flight as pilot of a fighter plane in Fighting Squadron Seventeen, in action against enemy

Japanese forces on New Britain, Solomon Islands, on January 28, 1944. Intercepted by a numerically superior force of enemy fighters while flying escort for a bomber strike against hostile installations at Rabaul, Lt. Cdr. (then Lt.) March closed with the enemy aircraft and, pressing home his attacks, succeeded in personally shooting down two of the enemy planes, thereby contributing to the frustration of the concentrated attack. His courage and devotion to duty throughout this hazardous operation were in keeping with the highest traditions of the U.S. Naval Service.

Harry March was also posthumously awarded a Gold Star in lieu of a second Air Medal for destroying two enemy aircraft during the period of June 10, 1942, to January 27, 1944.

Appendix 2

Biographies of "Dirty Eddie's" Guadalcanal Buddies

Ens. William Wolfe Wileman

Bill Wileman was the only son of William H. Wileman and Daisy Wileman and was born on May 4, 1917, in Bardsdale, California. He studied at Fillmore Union High School, Fillmore California and attended the University of California, completing 107 units out of 124 for a Bachelor of Science degree in Agriculture. He majored in plant pathology and worked as a student assistant in plant pathological research for three years while attending university. He completed C.A.A. primary and secondary courses at Oakland, California, and on his application for aviation training in the U.S.N.R. in December 1940, he listed his experience as follows:

"Two years in the Infantry Division of the Army R.O.T.C. taken at the University of California during the years 1936–1938. While studying at the University of California I was employed as a part-time laboratory assistant for 3½ years in the Department of Plant Pathology. This work included the keeping of scientific records, microscopic and chemical work, photography and photomicrography. Other occupational experience includes, oil well crewman, oil refinery worker, and insect control worker, these representing temporary jobs held during vacation periods while attending college. I have no previous military service."

In February 1941, he enlisted in U.S.N.R. as seaman second class, in Oakland California and on his application for aviation training in the U.S.N.R. he was assigned a mark of 3.5 in potential ability as an officer and naval aviator, and it was noted that he was: "above average officer material, splendid and respectful in personality and manner and above-average athletic appearance.".

He was appointed an aviation cadet on April 1, 1941, and commenced flying training at N.A.S. Pensacola and completed his training on November 5, 1941, at Miami, Florida. On September 6, 1941, he accepted his commission as an ensign and was on active duty flying until he reported to Advanced Carrier Training Group, N.A.S. San Diego on January 17, 1942. He was awarded the Navy Cross for his actions in the Battle of the Coral Sea with the following citation:

> For extraordinary heroism and utter disregard for his personal safety as pilot of a fighter plane in Fighting Squadron Two (VF-2), attached to the USS *Lexington*, in action against enemy Japanese forces in the Coral Sea on May 7, and May 8, 1942. With an accurate conception of his objective and dauntless perseverance in attaining it, Ensign Wileman destroyed one enemy fighter and courageously attacked several others. His strict devotion to duty in the performance of a difficult and dangerous task, contributed materially to the defense of our forces and was in keeping with the highest traditions of the United States Naval Service.

Ensign Wileman reported to Fighting Squadron Six (VF-6) on May 28, 1942, and was shot down and killed on September 13, 1942, a few days after arriving at Guadalcanal.

Decorations:

Navy Cross
Purple Heart

Presidential Unit Citation (USS *Enterprise*)
American Defense Service Medal (Fleet Clasp)
World War II Victory Medal.[1]

The USS *Wileman* (DE-22) was named in honor of Ensign Wileman and saw service as a destroyer escort in the Pacific Theater from August 1943 until the end of hostilities. The USS *Wileman* earned four battle stars during World War II and was decommissioned in November 1945.[2]

Ens. Joseph Donald "Dutch" Shoemaker

Joseph Donald Shoemaker was born on August 29, 1920, in Lyons, Kansas, and was the son of Wilbert and Selma Shoemaker. He studied at the Southern Methodist University in Dallas, Texas, and also attended the University of Wichita in Wichita, Kansas from 1939 to 1941. He passed the Civilian Pilot Training Program Secondary Course at the University of Wichita and enlisted in the U.S. Naval Reserve, as seaman second class on March 31, 1941. At the Naval Reserve Flight Selection Board, U.S.N.R.A.B. Kansas City on March 31, 1941, he was given a mark of 3.0 and noted that he was "good officer material, with a pleasant, reserved manner and good, ambitious appearance."

On May 16, 1941, he was appointed an aviation cadet, U.S.N.R. and he reported for active duty undergoing training to N.A.S. Pensacola on May 16, 1941. He accepted his commission as ensign on October 10, 1941, and reported to N.A.S. Miami the same day. On October 31, 1941, he was appointed a naval aviator. Following completion of his training, his final course mark was 3.18 and he stood 38 out of 90 with a total of 193 hours flight time. Shoemaker reported to Fighting Squadron Six on the *Enterprise* on June 15, 1942. He was awarded the Air Medal for his actions on August 7, 1942, with the following citation:

For meritorious achievement in aerial flight as pilot of a fighter plane in Fighting Squadron Six, attached to the USS Entèrprise, in action against the enemy Japanese forces in the Guadalcanal Area on August 7, 1942. Participating in a strike against the enemy, Ensign

Shoemaker skilfully shot down one hostile plane. His airmanship and devotion to duty were in keeping with the highest traditions of the United States Naval Service.

Ensign Shoemaker was shot down and killed on September 29, 1942.

Decorations:

Purple Heart
Air Medal
Presidential Unit Citation with two Stars (USS *Enterprise*, 1st Marine
    Division)
American Defense Service Medal
World War II Victory Medal.[3]

Lt. John Milton Kleinman

John Milton Kleinman was born on October 3, 1919, in Kissimmee, Florida. He attended Osceola High School and while there he worked through the summer months at the Broadway Pharmacy preceding his first year at the University of Florida. During the two years that he attended the University of Florida, he received an Associate of Arts Certificate. He also completed three semesters of Military Science in Field Artillery. He attended a C.A.A. flying school course in Orlando, Florida, which he completed in thirty-five hours of flying time, the average for the course being over ninety. He was a junior when he enlisted in the Navy and he became an aviation cadet at N.A.S. Pensacola and was then ordered to N.A.S. Miami. He was designated a naval aviator on November 6, 1941, and commissioned as an ensign on October 8, 1941. He reported on January 2, 1942, to the Advanced Carrier Training Group and on February 26, 1942, to Fighting Squadron Five. Ens. John Kleinman was recommended for the Navy Cross for his actions on August 24, 1942, in the Solomon Islands area with the following citation:

For extraordinary heroism and distinguished service in the line of his profession as a pilot in the sixth division, Fighting Squadron Five

(USS *Saratoga*), during the air attack by the Japanese on the USS *Enterprise* on August 24, 1942, in the Solomon Islands Area. Ensign Kleinman, flying as wingman on Lt. Hayden M. Jensen, leading the Sixth Division intercepted the second enemy division of nine dive bombers as they entered their dives upon the *Enterprise*, following them down and personally destroying two of them before they could release their bombs, thereby saving the *Enterprise* from possible bomb hits and contributing greatly toward demoralizing the entire enemy attack. His unyielding devotion to duty, maintained with complete disregard for his personal safety, was in keeping with the highest traditions of the United States Naval Service.

He was awarded the Distinguished Flying Cross, instead of the Navy Cross, and Presidential Unit Citation for VF-5 attached to the 1st Marine Division (August 7, 1942 to December 9, 1942). He was promoted to lieutenant junior grade on October 1, 1942, and reported to *Fighting Seventeen* on January 1, 1943, at N.A.S. Norfolk. John Kleinman married Frances Greene Gainey on August 14, 1943, in Norfolk, Virginia, and on October 1, 1943, he was promoted to lieutenant. He was one of the few experienced combat veterans that *Fighting Seventeen* relied on when they first saw action in the Solomon Islands. On November 11, 1943, he played his part in the success of *Fighting Seventeen*'s mission as cover for the carriers, when he shot down a Japanese Kate torpedo bomber. He made a run on another Kate, but was hit by a 40 mm shell from one of his own ships. The shell exploded, blew up his instrument panel, and wounded him in the face. As he turned to get away, he was jumped by two U.S. Navy Hellcats, who scored hits on his wing. Injured and with no instruments, Kleinman navigated by the sun back to base. He was awarded the Purple Heart for this mission and credited for one Kate shot down and one Kate damaged.

In letters Kleinman wrote home, he couldn't give out any details of where he was or what he was doing, so he would say things like "We went hunting yesterday and I shot two turkeys." Kleinman had served the squadron with distinction and was ready to go home. He was detached from *Fighting Seventeen*

on December 17, 1943, and reported on December 27, 1943, to Fleet Air
Coast, Jacksonville, and then N.A.A.S. Melbourne reporting on January 30,
1944. Johnny Kleinman was killed in a crash after take-off for a gunnery
flight on February 18, 1944.

Decorations:

Distinguished Flying Cross
Purple Heart
Presidential Unit Citation (1st Marine Division)
Navy Unit Commendation
American Defense Service Medal
Asiatic-Pacific Area Campaign Medal
World War II Victory Medal.[4]

Lt. Donald Allan "Stinky" Innis

Donald Allan Innis was born on November 14, 1915, in Nevada, Missouri.
He entered Nevada High School in September 1929 and graduated from there
on May 17, 1933. He was then educated at the University of Missouri starting
there in September 1934 and worked his way through college as a waiter at
the Daniel Boone Tavern, Columbia, and during the summer months worked
for three seasons for the Radio Springs Park, Nevada, Missouri, as a life
guard. He also worked two summers on construction jobs; one for the Pan
Handle Eastern Pipeline Co., of Kansas City, Missouri, and the other for a
company in North Carolina. Upon leaving the University of Missouri, he was
employed for two and a half years as a Credit Correspondent by the Liquid
Carbonic Corporation of Chicago, Ill. Other than the basic R.O.T.C. training
that he received at the University of Missouri, he had no previous military or
Navy training. Innis joined the Naval Reserve, enlisting on October 29, 1940,
and on February 1, 1941, his enlisted service was terminated to accept his
appointment as an aviation cadet. He reported to N.A.S. Pensacola and then
N.A.S. Miami for training and was commissioned as an ensign on July 16,
1941. He was designated a naval aviator on September 8, 1941 and reported

to Advanced Carrier Training Group, N.A.S. Norfolk, Virginia, on October 24, 1941. He was ordered on January 3, 1942, to Fighting Squadron Five and on May 20, 1942, along with VF-5, was ordered to Commander Aircraft South Pacific and reported on September 2, 1942. He was wounded in action on September 13, 1942, following air combat against Japanese aircraft at Guadalcanal. He was hit by gunfire and his aircraft burst into flames, resulting in burns. The medical report stated: "He had first- and second-degree burns of the face, neck, right ear, right arm and forearm, left wrist and both legs." Ensign Innis was admitted to U.S. Naval Base Hospital, Number Two, ROSES on September 14, 1942. On September 29, 1942, he was transferred to hospital from the USS *Solace* (AH-5) for an indefinite duration of stay in hospital.

He was promoted to lieutenant junior grade on October 1, 1942 and was detached from VF-5 on December 24, 1942. He reported to U.S. Navy Camden, New Jersey, for duty in connection of fitting out a vessel on January 1, 1943, and then reported to VF-24 on March 31, 1943. He was promoted to lieutenant on October 1, 1943, and detached from VF-24 and assigned to VF-17 on October 13, 1943. He served two tours with *Fighting Seventeen* and after being injured in an accident, was given the role as Squadron Duty Officer.

Once VF-17 had returned home and Innis had received a well-earned leave he reported to N.A.S. San Diego. His duties involved flying in the Aircraft Ordnance Development Unit at Inyokern, California. On June 20, 1944, "Stinky" was killed in a crash over the Salton Sea in Southern California.

Decorations:

Purple Heart

Presidential Unit Citation with two stars (1st Marine Division, USS *Belleau Wood*)

American Defense Service Medal

Asiatic–Pacific Campaign Medal

World War II Victory Medal.[5]

Lt. Cdr. James Alexander Halford, Jr.

James Alexander Halford was born in Taurusa, California, on February 7, 1919, and was educated at Orosi Grammar and Orosi High School, both in the Central Valley of California. He attended the College of the Sequoias (then Junior College, Visalia) California, and Fresno State University, Fresno, California. Halford completed private pilot courses from the Department of Commerce and applied for aviation training on November 20, 1940, where it was noted that he had a "quiet, determined personality, good, and ambitious appearance."

On January 14, 1941, he entered the U.S. Naval Reserve in Oakland, California, and had preliminary flight training at the Naval Reserve Aviation Base there. He was appointed an aviation cadet on April 11, 1941, and had flight training at the Naval Air Station, Corpus Christi, Texas. He was commissioned ensign, U.S.N.R., on September 6, 1941, and was ordered to active duty in a Fighting Squadron attached to a carrier. From May to June 1942, Ensign Halford was with VF-3 as a wingman then was assigned to VF-6 during the Battle of Midway, where he was awarded the Distinguished Flying Cross with the citation:

> For heroic achievement in aerial flight as a pilot of a Fighting Squadron in action against enemy Japanese forces in the Battle of Midway, June 4–6, 1942. While engaged in combat patrol, Ensign Halford, at great personal risk, made a determined attack against enemy aircraft approaching the USS *Yorktown* and assisted in the destruction of at least one enemy airplane. On June 6, 1942, he delivered an effective strafing attack against two enemy Japanese heavy cruisers and two destroyers, inflicting heavy damage on those enemy vessels. His skill as an airman, his courageous perseverance and devotion to duty were in keeping with the highest traditions of the United States Naval Service.

Following the Battle of Midway, Jim Halford served with VF-6 as a section leader and was then assigned to VF-5 as a division leader for the invasion of Guadalcanal as part of the first naval air group to be stationed there. One of the actions on August 24, 1942, was reported in a press release at the time:

> There was a lone Aichi dive bomber getting close to the task force when Lt. L. H. Bauer, VF-6's Squadron Commander, spotted it and shot it down. He soon found himself tangled with a Zero and scored a hit. The Zero dove for the water in evasive action and Ens. J. A. Halford, Jr., came down and finished it off.

Halford was awarded the Distinguished Flying Cross for his actions at Guadalcanal, which was personally presented to him by Adm. Chester Nimitz, with the Citation:

> For heroism and extraordinary achievement while participating in aerial combat against the enemy. As a member of a naval air squadron based at Guadalcanal, Solomon Islands, Ensign Halford, with complete and utter disregard for personal safety, attacked enemy planes in actions occurring in this area. On September 14, 1942, Ensign Halford shot down one enemy fighter and on September 28, 1942, he shot down one enemy bomber. His great courage, fortitude and skill were in keeping with the highest traditions of the Naval Service.

During the Battle of Guadalcanal, Halford was promoted to lieutenant junior grade and he finished his heroic service with 3.5 confirmed victories and was sent home for a deserved rest. He was then assigned to *Fighting Seventeen* as a flight leader and one of the few experienced combat pilots in the squadron. He was promoted to lieutenant on October 1, 1943, just prior to going into combat with VF-17. Following his sterling service with *Fighting Seventeen*, he was assigned as a flight instructor at N.A.S. Melbourne, Florida, and then ground training officer at the same base. His last assignment before the war ended was at Maui, Hawaii, where he was later promoted to lieutenant commander on October 3, 1945. After his war service, he returned to the family farm in California. He continued in the Navy Reserves and retired on November 1, 1959. He died on June 7, 1987.

Decorations:

Distinguished Flying Cross plus one Star

Air Medal

Presidential Unit Citation with two Stars (USS *Enterprise*, 1st Marine
    Division)

Navy Unit Commendation

American Defense Service Medal

American Campaign Medal

Asiatic–Pacific Area Campaign Medal with five stars

World War II Victory Medal

Philippine Independence Ribbon.[6]

Endnotes

Frequently cited archives and collections have been noted by the following abbreviations:

HMFL   Harry Andrew March, Jr., flight logbooks—April 22, 1941 to February 18, 1946.

HMPD   Personal diary of Harry Andrew March, Jr.—July 13, 1942 to November 17, 1942, and September 4, 1943 to March 30, 1944.

NARA   National Archives and Records Administration.

NHHC   Naval History and Heritage Command.

NHC/OAB Department of the Navy, Naval Historical Center, Operational Archives Branch, Washington Navy Yard, Washington, D.C.

NPRC   National Personnel Records Center, Military Personnel Records.

OMPF   Official Military Personnel File.

USSE   USS Enterprise CV-6 Association.

VFWD   VF-17 War Diary—September 28, 1943 to March 31, 1944.

The Official Military Personnel Files were obtained from the National Personnel Records Center, Military Personnel Records, 9700 Page Avenue, St. Louis, Missouri 63132-5100, U.S.A.

Notes for Foreword

1. I received the foreword for the book on March 15, 2011.

Notes for Introduction

1. Two books covering these events are the Pulitzer Prize-winning masterpiece by John Toland, *The Rising Sun: The Decline and Fall of the Japanese Empire* (Random House Inc., 1970) and the excellent Samuel Eliot Morison, *History of United States Naval Operations in World War II: The Rising Sun in the Pacific, 1931–April 1942 Volume III* (Little, Brown and Company, 1948).

2. www.loc.gov/law/help/us-treaties/bevans/m-ust000002-0351.pdf.

3. www.loc.gov/law/find/hearings/pdf/00032588311.pdf.

4. Toland, *The Rising Sun*; Morison, *History of United States Naval Operations in World War II, Volume III*.

5. Toland, *The Rising Sun*; Morison, *History of United States Naval Operations in World War II, Volume III*.

6. Toland, *The Rising Sun*; Morison, *History of United States Naval Operations in World War II, Volume III*.

7. For the classic work on Pearl Harbor, see Gordon W. Prange, *At Dawn We Slept—The Untold Story of Pearl Harbor* (McGraw-Hill Book Company, 1981; reprint Penguin Books, 1983); Also see Toland, *The Rising Sun*; Morison, *History of United States Naval Operations in World War II, Volume III*;.

8. 'Land of Liberty' was a 1939 American documentary film telling the history of the United States from pre-Revolution through 1939—see www.IMDb.com

9. Toland, *The Rising Sun*; Morison, *History of United States Naval Operations in World War II, Volume III*; Prange, *At Dawn We Slept*.

10. For a highly regarded work on the land battles in the Pacific see Eric Bergerud, *Touched with Fire—The Land War in the South Pacific* (Viking Penguin, 1996; reprint Penguin Books, 1997).

11. For the definitive history of the Battle of Midway, see Jonathan Parshall and Anthony Tully, *Shattered Sword: The Untold Story of the Battle of Midway* (Potomac Books, 2005).

12. Parshall & Tully, *Shattered Sword*, p. 421.

13. Parshall & Tully, *Shattered Sword*.

14. www.history.navy.mil/content/history/nhhc/research/library/online-reading-room/title-list-alphabetically/n/navy-depart-communiques-1-300-pertinent-press-releases.html.

15. For two outstanding accounts of the struggle at Guadalcanal see Samuel Eliot Morison, *History of United States Naval Operations in World War II: Struggle for Guadalcanal August 1942–February 1943, Volume V* (Little, Brown and Company, 1949) and John B. Lundstrom, *First Team and the Guadalcanal Campaign: Naval Fighter Combat from August to November 1942* (Naval Institute Press, 1994; reprint 2005).

16. An excellent account of the Bougainville and Rabaul operations is Samuel Eliot Morison, *History of United States Naval Operations in World War II: Breaking the Bismarck's Barrier, 22 July 1942–1 May 1944, Volume VI* (Little, Brown and Company, 1950; reprint 1994).

17. NARA/NPRC/OMPF—Harry Andrew March, Jr.; www.sports-reference.com/olympics/athletes/co/roy-cochran-1.html; www.msfame.com/roy-cochran-a-mississippi-olympic-story.

18. Telephone conversation Dora Taylor, April 18, 2009.
19. NARA/NPRC/OMPF—Harry Andrew March, Jr.

Notes for Prologue

1. Dr. Rhett Youmans Winters researched and wrote out by hand the ancestral heritage of five of the families that made up his family tree in America, 1957; Emails from Dora Taylor dated Apr 24, 2014.
2. The *Daily Tar Heel Sports*, May 24, 1939.
3. Emails from Dora Taylor dated March 31, 2012, April 24, 2012, April 22, 2014, October 13, 2014, October 18, 2014, & November 29, 2014.
4. NARA/NPRC/OMPF—Harry Andrew March, Jr.
5. The *Daily Tar Heel Sports*, October 23, 1936.
6. Telephone conversation Dora Taylor, April 18, 2009.
7. For a fascinating account of Bill Tilden, see Frank Deford, *Big Bill Tilden: The Triumphs and the Tragedy* (Simon & Schuster, 1976).
8. Email from Dora Taylor dated February 26, 2011.
9. Extract from the *Daily Tar Heel Sports*, May 22, 1937.
10. University of North Carolina at Chapel Hill Yearbook,1940.
11. Extract from the *Daily Tar Heel Sports*, February 3, 1939.
12. Extract from the *Daily Tar Heel Sports*, Chapel Hill, NC, October 11, 1940.
13. University of North Carolina at Chapel Hill Year book, 1940.
14. Extracts from the *Daily Tar Heel Sports*, May 13, 1939.
15. www.ustfccca.org/2020/02/featured/meet-recap-2020-nyrr-millrose-games.
16. Extracts from the *Daily Tar Heel Sports*, February 6, 1940 and December 10, 1940.
17. NARA/NPRC/OMPF—Harry Andrew March, Jr.
18. Newspaper Cutting from Elsa March's Scrapbook provided by Dora Taylor email April 10, 2012.
19. www.trackandfieldnews.com.
20. Extracts from the *Daily Tar Heel Sports*, September 25, 1940.
21. *Spalding's Official Athletic Almanac 1940* (American Sports Publishing Co., 1940) via Tony Staley (A.A.U.) email, Feb 24, 2010.
22. NARA/NPRC/OMPF—Harry Andrew March, Jr.
23. Telephone conversation Dora Taylor, April 18, 2009.
24. NARA/NPRC/OMPF—Harry Andrew March, Jr.

25. NARA/NPRC/OMPF—Harry Andrew March, Jr.
26. Correspondence with William "Country" Landreth, November 24, 1993.
27. www.trackandfieldnews.com.
28. *Shreveport Times*, January 14, 1947.
29. NARA/NPRC/OMPF—Harry Andrew March, Jr.
30. Email from Steve and Mary-Anne McAfee, June 11, 2020.
31. Recorded interview with Wilbert Peter Popp, May 9, 1995.
32. Email from Dora Taylor dated April 24, 2014 & October 18, 2014, including extracts from Dr Rhett Youmans Winters' family history.
33. NARA/NPRC/OMPF—Harry Andrew March, Jr. and HMFL.
34. Recorded interview with Wilbert Peter Popp, May 9, 1995.

Notes for Chapter 1

1. www.loc.gov/resource/afc1986022.afc1986022_ms2201/?st=text&r= 0.014,-0.238,1,1.052,0.
2. HMFL.
3. www.navsource.org/archives/02/06.htm.
4. www.history.navy.mil/research/histories/ship-histories/danfs/e/ enterprise-cv-6-vii.html.
5. NARA/NPRC/OMPF—Harry Andrew March, Jr., and Joseph Donald Shoemaker.
6. USSE; NHHC; www.history.navy.mil/research/histories/ship-histories/ danfs/e/enterprise-cv-6-vii.html; www.navsource.org/archives/02/06. htm.
7. Eric Bergerud, *Touched with Fire—The Land War in the South Pacific* (Viking Penguin, 1996; reprint Penguin Books, 1997).
8. USSE.
9. A fascinating book on the Pacific Air War, covering both sides, is Eric Bergerud, *Fire in the Sky—The Air War in the South Pacific* (Westview Press, 2000; reprint Basic Books, 2009).
10. www.pearlharboraviationmuseum.org/exhibits/grumman-f4f-3- wildcat-fighter.

Notes for Chapter 2

1. www.history.navy.mil/content/history/nhhc/research/library/online- reading-room/title-list-alphabetically/n/navy-depart-communiques-1- 300-pertinent-press-releases.html.

2. Samuel Eliot Morison, *History of United States Naval Operations in World War II: Struggle for Guadalcanal August 1942-February 1943, Volume V* (Little, Brown and Company, 1949); John B. Lundstrom, *First Team and the Guadalcanal Campaign: Naval Fighter Combat from August to November 1942* (Naval Institute Press, 1994; reprint 2005); Eric Bergerud, *Touched with Fire—The Land War in the South Pacific* (Viking Penguin, 1996; reprint Penguin Books, 1997).
3. www.cv6.org/ship/logs/action19420807.htm#action0807.
4. USSE.
5. USSE.
6. Courtesy of Watertown Historical Society by email December 11, 2014.
7. USSE; Morison, *History of United States Naval Operations in World War II*, *Volume V* and Lundstrom, *First Team and the Guadalcanal Campaign*.
8. Morison, *History of United States Naval Operations in World War II*, *Volume V*.
9. Bergerud, *Touched with Fire*, 175.
10. USSE; Morison, *History of United States Naval Operations in World War II*, *Volume V*; Lundstrom, *First Team and the Guadalcanal Campaign*.
11. NARA/NPRC/OMPF—Harry Andrew March, Jr.
12. NARA/NPRC/OMPF—Harry Andrew March, Jr.
13. NARA/NPRC/OMPF—Harry Andrew March, Jr.

Notes for Chapter 3

1. USSE.
2. NHHC; www.history.navy.mil/research/histories/ship-histories/danfs/s/saratoga-v.html; www.navsource.org/archives/02/03.htm.
3. NARA/NPRC/OMPF—William Wolfe Wileman.
4. NARA/NPRC/OMPF—James Alexander Halford, Jr.
5. Eric Bergerud, *Touched with Fire—The Land War in the South Pacific* (Viking Penguin, 1996; reprint Penguin Books, 1997).

Notes for Chapter 4

1. NHHC; www.johnkellynightfighterpilot.wordpress.com/2017/09/10/captain-leroy-coard-simpler-1905-1988.
2. *"Ramblin" Wreck from Geo Tech'* is Georgia University's official fight song, www.traditions.gatech.edu/gtsongs.html.

3. Eric Bergerud, *Touched with Fire—The Land War in the South Pacific* (Viking Penguin, 1996; reprint Penguin Books, 1997).
4. NARA/NPRC/OMPF—William Wolfe Wileman.
5. Correspondence with Lennard "Red" Edmisten February 8, 1994.
6. Wilbert P. Popp. "Beads." *The Survival of a WWII Navy Fighter Pilot* (Privately published, 2003), 33.
7. *Star Bulletin* newspaper cutting, March 23, 1944, provided by Del and Pat May by email March 9, 2009.
8. NARA; www.army.mil/medalofhonor/keeble/medal/citations21.htm-Robert E Galer; www.cmohs.org-RobertEGaler; www.themedalofhonor. com-Robert Galer.
9. The *Seattle Times* Obituary, August 16–17, 2007.
10. NARA/NPRC/OMPF—Joseph Donald Shoemaker.

Notes for Chapter 5

1. Samuel Eliot Morison, *History of United States Naval Operations in World War II: Struggle for Guadalcanal August 1942-February 1943, Volume V* (Little, Brown and Company, 1949) and John B. Lundstrom, *First Team and the Guadalcanal Campaign: Naval Fighter Combat from August to November 1942* (Naval Institute Press, 1994; reprint 2005).
2. www.britannica.com/event/Bataan-Death-March/The-march-and-imprisonment-at-Camp-ODonnell.
3. NARA/NPRC/OMPF—Harry Andrew March, Jr.
4. Correspondence with Roger Hedrick and Alida Christinaz, 1994 to 2020.
5. www.homeofheroes.com/distinguished-service-cross/service-cross-world-war-ii/navy-cross-world-war-ii/navy-cross-world-war-ii-marine-corps/navy-cross-world-war-ii-marine-corps-c-d/.

Notes for Chapter 6

1. Eric Bergerud, *Touched with Fire—The Land War in the South Pacific* (Viking Penguin, 1996; reprint Penguin Books, 1997).
2. Samuel Eliot Morison, *History of United States Naval Operations in World War II: Struggle for Guadalcanal August 1942–February 1943, Volume V* (Little, Brown and Company, 1949).
3. Bergerud, *Touched with Fire*, 391.
4. Interview with George Mauhar St Louis, April 20, 1996.

5. NHHC; USSE; see www.history.navy.mil/research/histories/ship-histories/danfs/e/enterprise-cv-6-vii.html; www.navsource.org/archives/02/06.htm.
6. www.cv6.org/1942/1942.htm.
7. www.IMDb.com/Frances Dee.
8. Morison, *History of United States Naval Operations in World War II, Volume V*.

Notes for Chapter 7

1. HMFL.
2. Email from Dora Taylor dated May 12, 2011.
3. NARA/NPRC/OMP—Harry Andrew March, Jr.
4. NARA/NPRC/OMP—Harry Andrew March, Jr.
5. NHHC; www.history.navy.mil/research/histories/ship-histories/danfs/b/belleau-wood-cv-24-i.html; www.navsource.org/archives/02/24.htm.
6. NHHC; www.history.navy.mil/research/histories/ship-histories/danfs/b/belleau-wood-cv-24-i.html; www.navsource.org/archives/02/24.htm.
7. For an accomplished account of *Fighting Seventeen*, see Tom Blackburn, *The Jolly Rogers* (Orion, 1989); For a superb story of the F4U's development into an excellent carrier aircraft, see Boone T. Guyton. *Whistling Death: The Test Pilot's Story of the F4U Corsair* (Schiffer, 1994); For the remarkable story of an aircraft that became a legend see Barrett Tillman *Corsair—The F4U in World War II and Korea* (Naval Institute Press, 1979; UK edition: Patrick Stephens Limited, 1979).
8. Transcript of radio interview WINS Program with Bob Dryfoos, February 10, 1943 via Dora Taylor email February 22, 2009.

Notes for Chapter 8

1. NHHC; www.history.navy.mil/research/histories/ship-histories/danfs/b/belleau-wood-cv-24-i.html; www.navsource.org/archives/02/24.htm.
2. Boone T. Guyton, *Whistling Death: The Test Pilot's Story of the F4U Corsair* (Schiffer, 1994); Harold J. Bitzegaio interview on DVD *VF-17 Remembered*, RDR Video Productions. Northbrook, Illinois (1984).
3. NARA/NPRC/OMPF—Harry Andrew March, Jr.
4. HMFL.
5. NARA/NPRC/OMPF—Harry Andrew March, Jr.
6. HMFL.
7. HMFL.

Notes for Chapter 9

1. Correspondence with Department of the Navy, Naval Historical Center, Washington Navy Yard, March 5, 1998; www.history.navy.mil/research/histories/ship-histories/danfs/b/bunker-hill-i.html and www.navsource.org/archives/02/17.htm.
2. NHHC; www.history.navy.mil/research/histories/ship-histories/danfs/b/bunker-hill-i.html; www.navsource.org/archives/02/17.htm; Correspondence with Department of the Navy, Naval Historical Center, Washington Navy Yard, March 5, 1998.
3. www.vought.org/products/html/f4u.html.
4. www.history.navy.mil/content/history/nhhc/research/histories/naval-aviation-history/naval-aircraft/aircraft-in-the-korean-conflict/f4u-corsair.html.
5. Danny Cunningham interview on DVD *VF-17 Remembered*; Danny Cunningham interview on DVD *Fighting 17, The Jolly Rogers* (Kenwood Productions, Minneapolis, 1990); Interview with Danny Cunningham, St. Louis, April 20, 1996.
6. NHHC; www.history.navy.mil/research/histories/ship-histories/danfs/b/bunker-hill-i.html; www.navsource.org/archives/02/17.htm; Correspondence with Department of the Navy, Naval Historical Center, Washington Navy Yard, March 5, 1998.
7. Interview with Danny Cunningham, St. Louis, April 20, 1996; Interview with Roger Hedrick on DVD *Fighting 17*; Correspondence with Roger Hedrick and Alida Christinaz 1994 to 2020.
8. Ray DeLeva on DVD *VF-17 Remembered*.
9. VFWD.
10. DVD *Fighting 17*.
11. VFWD.

Notes for Chapter 10

1. Morison, *Vol VI*.
2. Lee Cook, *The Skull and Crossbones Squadron—VF-17 in World War II*, (Schiffer Publishing Ltd. 1998).
3. Morrison, *Vol VI*.
4. Morison, *Vol VI*.
5. Popp, 33.
6. HMFL.
7. Roger Hedrick on DVD *VF-17 Remembered*.

8. DVD *Fighting 17*.
9. VFWD & NARA/NPRC/OMP—John Henry Keith.

Notes for Chapter 11

1. Morison, *Vol VI*.
2. VFWD.
3. VFWD.
4. VFWD.
5. Morison, *Vol VI*.
6. VFWD.
7. VFWD.
8. HMFL; VFWD; NARA/NPRC/OMPF—Harry Andrew March, Jr.
9. Gurney & Friedlander, p. 110; U.S.N. Fighter Squadron notes, Victory Credits in World War 2 (Units) VF-17, and Comments on U.S.N. Aces, (Frank J. Olynyk) received from Department of the Navy, Naval Historical Center, Operational Archives Branch, August 19 1994; HMFL; Fighting Squadron Seventeen Combat Statistics dated February 23, 1944, received from Department of the Navy, Naval Historical Center, Operational Archives Branch, August 19 1994.
10. VFWD; DVD *Fighting 17*.
11. Blackburn, 135.
12. Correspondence with William "Country" Landreth, November 24, 1993.
13. Ray DeLeva on DVD *VF-17 Remembered*.
14. VFWD.
15. VFWD.
16. VFWD.
17. Interview with Walter Schub, St. Louis, April 20, 1996.
18. VFWD.
19. Henry Sakaida, *The Siege of Rabaul*, (Phalanx Publishing Co., Ltd. 1996), 11–12.
20. Merl "Butch" Davenport on DVD *VF-17 Remembered*.

Notes for Chapter 12

1. Lyle Herrmann on DVD *VF-17 Remembered*.
2. VFWD.
3. NARA/NPRC/OMPF—Charles Alfred Pillsbury; Correspondence from George Pillsbury November 4, 2008.
4. VFWD; DVD *Fighting 17*.

Notes for Chapter 13

1. NARA/NPRC/OMPF—Harry Andrew March, Jr.

Notes for Chapter 14

1. Morison, *Vol VI*.
2. VFWD.
3. Popp, 33.
4. Popp, 34.
5. Correspondence with Milly DeLeva, February 27 1995—July 27 1995.
6. VFWD.
7. Blackburn, 181–86.
8. www.IMDb.com/Claudia1943.

Notes for Chapter 15

1. Morison, *Volume VI*.
2. Blackburn and Hedrick interviews on DVD *Fighting 17*.
3. VFWD.
4. VFWD.
5. VFWD.
6. VFWD; Interview with Danny Cunningham, St Louis, April 20, 1996.
7. Blackburn, 201.
8. VFWD.
9. NARA/NPRC/OMP—Harry Andrew March, Jr.
10. VFWD; NARA/NPRC/OMPF—Howard McClain Burriss; Correspondence with Kraeg Kepford, 1993–2019.
11. NARA/NPRC/OMPF—Douglas Hugo Charles Gutenkunst.
12. NARA/NPRC/OMPF—Thomas Frederick Kropf.
13. Recorded interview with Wilbert Peter Popp, May 9, 1995.
14. Emails from Kelly Burriss, February 9, 2009 to April 28, 2010.
15. NARA/NPRC/OMPF—Howard McClain Burriss; Emails from Christine Silengo, September 4, 2009 to September 29, 2011.
16. www.IMDb.com/airforce1943.
17. NARA/NPRC/OMPF—Percy Eugene Divenney.
18. NARA/NPRC/OMPF—Donald Thomas Malone.
19. Interview with George Mauhar, VF-17 reunion, St Louis, April 20, 1996.
20. VFWD.
21. NARA/NPRC/OMPF—Jack Evans Diteman, Richard Martin Einar, Jr., and Harvey Matthews; Emails with Joanie Diteman, March 7, 2009

to April 21, 2020; Emails from Rick Einar, March 2, 2009 to May 6, 2011; Emails from Paul Matthews, September 14, 2009 to December 22, 2014.

22. NARA/NPRC/OMPF—James Miller; Emails from Roger Mansell, December 20, 2007 to June 19, 2009; For two harrowing accounts of prisoners of war at Rabaul, see John B. Kepchia, *Missing in Action over Rabaul*, (The Palace Printer, 1986). Joseph G. Nason, *Horio, You Next Die!* (Pacific Rim Press, Inc., 1987).

23. NARA/NPRC/OMPF—Clyde Howard Dunn.

24. Recorded interview with Wilbert Peter Popp, May 9, 1995.

25. VFWD.

26. Correspondence with Kraeg Kepford, 1993–2019.

27. VFWD; Correspondence with Kraeg Kepford, 1993–2019.

Notes for Chapter 16

1. Morison, *Volume VI*, 403.

2. Morison, *Vol VI*.

3. VFWD.

4. VFWD.

5. VFWD.

6. VFWD.

7. Blackburn, 255.

8. VFWD.

9. Bergerud, *Touched with Fire*.

10. VFWD.

11. Morison, *Vol VI*; Bergerud, *Touched with Fire*.

Notes for Chapter 17

1. Correspondence with Kraeg Kepford, 1993–2019.

2. VFWD.

3. VFWD; Chance Vought Aircraft letter of congratulations, June 13, 1944, via emails from Rick Einar, March 2, 2009—April 23, 2009.

4. www.vought.org/products/html/f4u.html.

5. U.S.N. Fighter Squadron notes, Victory Credits in World War 2 (Units) VF-17, and Comments on U.S.N. Aces, (Frank J. Olynyk) received from Department of the Navy, Naval Historical Center, Operational Archives Branch, August 19, 1994; Cook, *The Skull and Crossbones*; Lee Cook, *Fighting Seventeen A Photographic History of VF-17 in*

World War II, (Schiffer Publishing Ltd, 2011); Lee Cook, *The Aces of Fighting Seventeen*, (Schiffer Publishing Ltd, 2011).

6. VFWD; USS Bunker Hill magazine '*The Monument*', April 22, 1944; Correspondence with Department of the Navy, Naval Historical Center, Washington Navy Yard, March 5, 1998.

7. VFWD.

8. NARA/NPRC/OMPF—Donald Allan Innis.

Notes for Chapter 18

1. For a highly acclaimed one-volume account of WWII in the Pacific, see John Costello, *The Pacific War, 1941–1945*, (HarperCollins, 1981; reprint Harper Perennial, 2009).

2. NARA/NPRC/OMPF—Harry Andrew March, Jr.

3. Chance Vought Aircraft letter of congratulations, June 13, 1944, via emails from Rick Einar, March 2, 2009–April 23, 2009.

4. NARA/NPRC/OMPF—Harry Andrew March, Jr.

5. www.museumoffloridahistory.com/exhibits/permanent-exhibits/world-war-ii/florida-remembers-world-war-ii/military-training-in-florida-aviation/.

6. "Hap" Bowers Letters via Alexandra Bowers, September 17, 2009.

7. NARA/NPRC/OMPF—Harry Andrew March, Jr.

8. Costello.

9. www.trackandfieldnews.com; trackfield.brinkster.net.

10. www.trackandfieldnews.com.

11. Email from Dora Taylor dated October 29, 2008.

12. Costello; Correspondence with "Country" Landreth and Linda Landreth-Phelps, 1993 to 2020.

13. www.history.navy.mil/research/histories/ship-histories/danfs/m/midway-iii.html; www.navsource.org/archives/02/41.htm; www.midway.org/.

14. www.history.navy.mil/research/histories/ship-histories/danfs/m/midway-iii.html; www.navsource.org/archives/02/41.htm; www.midway.org/.

15. www.midway.org/about-us/midway-history; www.history.navy.mil/research/histories/ship-histories/danfs/m/midway-iii.html.

16. NARA/NPRC/OMPF—Harry Andrew March, Jr.

17. NARA/NPRC/OMPF—Harry Andrew March, Jr.

18. NARA/NPRC/OMPF—Harry Andrew March, Jr.

Notes for Epilogue

1. Email from Dora Taylor dated October 29, 2008.
2. Extracts from *the Daily Tar Heel*, February 12, 19, & 23, 1946.
3. NARA/NPRC/OMPF—Harry Andrew March, Jr.; Dr Rhett Youmans Winters family history, 1957 provided by Dora Taylor by email April 24, 2014.
4. NARA/NPRC/OMPF—Harry Andrew March, Jr.
5. Extracts from *the Daily Tar Heel*, March 3, 1946.
6. NARA/NPRC/OMPF—Harry Andrew March, Jr.
7. NARA/NPRC/OMPF—Harry Andrew March, Jr.
8. www.uclabruins.com/news/2015/10/15/210446587.aspx.
9. www.sports-reference.com/olympics/athletes/co/roy-cochran-1.html; www.msfame.com/roy-cochran-a-mississippi-olympic-story.
10. www.njsportsheroes.com/johnboricantf.html; www.spectatorarchive. library.columbia.edu/cgi-bin/columbia; www.books.google.co.uk/books/ JohnBorican; www.ciaa.com/hof.aspx?hof=25.
11. Courtesy of Watertown Historical Society by email December 11, 2014.
12. San Diego Union Tribune May 11, 2008.
13. www.homeofheroes.com/distinguished-service-cross/service-cross-world-war-ii/navy-cross-world-war-ii/navy-cross-world-war-ii-navy/ navy-cross-world-war-ii-navy-b; Gene Gurney and Mark P. Friedlander, Jr., *Five Down and Glory—A History of the American Air Ace*, (Putnam, 1958), 106; https://www.findagrave.com/memorial/56116296.
14. www.airandspace.si.edu/support/wall-of-honor/capt-howard-w-crews-usn-ret; www.findagrave.com-Crews.
15. www.findagrave.com-Currie.
16. www.findagrave.com-Dibb.
17. NARA; www.obits.dallasnews.com/obituaries/dallasmorningnews/ obituary; www.army.mil/medalofhonor/keeble/medal/citations21.htm-Robert E Galer; www.cmohs.org-RobertEGaler; www.themedalofhonor. com-Robert Galer.
18. www.findagrave.com-Hartmann.
19. www.findagrave.com-Loesch; Seattle Times Obituary, August 16–17, 2007.
20. Navy.togetherweserved.com.
21. NHHC—Melvin C. Roach.
22. www.findagrave.com-Runyon.

23. www.johnkellynightfighterpilot.wordpress.com/2017/09/10/captain-leroy-coard-simpler-1905–1988; www.findagrave.com-Leroy Coard-Simpler.

24. www.homeofheroes.com/distinguished-service-cross/service-cross-world-war-ii/navy-cross-world-war-ii/navy-cross-world-war-ii-navy/navy-cross-world-war-ii-navy-v-to-z; www.history.navy.mil/research/library/research-guides/modern-biographical-files-ndl/modern-bios-v/vorse-albert-ogden-jr.; www.cv14.com/scoop_vorse.html.

25. *The Star-News Feb 22, 1992, Chula Vista, California.*

26. Correspondence with Joy Anderson Schroeder, December 27, 1995 to 2018.

27. NHC/OAB/NPRC; Emails from Blackburn family, 2008 to 2020.

28. NARA/NPRC/OMPF—Lemuel Doty Cooke.

29. NHC/OAB/NPRC; Emails from Toni Sennott, 2008 to 2020.

30. Correspondence with Roger Hedrick and Alida Christinaz, 1994 to 2020.

31. Correspondence with Alison Henning, March 15, 1994 to May 21, 1998.

32. Email from Lyle Herrmann, Jr., September 26, 2009.

33. Correspondence with Kraeg Kepford, 1993 to 2019.

34. *Tom Killefer, 1917–1996,* book produced for family and special friends, December 1999.

35. Correspondence with "Country" Landreth and Linda Landreth-Phelps, 1993 to 2020.

36. Interview with George Mauhar, St Louis, April 20, 1996. www.coronadonewsca.com/obituariesgeorge-mauhar.

37. Recorded interview with Wilbert Peter Popp, May 9, 1995.

38. www.findagrave.com/memorial/36329891/wilbert-peter-popp.

39. Correspondence with Joyce Wharton, January 1995 to April 1998.

40. Emails from Mary Anne Hampton-McAfee, May 31, 2020–October 19, 2020.

41. Telephone conversation, April 18, 2009 and emails from Dora Taylor dated March 31, 2012, October 13, 2014, and October 18, 2014.

Notes for Appendix 1

1. HMFL; Gurney & Friedlander, 110; U.S.N. Fighter Squadron notes, Victory Credits in World War 2 (Units) VF-17, and Comments on U.S.N. Aces, (Frank J. Olynyk) received from Department of the Navy, Naval Historical Center, Operational Archives Branch,

August 19, 1994; HMFL; Fighting Squadron Seventeen Combat Statistics dated February 23, 1944, received from Department of the Navy, Naval Historical Center, Operational Archives Branch, August 19, 1994.

2. NARA/NPRC/OMPF—Harry Andrew March, Jr.

Notes for Appendix 2

1. NARA/NPRC/OMPF—William Wolfe Wileman.
2. NHHC; www.history.navy.mil/research/histories/ship-histories/danfs/ w/wileman.html; www.navsource.org/archives/06/022.htm.
3. NARA/NPRC/OMPF—Joseph Donald Shoemaker.
4. NARA/NPRC/OMPF—John Milton Kleinman. Emails with Kleinman family May 29, 2009 to December 25, 2018.
5. NARA/NPRC/OMPF—Donald Allan Innis.
6. NARA/NPRC/OMPF—James Alexander Halford, Jr. Emails from Mike DeBorde, October 23, 2008–November 23, 2018.

Glossary

AA. Antiaircraft fire.

A.A.U. Amateur Athletic Union.

A.B. degree. Bachelor's degree.

A.C.T.G. Advance Carrier Training Group.

Air Group. A carrier air group, usually consisting of a fighter squadron, a dive-bombing squadron, a torpedo squadron and a scouting squadron.

Air Solomons (AirSols). A combined joint command of Allied air units in the Solomon Islands Campaign.

America First. Anti-war organization.

AP. Transport operated by the Navy.

AP1c. Aviation Pilot 1st Class (enlisted rank).

APA. Transport, Attack.

APV. Transport and Aircraft Ferry.

Astoria. *New Orleans*-class cruiser (CA-34).

AvCad. Aviation Cadet.

B-17. Boeing Flying Fortress four-engine bomber.

B-24. Consolidated Liberator four-engine bomber.

B-25. North American Mitchell medium bomber.

Bail out. Jump out of aircraft.

Barnes. *Bogue*-class escort carrier (CVE-20).

Bataan. Province of the Philippines, known for the forced march of U.S. prisoners in WWII.

Battlebuggies. Battleships.

Belleau Wood. *Independence*-class light aircraft carrier (CVL-24).

Betty. Mitsubishi G4M Japanese twin-engine bomber.

Blitz. German bombing campaign against Great Britain in 1940–1941 during WWII.

Bremerton. Bremerton Navy Yard, Washington State, known as Puget Sound Naval Shipyard after WWII.

Bogey. Fighter direction code for unknown aircraft.

Broad jump. Long Jump.

Bull session. Informal discussion, usually involving a group of people.

Bunker Hill. *Essex*-class carrier CV-17.

BUTTON. Code name for Espiritu Santo, largest island in the nation of Vanuatu.

Buttons. The name Harry used for BUTTON.

CA. Heavy Cruiser.

C.A.A. Civil Aviation Authority.

CACTUS. Code name for Guadalcanal.

Cactus. The name Harry used for CACTUS.

Cactus Air Force. Slang for the air group defending Guadalcanal.

C.A.G. Carrier Air Group.

Canberra. Royal Australian Navy heavy cruiser (D-33).

Can/cans. Destroyers.

C.A.S.U. Carrier Air Service Unit.

Ceiling. Lowest broken or overcast cloud layer.

CHERRY BLOSSOM. Code name for Empress Augusta Bay, Bougainville and the operation on the island.

Chow. Food.

CL. Light cruiser.

Club. Officers' Club.

COMAIRSOPAC. Commander Air Forces South Pacific.

Combat Air Patrol. Flying mission, usually to protect an aircraft carrier or specific forces from enemy attack.

Condition Red. Air raid imminent.

Cooking/cooks. Happens.

Crap/craps. Dice game in which players bet on the roll of the dice.

Cribbage. Card game.

Curtiss. *Curtiss*-class seaplane tender (AV-4).

CV. Aircraft carrier.

CVB. Aircraft Carrier, Large.

CVE. Aircraft Carrier, Escort.

CVL. Aircraft Carrier, Small.

DE. Destroyer escort.

Dead End Kids. Group of young actors who made films in the late 1930s.

Decommissioned. Withdraw from service.

Detached. Transferred.

D.F.C. Distinguished Flying Cross.

Dog Day. The unnamed day on which a particular operation commences or is to commence.

Dope. News/information.

Dough. Money.

Duck. Single-engine Navy utility (VJ) biplane, Grumman (J2F).

Dumbo. Consolidated PBY Catalina twin-engine seaplane.

E-Base. Elimination Training Base.

Efate. Island in the nation of Vanuatu.

Ens. Ensign.

Enterprise. *Yorktown*-class aircraft carrier (CV-6).

Espiritu Santo. Largest island in the nation of Vanuatu.

Essex. Leading ship in *Essex*-class aircraft carriers (CV-9).

Ewa. Marine Corps Air Station Ewa (M.C.A.S. Ewa) was located 17 miles (27 km) west of Pearl Harbor on the island of Oahu, Hawaii. It served as a hub for all Marine aviation units heading into combat in the Pacific Theater during World War II.

F4F. Grumman Wildcat.

F4U. Chance Vought Corsair.

F6F. Grumman Hellcat.

Fish. Torpedo.

Flat top. Slang for aircraft carrier.

Fleet of the Rising Sun. Nickname for Japanese Navy.

Flying Tigers. The American Volunteer Group (A.V.G.)—American pilots flying with Chinese markings (but under American control) against the Japanese.

FM Wildcat. Single-engine Navy fighter manufactured by General Motors.

Foxhole. A hole dug in the ground as a shelter from enemy fire.

Friedlander's Bacillus. A bacterial organism that causes pneumonia.

General Quarters/GQ. General quarters or battle stations is an announce-ment made aboard a naval warship to signal the crew to prepare for battle.

Gravy train. Nickname for the roving high cover tactic.

Ground school. Non-flying basics of flight training.

Guadalcanal. Island in the Solomon Islands.

Hamp/Hamps. Mitsubishi A6M Japanese fighter.

Higgins boat. Landing craft named after its designer, Andrew Higgins.

Highball. Alcoholic drink, commonly scotch and soda.

H.M.A.S. Her Majesty's Australian Ship.

Hog. Slang for the F4U Corsair.

Hop. Mission.

Hornet. *Yorktown*-class aircraft carrier (CV-8).

Hose nose. Slang for the F4U Corsair.

Independence. Leading ship in *Independence*-class aircraft carriers (CVL-22).

International Date Line. An imaginary line that runs from the North Pole to the South Pole which demarcates the change of one calendar day to the next.

Japs. Extremely offensive term for the Japanese used in WWII.

JG/jg. Lieutenant Junior Grade.

Jim the works. Mess things up.

Kamikaze. Japanese aircraft loaded with explosives making a suicidal crash on an enemy target.

Kate. Nakajima B5N2 Type 97 torpedo bomber.

Kitty Hawk. Aircraft transport ship (APV-1).

Koro Island. An island of Fiji in the Pacific.

Lex. Nickname for *Lexington* (CV-2 and CV-16) aircraft carriers.

Lexington **(CV-2)**. Lead ship in *Lexington*-class aircraft carriers.

Lexington **(CV-16)**. *Essex*-class aircraft carrier, renamed while under construction to commemorate the earlier ship (CV-2) that was lost in the Battle of the Coral Sea.

Limey. American slang for people from England.

Long Island. Lead ship in *Long Island*-class escort carriers. Originally AVG-1 and then ACV-1. Later re-classified as CVE-1.

LST. Landing Ship, Tank.

Lt. Lieutenant.

Lt. (jg). Lieutenant Junior Grade.

Lt. Cdr. Lieutenant Commander.

Lt. Col. Lieutenant Colonel.

MacArthur. General Douglas MacArthur, Commander of U.S. Forces in the Pacific.

Mach./Machinist. Enlisted rating.

Make the cheese more binding. To add complication to the situation.

Mess. An area where military people eat and socialize.

Midway. Lead ship in *Midway*-class aircraft carriers (CVB-41).

Missouri. *Iowa*-class battleship (BB-63).

N2S Stearman. Boeing training plane.

N.A.A.S. Naval Auxiliary Air Station.

N.A.S. Naval Air Station.

N.A.T.S. Naval Air Transport Service.

NavCad. Naval Aviation Cadet program.

New Hebrides. Colonial name for the island group in the South Pacific now called Vanuatu.

Nips. Extremely offensive term for the Japanese used in WWII.

Nuggets. New useless guy/guys.

O' Club. Officers' Club.

Ondonga/Ondongo. WWII airfield on the island of New Georgia. The spelling varies in different sources.

Overhead. Steep diving run from above target.

P-38. Lockheed Lightning twin-engine fighter.

P-39. Bell Airacobra single-engine fighter.

P-47. Republic Thunderbolt single-engine fighter.

Pan American Clipper. Boeing long-range flying boat.

PBJ. Mitchell, twin-engine Navy patrol-bomber (VPB(MS)), manufactured by North American.

PBY. Consolidated Catalina twin-engine seaplane ("Dumbo").

Pearl. Pearl Harbor, Hawaii.

Pee Willie. Nickname for *Prince William* (CVE-31).

Plank owner. Member of ship or squadron complement from date of commissioning.

Pollywogs. Seamen who have not crossed the equator.

President Jackson. *President Jackson*-class Transport (APA-18).

Princeton. *Independence*-class light aircraft carrier (CVL-23).

Prince William. Bogue-class escort carrier (CVE-31).

PT boats. Motor torpedo boats.

PV-1. Lockheed Ventura twin-engine medium bomber.

Quincy. *New Orleans*-class cruiser (CA-39).

Quonset hut. Prefabricated, lightweight building.

R & R. Rest and recreation.

Red Dog. Poker game.

Reuters. International news organization.

ROSES. Code name for Efate.

R.O.T.C. Reserve Officer Training Corps.

Ruth. Fiat BR.20 Italian-built, twin-engine bomber used by the Japanese Air Force.

Santos. Harry's name for Espiritu Santo.

Sara. Nickname for USS *Saratoga*.

Saratoga. *Lexington*-class aircraft carrier (CV-3).

SBD. Douglas Dauntless dive-bomber aircraft.

S.C.A.T. Southern Cross Air Transport (Army Air Force Transport Service South Pacific).

Scuttlebutt. Rumor.

Seabees. U.S. Navy Construction battalions (CB).

Shakedown cruise. First operations of a new ship.

Shellbacks. Seamen who have crossed the equator.

Shoot the bull. Casual conversation.

Short snorter. A banknote inscribed by people traveling together on an aircraft.

Shot the fat. Casual conversation.

Slant-eye. Extremely offensive term for the Japanese used in WWII.

SNJ. U.S. Navy designation for a North American advanced trainer aircraft.

SNV. Vultee BT-13 Valiant training aircraft.

Solace. Hospital ship (AH-5).

Sortie. Deployment of an aircraft.

Spam. Specially Processed American Meat.

Staphylococcus. A group of bacteria that cause a large number of diseases.

Strafe/strafing. Attack by a low-flying aircraft.

Tar Heel. Nickname applied the U.S. State of North Carolina.

Tau Island. Island in American Samoa, South Pacific.

TBF. Grumman Avenger torpedo plane.

Thach Weave. Aerial combat tactic developed by Navy pilot, Lt. Cdr. John S. Thach, also known as beam defense position

The Big E. Nickname for USS *Enterprise*.

The Line. Equator.

The Slot. A narrow channel in New Georgia Sound named by the Allied Forces due to its shape, that was regularly used by Japanese ships going to Guadalcanal.

Tojo. The surname of the General of the Imperial Japanese Army, Hideki Tojo, which was used as a derogatory nickname for any Japanese enemy in World War II.

Tokyo Express. Allied forces nickname for Japanese ships re-supplying Guadalcanal at night.

Tongatapu. Main island of the Kingdom of Tonga, South Pacific, also known as Tongatabu, Tongataboo, and Tonga Taboo.

Tulagi. Island in the Solomon Islands, South Pacific.

Type 97 bomber. Nakajima B5N Kate torpedo bomber.

U.N.C. University of North Carolina.

Uncle Sugar. Nickname for United States.

U.S.N.R. United States Naval Reserve.

U.S.N.R.A.B. United States Naval Reserve Air Base.

U.S.O. United Service Organization.

USS. United States Ship.

V-5 Program. Naval Aviation Cadet (NavCad) program.

Val/Vals. Aichi D3A1 Type 99 dive bomber.

VB. Bomber—aircraft type and squadron designation.

VBF. Navy Bombing-Fighting aircraft/Navy Bomber-Fighting Squadron.

VF. Fighter—aircraft type and squadron designation.

Vienna sausages. Frankfurter, German sausage.

Vincennes. *New Orleans*-class cruiser (CA-44).

V-mail. Victory Mail, letters transmitted by microfilm.

VMF. Marine Fighter Squadron Designation.

VS. Scouting—aircraft type and squadron designation.

VSB. Scout bombing—aircraft type and squadron designation.

VT. Torpedo—aircraft type and squadron designation.

Wake (Island). A coral atoll in the western Pacific which lies 2300 miles west of Honolulu.

Washing Machine Charlie. Japanese night bomber over Solomon Islands.

Wasp. Reduced-size version of the *Yorktown*-class aircraft carrier (CV-7).

WHITE POPPY. Code name for Noumea, New Caledonia.

White Poppy. The name Harry used for WHITE POPPY.

Yorktown. Lead ship in *Yorktown*-class aircraft carrier (CV-5).

Zeke. Allied code name for Zero.

Zero. Mitsubishi A6M principal Japanese fighter plane.

Bibliography

Documents

Personal diary of Harry Andrew March, Jr., July 13, 1942 to November 17, 1942 and September 4, 1943 to March 30, 1944.

Flight Logbooks—Harry Andrew March, Jr.

Archival Official Military Personnel Files: Harry Andrew March, Jr., Donald Allan Innis, John Milton Kleinman, Joseph Donald Shoemaker, William Wolfe Wileman, John Henry Keith, Charles Alfred Pillsbury, Howard McClain Burriss, Douglas Hugo Charles Gutenkunst, Thomas Frederick Kropf, Percy Eugene Divenney, Donald Thomas Malone, James Miller, and Clyde Howard Dunn.

Official Military Personnel Files: James Alexander Halford, Jr., Lemuel Doty Cooke, Jack Evans Diteman, Richard Martin Einar, Jr., and Harvey Matthews.

VF-17 Action Reports and Combat Statistics.

VF-17 War Diary.

Publications

Bergerud, Eric. *Touched with Fire—The Land War in the South Pacific.* New York: Viking Penguin, 1996.

Bergerud, Eric. *Fire in the Sky—The Air War in the South Pacific.* New York: Westview Press, 2000.

Blackburn, Tom. *The Jolly Rogers.* New York: Orion, 1989.

Cook, Lee. *The Skull and Crossbones Squadron—VF-17 in World War II.* Atglen: Schiffer Publishing Ltd, 1998.

Cook, Lee. *Fighting Seventeen A Photographic History of VF-17 in World War II.* Atglen: Schiffer Publishing Ltd, 2011.

Cook, Lee. *The Aces of Fighting Seventeen.* Atglen: Schiffer Publishing Ltd, 2011.

Costello, John. *The Pacific War 1941—1945.* New York: HarperCollins, 1981.

Deford, Frank. *Big Bill Tilden: The Triumphs and the Tragedy.* New York: Simon & Schuster, 1976.

Gurney, Gene and Friedlander, Mark P., Jr. *Five Down and Glory—A History of the American Air Ace.* New York: Putnam, 1958.

Guyton, Boone T. *Whistling Death: The Test Pilot's Story of the F4U Corsair.* Atglen: Schiffer, 1994.

Kepchia, John B. *Missing in Action over Rabaul.* Privately published: The Palace Printer, 1986.

Lundstrom, John B. *The First Team and the Guadalcanal Campaign: Naval Fighter Combat from August to November 1942.* Annapolis: Naval Institute Press, 1994.

Morison, Samuel Eliot. *History of United States Naval Operations in World War II: The Rising Sun in the Pacific, 1931–April 1942, Volume III.* Boston: Little, Brown and Company, 1948.

Morison, Samuel Eliot. *History of United States Naval Operations in World War II: Struggle for Guadalcanal August 1942–February 1943, Volume V.* Boston: Little, Brown and Company, 1949.

Morison, Samuel Eliot. *History of United States Naval Operations in World War II: Breaking the Bismarck's Barrier 22 July 1942–1 May 1944, Volume VI.* Boston: Little, Brown and Company, 1950.

Nason, Joseph G. *Horio, You Next Die!* Carlsbad: Pacific Rim Press Inc., 1987.

Parshall, Jonathan and Tully, Anthony. *Shattered Sword: The Untold Story of the Battle of Midway.* Washington: Potomac Books, 2005.

Popp, Wilbert P. "Beads." *The Survival of a WWII Navy Fighter Pilot.* Privately published, 2003.

Prange Gordon W. *At Dawn We Slept: The Untold Story of Pearl Harbor.* New York: McGraw-Hill Book Company, 1981.

Sakaida, Henry. *The Siege of Rabaul.* St Paul: Phalanx Publishing Co. Ltd, 1996.

Spalding's *Official Athletic Almanac 1940.* New York: American Sports Publishing Co., 1940.

Tillman, Barrett. *Corsair: The F4U in World War Two and Korea.* Annapolis: Naval Institute Press, 1979.

Toland, John. *The Rising Sun: The Decline and Fall of the Japanese Empire.* New York: Random House Inc., 1970.

DVD/Videos

Fighting 17, The Jolly Rogers. Kenwood Productions, Minneapolis, 1990.

VF-17 Remembered. RDR Video Productions. Northbrook, Illinois, 1984.

Index

Military ranks shown are the rank held for the majority of the period covered, with exception of Lt. Cdr. Harry March, Jr. Page references in boldface indicate illustrations.

A

A.A.U. National Championships, 7, 8, 11, 246–47
accidents, air, 22, 118, 121, 166–67, 182, 203, 239–40, 256–57
Achten, Machinist Julius A., 28, 32, 255
Advanced Carrier Training Group, 14, 270, 272, 275
aerial combat, description of, 32, 168–69, 200–201
    See also under March, Harry
aerial tactics
    against the Japanese Zero, 22–23, 28
    gunnery runs, 22, 132, 189
    roving high cover, 200–201, 203, 211, 213
Aichi D3A1 Type 99 dive bomber. *See* Val
aircraft, training, 11
Air Group 17, 131, 132
Air Group 24, 113, 116, **123**
Air Solomons, 145, 181
Akagi (Japanese carrier), xvii
Allard, Machinist Clayton, 22
America's Navy in World War II (Cant), 128
Anderson, Lieutenant (jg) Robert, 163–64, 246, 257
Arlington National Cemetery, 253, 256, 257, 262
Astoria (CA-34), 29, 33
aviation training (naval), description of, 11, 12, 17, 107
awards. *See* medals/awards

B

B-17 bomber, 29, 33, 44, 49, 68, 82
B-24 bomber, 86, 119, 148, 204, 209, 211, 217
B-25 bomber, 148, 155, 162, 199, 211, 213
B-29 bomber, 246
Baker, Ensign Bradford Warren, 163, 169
Baker Island, 116, 117, 118, 265